HOT ROD
volume 11
TECHNICAL LIBRARY

The Best of

HOT ROD
MAGAZINE

High Peformance
CAMSHAFTS

D1737440

CarTech
Auto Books & Manuals

Published by CarTech, Inc.
11605 Kost Dam Road
North Branch, MN 55056 U.S.A.
United States of America
Tel: 800-551-4754, Fax 651-583-2023

Published and Distributed under
license from Petersen Publishing Company,
L.L.C. © 2000 and
® Petersen Publishing Company, L.L.C.
All Rights Reserved

ISBN 1-884089-50-X

Book Trade Distribution by
Voyageur Press, Inc.
123 North Second Street
P.O. Box 338
Stillwater, MN 55082 U.S.A.
Tel: 651-430-2210, Fax 651-430-2211

Distributed in England by
Brooklands Books Ltd
P.O. Box 146, Cobham
Surrey KT11 1LG
England
Tel: 01932 865051, Fax 01932 868803

Distributed in Australia by
Brooklands Books Ltd
1/81 Darley St, P.O. Box 199
Mona Vale, NSW 2103
Australia
Tel: 02 9997 8428, Fax 02 9979 5799

Printed in Hong Kong

CONTENTS

CAM TALK

ONCE YOU UNDERSTAND CAMSHAFT BASICS, YOU'LL BE ABLE TO SPEAK THE LANGUAGE

By Pat Ganahl

To most hot rodders, cam science is a black art practiced by a few cognoscenti who speak a strange idiom so nobody can learn their secrets.

The major problem is that there is little standardization of terms among camshaft manufacturers. But once you see how cams work and know what the terms really mean, you'll be talking "cam" in no time.

WHAT CAMS DO

We all know that the camshaft opens and closes the valves to let the air/fuel mixture into the cylinder and the exhaust out. The cam itself is an age-old mechanical device that converts rotary motion to linear motion. Most of us also know that the bigger and fatter the lobes on the cam, the higher and longer it will lift the valves, allowing more air/fuel into the engine and more exhaust out—both of which should make the engine run better. The height of the lobe, or the distance it opens the valve, is known as **lift** and is given in thousandths of an inch. The width or fatness of the lobe determines the amount of time (relative to the crankshaft cycle) it will keep the valve open; this is known as **duration** and is given in degrees of crankshaft rotation.

There's much more to making power in an engine than getting lots of good fuel and air in and getting the burned gases out. Yes, we want to get as much air into the cylinder as we can on the intake stroke and the correct percentage of fuel. But it is the *pressure* of the heated air in the closed cylinder that pushes the piston. The amount of air pressure and the period it acts on the piston (known as mean effective pressure or MEP) determine the power of the engine. The lift and duration of the intake valve—along with the efficiency of the rest of the intake system—will control the amount of air/fuel that gets into the cylinder. Other things being equal, this would determine the volume of the charge in the cylinder, and thus the peak cylinder pressure after combustion. However, it is the amount of time the two valves are *closed*, thus sealing the cylinder, that determines how long that pressure pushes on the piston. The point at which the intake valve closes and the point at which the exhaust valve opens are both critical to making power in the engine. These are just two of the timing events that can be altered on a cam.

When the intake valve opens, it takes a little while to get the column of air in the port to start flowing through it. The exhaust has a similar problem, but to a much lesser degree because the cylinder is pressurized when the exhaust valve opens. While the rpm of the engine increases, the "lag time" of the intake

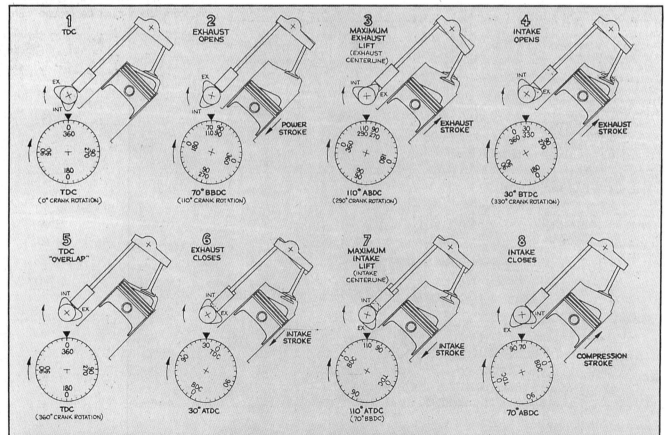

This diagram shows the major cam events through one full cylinder cycle (two crank revolutions or 720 degrees), beginning at TDC firing. The exhaust lobe and valvetrain is closer to the front, and both the crank and the cam rotate clockwise. Cumulative crank degrees are given through the first revolution, but valve events are given in degrees before or after top or bottom dead center.

4

charge tends to remain the same. And once the charge is moving, its momentum will keep it flowing into the cylinder even after the end of the intake stroke (as the piston begins to rise on the compression stroke)—if the intake valve is kept open a little longer. Therefore, as an engine runs faster and faster, the camshaft timing should occur later and later to keep pace with the air/fuel charge, which gets moving slower and keeps moving longer relative to engine speed.

CAM TIMING AND TUNING

We must decide which operating range we want to optimize in our engine and then select a camshaft that will optimize airflow and cylinder pressure in that range, given our specific engine-and-vehicle combination. The problem is once that cam is selected and installed, it optimizes one driving range, not others.

There are three basic ways to alter camshaft timing or tuning: **lobe profile, lobe separation**, and the **camshaft installation position**. The first two are determined when the cam is manufactured and cannot be changed without regrinding it. The latter is determined by the alignment of the timing gears on the crank and cam, and it can be altered. Let's look at each of these cam timing variables, in order.

LOBE PROFILE

The size and shape of the cam lobe determines how high and how long the valve opens. **Lobe lift** is the actual height of the lobe above the base circle, or the distance the cam will lift the lifter. **Gross lift** is the lobe lift multiplied by the rocker arm ratio, giving the theoretical **valve lift** (also called the lift "at valve"). In a stock small-block Chevy, the rocker ratio is 1.5:1. Thus a cam with a lobe lift of .300 inch would produce a gross lift of .450 inch at the valve. In flatheads and overhead-cam engines without rocker arms, the lobe must generate all the valve lift. **Net lift**, a term not often used in discussing street cams, is the true distance the valve actually lifts off its seat. This is equal to gross lift minus valve clearance (on solid-lifter cams), pushrod flex, and other losses. Obviously you want as much valve lift as you can get. Maximum lift is limited, however, by available valve-to-piston clearance, valvespring capability, and camshaft journal size (the lobes can't be bigger

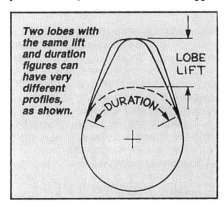

Two lobes with the same lift and duration figures can have very different profiles, as shown.

LOBE LIFT

DURATION

than the journals, or the cam won't go in the block).

Duration is the period during the cylinder cycle that the valve is open. It is expressed in degrees of crankshaft rotation. Remember that the camshaft rotates at one-half crank speed. It has to, because this is a four-cycle engine. Each valve opens once during two crankshaft revolutions. (Refer to the accompanying diagram, which should make cam operation much clearer.) Beginning at top dead center (TDC) before the power stroke (ignition) in one cylinder, both valves are closed. Then we have the power stroke and the exhaust stroke (one crank revolution), during which the exhaust valve opens and nearly closes. At TDC between the exhaust stroke and intake stroke (called "TDC overlap"), the exhaust valve is still closing and the intake valve is already beginning to open on most cams. That is, both valves are open at the same time briefly. This is called **overlap.** The next two cylinder cycles are the intake stroke, during which the intake valve is open, and the compression stroke, which completes the second crank revolution. Understanding this sequence is crucial to understanding cam timing.

Advertised duration is the term we have traditionally used to describe how "big" a cam is: a "272-degree cam." This term should describe the actual duration that the valve is off the seat. However, cam lobes must be ground with

CAM SHOP

STREET GRIND RECOMMENDATIONS FROM THE EXPERTS

We made up five different vehicle "combinations," giving them some variety, yet trying to keep them representative of typical street-driven rods. Then we sent them to nine of the major cam manufacturers, asking them to recommend one of their grinds for each combo. Other than Lunati (these guys want to be first to the grocery store), there is amazing consistency between manufacturers (look at duration at .050).

Also note differences between advertised and .050 duration numbers between brands. All combinations are for street-driven cars with 28- to 30-inch-tall tires and street converters.

Next we cooked up a typical street-rod combination and sent it out to a bunch of professional rod builders, figuring they'd have the most experience in which cams work and which don't. Several admitted they knew little about cams; but those

COMBINATION 1: 350 Chevy small-block, 600-cfm 4-barrel, dual-plane intake, 9.0:1 compression, 3500-pound car, 3.50:1 rear, auto trans.

Manufacturer	Cam Name or Grind No.	Cat. No.	Lifter Type	Advert. Duration Int.	Advert. Duration Exh.	Dur. @ .050 Int.	Dur. @ .050 Exh.	Lobe Lift Int.	Lobe Lift Exh.	Gross Lift Int.	Gross Lift Exh.	Lobe Separation	Rec. Install
Competition Cams	CS268H-10	12-210-2	Hyd.	268°	268°	218°	218°	.303	.303	.455	.455	110°	Cam ground 4° Advanced
Crane	Max Velocity HMV-260-2-NC	113901	Hyd.	260°	272°	204°	216°	.285	.303	.427	.455	112°	Cam ground 5°Advanced
Cam Dynamics	Energizer 266H10	10003	Hyd.	266°	266°	210°	210°	.285	.285	.427	.427	110°	
Crower	Power Compu-Pro 270-HDP	00240	Hyd.	270°	276°	209°	218°	.281	.296	.421	.444	112°	Advance 4°
Engle	EP18/20 Hyd.	1018-H	Hyd.	260°	268°	216°	226°	.305	.310	.458	.468	112°	Cam ground 2° Advanced
Erson	HI-FLO-AH	E-110-321	Hyd.	284°	284°	218°	218°	.315	.315	.472	.472	108°	Advance 2-4°
Iskenderian	262-Hyd Super Cam	201262	Hyd.	262°	262°	208°	208°	.290	.290	.435	.435	108°	Advance 3°
Lunati	Bracket Master II	00010	Hyd.	292°	292°	230°	230°	.320	.320	.480	.480	109°	Straight up
Schneider	135H Hi Torque	02001	Hyd.	270°	270°	218°	218°	.305	.305	.460	.460	110°	Advance 4°

very gradual opening and closing "ramps" to keep the lifter from "slamming" on the cam and to reduce shock in the valvetrain. Thus it is very difficult to measure, with a degree wheel on the crank and a dial gauge on the lifter, the exact point in crank rotation where the lifter begins to move. Consequently, most grinders measure advertised duration at approximately .004-inch lifter rise. But this is not a standard, nor is it an easy point to measure. Advertised duration for camshafts is as meaningful as "suggested retail price" for new cars.

A much more accurate measuring point, and the new standard for the industry, is **duration at .050**. It is measured in crank degrees from the point where the lifter rises .050 inch from the base circle to the point where it drops back down to .050 above the base.

Even duration at .050 is an inaccurate comparison figure for cams. Two camshafts can have the same lift and duration at .050 specs, yet have different profiles. As shown in diagrams here, one lobe could have steeper flanks and a broader nose (known as a "fast acting" profile), lifting the valve higher sooner and keeping it open higher longer. Unfortunately, you can't tell this difference from cam specs in the catalogs. (One indicator is the difference between advertised duration and duration at .050. A cam with less difference between these two figures should be a "faster acting" cam. But this depends largely on how, and where, the advertised duration was measured on the two cams.) One way to compare cams is to measure actual lifter rise per every 20 or 40 degrees of crank rotation in the engine and plot it as a curve on a graph. Plotting the entire lift sequence is the only way to really compare two different profiles.

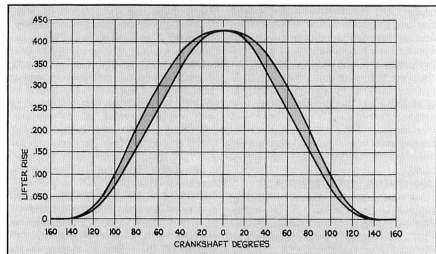

The only way to see the true difference between two cam profiles is to measure the lifter rise at given degrees of crank rotation and plot these figures on a graph. These two cams have the same lift and duration at .050 specs, but one has a "fatter" profile.

A **dual-pattern** camshaft is one on which the intake and exhaust lobe profiles differ, which is often the case. An **asymmetric profile** has lobes that differ from the opening to the closing sides; this is rare, especially for street cams.

Obviously you want the broadest, fastest-acting lobe profile you can get. The two primary limitations to lobe profile are lifter size and type, and spring pressure. With a flat tappet (solid or hydraulic), the cam rise is limited by the contact surface of the lifter. If the lobe rises too steeply, the lifter edge would "dig into" the lobe surface, destroying it. The broader the base of the lifter, the steeper the lobe it can remain in contact with. A roller lifter allows much more radical lifter rise because of its physical design. This is why roller lifters were invented and why they are used in all-out racing engines. Sav-

who answered obviously do, because—again—the choices are all close.

Jerry Slover of Pete & Jake's, who has run a speed shop for years, added some comments we thought pertinent. He selected the given Comp Cam because he: (1) carb tuning isn't normally required, (2) it has broad range; will work well even with different compression, gear ratio or other misapplications, (3) vacuum accessories are not affected, (4) it has some "hot rod sound," which most rodders want, (5) most people don't degree their cams, and this one has four degrees advance ground in, so the possibility of installing it retarded is unlikely, and (6) it gives a fair power increase. If a customer doesn't care about idle quality or fuel economy and wants that race car "quick rap," he recommends Cam Dynamics part No. 10017, with 218-degree duration at .050, .450 lift, and 106-degree lobe separation. If he wants a definite rough idle, try Comp Cams 280 Magnum (230 degrees at .050, .526 lift, 110-degree lobe separation). Neither cam works well with power brakes, and carb tuning is usually required. For a "low-price" cam, the Crane Fireball II (specs similar to Comp Cams Hi-Energy 268 and Magnum 280 series) is popular. And the GM factory 350-hp 327 cam (part No. 3863151) is often on sale.

COMBINATION 2: 350 Chevy small-block, 750-cfm 4-barrel, single-plane intake, 10:1 compression, 2800-pound car, 4.11:1 rear, 4-speed.

Manufacturer	Cam Name or Grind No.	Cat. No.	Lifter Type	Advert. Duration Int.	Advert. Duration Exh.	Dur. @ .050 Int.	Dur. @ .050 Exh.	Lobe Lift Int.	Lobe Lift Exh.	Gross Lift Int.	Gross Lift Exh.	Lobe Separation	Rec. Install
Competition Cams	CS280H-10	12-212-2	Hyd.	280°	280°	230°	230°	.320	.320	.480	.480	110°	Cam ground 4° Advanced
Crane	Hi Intensity HIT-284-2-NC	113821	Hyd.	284°	292°	228°	236°	.327	.340	.490	.510	114°	
Cam Dynamics	Energizer 284H12	10007	Hyd.	284°	284°	228°	228°	.320	.320	.480	.480	112°	
Crower	Hi-Draulic Hauler 278-HDP	00210	Hyd.	278°	288°	220°	230°	.317	.303	.475	.454	108°	Advance 4°
Engle	EP25 Hyd.	1025-H	Hyd.	282°	282°	236°	236°	.327	.327	.494	.494	110°	Cam ground 2° Advanced
Erson	HI-FLO-IIH	E-110-521	Hyd.	306°	306°	235°	235°	.315	.315	.472	.472	108°	Advance 4°
Iskenderian	280 Mega Cam	201281	Hyd.	280°	280°	232°	232°	.323	.323	.485	.485	108°	Advance 3°
Lunati	Bracket Master II	00012	Hyd.	300°	300°	246°	246°	.343	.343	.515	.515	108°	Advance 4°
Schneider	Street Pro II	30002	Hyd.	284°	294°	224°	228°	.320	.320	.480	.480	110°	Advance 4°

ings in friction are minimal in comparison (flat tappets rotate in their bores as they ride on the lobe to reduce friction and wear). Given the difference in cost and complexity, there's little reason to use a roller cam on the street.

The more radical the lobe profile, the greater the valvespring pressure necessary to keep the lifter on the cam lobe. If the lobe shape changes too quickly, momentum will cause the lifter to fly off the lobe at higher rpm. Valve float is a side effect. This condition also leads to rapid cam wear. Increased valvespring pressure, however, increases drag, friction, cam wear, and stress on valvetrain components. Thus camshaft lobe profile is physically limited. Don't use more spring pressure than necessary.

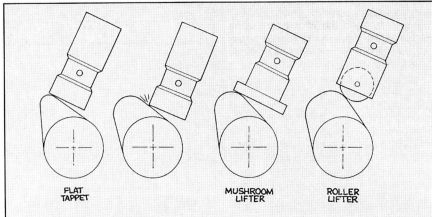

Lobe profile is limited by lifter size or type. A wide, or mushroom-tip, lifter will follow a steeper lobe without "digging in." A roller will follow a very radical lobe.

LOBE SEPARATION

The **lobe separation angle**, also known as the **lobe centerline displacement angle** or—more commonly but not necessarily correctly—the cam's **lobe centers**, is the angle between the centerline of the intake lobe and the centerline of the exhaust lobe for one cylinder, as measured on the cam. In other words, it is the timing of the intake lobe relative to the exhaust lobe as determined by the placement of the lobes on the camshaft. The standard lobe separation angle is 110 degrees (these are cam degrees). When a cam is made, it can be ground with "narrower" (say, 108- or 106-degree) or "wider" (112-, 114-degree) lobe separation. Once ground, it's set.

Lobe separation angle is a relatively new term, replacing the once more common, but misleading, "overlap" spec. Reducing the separation angle does increase overlap—the time that both valves are open. But it also increases the time that both valves are *closed*.

People find the lobe separation angle confusing for two reasons: First, many cam companies list the intake centerline (or both intake and exhaust centerlines) in similar-looking crank degrees, as a method for "degreeing in" the cam. We'll get to this in a minute. Second, the way the lobe separation angle is shown, and measured, on a cam card (and in this article) is really upside down. If you already understand lobe centers, don't let me confuse you. But if you're new to the concept, consider the cam turned over, so that the lobes point down, with the exhaust on the left and the intake on the right. This is how the cam actually sits, in relation to the lifters for a given cylinder, when the piston is at TDC at the beginning of the combustion cycle. Viewed from the front of the engine, both the crank and the cam rotate clockwise (in typical V8s).

Viewing the cam this way, you should readily see that narrowing the lobe separation angle will cause the exhaust valve to open later and the intake valve to close sooner. These points are critical valve events, because they determine the time the cylinder is sealed (with both valves closed), and cylinder pressure can push on the piston. Ed Iskenderian quotes Ed Winfield, "The intake closing point is the most important valve event of all." On the other hand, if you open

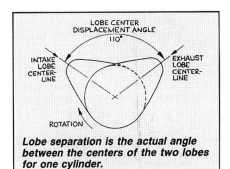

Lobe separation is the actual angle between the centers of the two lobes for one cylinder.

The lobe separation angle between the exhaust and intake lobes for the number-one cylinder (arrows) is apparent on this Chevy cam. Note the "fatter" lobe profile on the cam at left.

COMBINATION 3: 454 Chevy big-block, 750-cfm 4-barrel, dual-plane intake, 9.5:1 compression, 3200-pound car, 3.70:1 rear, auto trans.

Manufacturer	Cam Name or Grind No.	Cat. No.	Lifter Type	Advert. Duration Int.	Advert. Duration Exh.	Dur. @ .050 Int.	Dur. @ .050 Exh.	Lobe Lift Int.	Lobe Lift Exh.	Gross Lift Int.	Gross Lift Exh.	Lobe Separation	Rec. Install
Competition Cams	CB280H-10	11-208-3	Hyd.	280°	280°	230°	230°	.306	.306	.520	.520	110°	Cam ground 4° Advanced
Crane	Max Velocity HMV-272-2-NC	133841	Hyd.	272°	284°	214°	228°	.303	.300	.515	.510	112°	
Cam Dynamics	Energizer 272H10	10305	Hyd.	272°	272°	216°	216°	.303	.303	.515	.515	110°	
Crower	Power Compu-Pro 276-HDP	01241	Hyd.	274°	281°	211°	220°	.288	.304	.490	.517	112°	Advance 4°
Engle	RV-72 Hyd.	2212-H	Hyd.	272°	272°	225°	225°	.295	.295	.500	.500	112°	Cam ground 2° Advanced
Erson	HI-FLO-IH	E-120-421	Hyd.	296°	296°	228°	228°	.315	.315	.542	.542	111°	Advance 2-4°
Iskenderian	270 Mega Cam	396271	Hyd.	270°	270°	221°	221°	.310	.310	.565	.565	108°	Advance 3°
Lunati	Street Master	07202	Hyd.	285°	285°	235°	235°	.323	.323	.550	.550	108°	Straight up
Schneider	Street Pro 6H	30006	Hyd.	284°	294°	220°	228°	.300	.300	.510	.510	110°	Advance 4°

the exhaust valve too soon, you will "blow down" the cylinder, allowing cylinder pressure to escape out the exhaust unused. Narrowing the lobe centers increases low-end torque.

The problem is that narrowing the lobe centers also increases valve overlap. The longer the duration of the cam, the worse the problem. If both valves remain open together too long at the transition between the exhaust and intake strokes, exhaust will tend to blow out the intake valve and vice versa. This may be great for EGR, but it's terrible for idle quality, especially in a street engine. As one engine builder put it, "It's like a giant vacuum leak." That is why most street cams (as you can see in the charts) run lobe separation angles of 110 to 114 degrees—to reduce rough idle and increase vacuum for accessories such as power brakes. If you don't care about idle quality, narrow lobe centers (110, maybe 108) will give you lots of torque in the street-driving range. But it also depends on duration; the longer the duration of a street cam, the wider the lobe centers must be to maintain any idle quality.

Cam timing, relative to the crank, can be changed with offset cam gear buttons or offset crank gear keys.

CAM INSTALLATION TIMING

The third basic variable in cam timing is how the cam is installed in the engine relative to crank/piston position. If you "line up the dots" on the crank and cam timing gears as you install the camshaft, the number-one cylinder should be at TDC, and the cam will be positioned near the middle of overlap for that cylinder. (Bet you didn't know that. The num-

Roller lifters allow much more radical lobes.

COMBINATION 4: 302 Ford small-block, 600-cfm 4-barrel, dual-plane intake, 9.5:1 compression, 3000-pound car, 3.50:1 rear, auto trans.

Manufacturer	Cam Name or Grind No.	Cat. No.	Lifter Type	Advert. Duration Int.	Advert. Duration Exh.	Dur. @ .050 Int.	Dur. @ .050 Exh.	Lobe Lift Int.	Lobe Lift Exh.	Gross Lift Int.	Gross Lift Exh.	Lobe Separation	Rec. Install
Competition Cams	FS260H-10	31-216-2	Hyd.	260°	260°	212°	212°	.280	.280	.447	.447	110°	Cam ground 4° Advanced
Crane	Max Velocity HMV-260-2-NC	363901	Hyd.	260°	272°	204°	216°	.285	.303	.456	.484	112°	
Cam Dynamics	Energizer 266H10	13004	Hyd.	266°	266°	210°	210°	.285	.285	.456	.456	110°	
Crower	Power Compu-Pro 260-HDP	15209	Hyd.	260°	266°	204°	210°	.278	.281	.445	.450	112°	Advance 4°
Engle	EP18/20 Hyd	2118-H	Hyd.	260°	268°	216°	226°	.305	.310	.488	.496	112°	Cam ground 2° Advanced
Erson	HI-FLO-IH	E-210-421	Hyd.	296°	296°	228°	228°	.315	.315	.504	.504	108°	Advance 2-4°
Iskenderian	262-Hyd Super Cam	381262	Hyd.	262°	262°	208°	208°	.278	.278	.445	.445	108°	Advance 3°
Lunati	Street-Master	07601	Hyd.	275°	275°	225°	225°	.317	.317	.508	.508	108°	Straight up
Schneider	135 H Hi Torque	0306	Hyd.	270°	270°	218°	218°	.305	.305	.480	.480	110°	Advance 4°

COMBINATION 5: 351C Ford, 600-cfm 4-barrel, dual-plane intake, 9.0:1 compression, 3500-pound car, 3.50:1 rear, auto trans.

Manufacturer	Cam Name or Grind No.	Cat. No.	Lifter Type	Advert. Duration Int.	Advert. Duration Exh.	Dur. @ .050 Int.	Dur. @ .050 Exh.	Lobe Lift Int.	Lobe Lift Exh.	Gross Lift Int.	Gross Lift Exh.	Lobe Separation	Rec. Install
Competition Cams	FC268H-10	32-221-3	Hyd.	268°	268°	218°	218°	.285	.285	.494	.494	110°	Cam ground 4° Advanced
Crane	Max Velocity HMV-260-2-NC	523901	Hyd.	260°	272°	204°	216°	.285	.303	.493	.524	112°	
Cam Dynamics	Energizer 266H10 13303		Hyd.	266°	266°	210°	210°	.285	.285	.493	.493	110°	
Crower	Power Compu-Pro 270-HDP	15240	Hyd.	270°	276°	209°	218°	.281	.296	.486	.512	112°	Advanced 4°
Engle	RV-101/104 Hyd.	2910-H	Hyd.	262°	270°	214°	222°	.295	.295	.509	.509	112°	Cam ground 2° Advanced
Erson	TQ20H	E-220-121	Hyd.	292°	292°	214°	214°	.299	.299	.517	.517	110°	Cam ground 4° Advanced
Iskenderian	262-Hyd. Super Cam	431262	Hyd.	262°	262°	208°	208°	.278	.278	.488	.488	108°	Advance 3°
Lunati	Street Master	07112	Hyd.	285°	285°	235°	235°	.323	.323	.560	.560	108°	Straight up
Schneider	135H Hi Torque	0318	Hyd.	270°	270°	218°	218°	.305	.305	.525	.525	110°	Advance 4°

ber-six cylinder on a Chevy will be at TDC firing when the cam timing marks are aligned.)

If the cam is ground "straight up," and if the timing gears are accurate, the cam will be exactly in the middle of overlap when the number-one piston is at TDC. The only way to check if this is so (the marks can often be off several degrees) is to "dial in" the cam.

Some cam cards give an **intake centerline** figure as the checking point for cam installation timing. This number looks like, and is often the same as, the lobe separation angle for the cam. But the *intake centerline* (sometimes listed as "lobe centerline," or the "max lift" point, for intake and/or exhaust) is not the same as the *lobe center displacement angle*. The similarity is a coincidence. Let's say a cam with a lobe displacement angle of 110 degrees is installed "straight up" in the engine. At TDC on the number-one cylinder, the cam will be positioned in the middle of overlap below the lifters. There are 110 degrees between the two lobes; the center of the intake lobe is 55 degrees to the left of the lifters, and the exhaust lobe is 55 degrees to the right. If you turn the crankshaft 110 degrees past TDC, the camshaft (which turns at half crank speed) will turn 55 degrees, and the centerline of the intake lobe will be directly under the lifter, or at maximum lift. Thus the "intake centerline" checking spec

for this cam is 110 degrees after top dead center (ATDC). The exhaust centerline would be 110 degrees before TDC. The lobe-separation angle and the intake-centerline checking spec happen to be the same number only when the cam is installed "straight up."

If the cam is moved ahead in relation to crank/piston timing, we say it has been **advanced**; if it's moved back from "straight up," it's **retarded**. Both lobes are advanced or retarded the same amount, because they're fixed on the camshaft. If a cam with a 110-degree lobe-separation angle is specified to be installed on a 106-degree intake centerline, the cam would be four degrees advanced (the intake lobe would reach max lift four crank degrees sooner). If the card called for a 114-degree intake centerline, the cam would be installed four degrees retarded.

Cam installation timing or phasing can be altered two ways. The cam manufacturer can cut the keyway (or dowel pin) for the cam gear in a retarded or advanced position, so that the cam is advanced or retarded a given amount when you line up the timing dots on the gears. We would say this cam is "ground advanced" or "ground retarded." Today most cam makers grind their street cams about four degrees advanced to compensate for timing-chain stretch. As the chain stretches, it retards cam timing.

The engine builder can also advance

Continued on page 15

A great way to study cam operation is to install the components in an engine, with a degree wheel, and turn the crank to see what happens. Isky made this cutaway for this purpose. TDC overlap is shown.

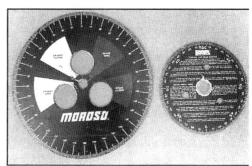

Even degree wheels vary. One reads 0-90-0-90-0; the other reads 0-180-0.

TYPICAL ROD COMBINATION: 350 Chevy small-block, 650-cfm 4-barrel, dual-plane intake, 9.0:1 compression, 2800- to 3000-pound car, 3.50:1 rear, 28- to 30-inch-tall rear tires, auto trans.

Builder	Cam Brand	Cat. No.	Dur. @ .050		Gross Lift		Lobe Separation	Comments
			Int.	Exh.	Int.	Exh.		
Jerry Slover Pete & Jake's Grandview, MO	Competition Cams	CS268H-10 12-210-2	218°	218°	.455	.455	110°	
Chuck Lombardo California Street Rods Huntington Beach, CA	GM/ Chevrolet	PN 3896962	224°	224°	.450	.460	114°	"LT-1" Chevy 350 cam
Ed Moss TCI Engineering Ontario, CA	Engle	1018-H	216°	226°	.458	.468	112°	
Jerry Kugel Kugel Komponents La Habra, CA	Isky or Erson		210° to 215°	220° to 225°	.472	.496	112°	Install 5° Advanced
Boyd Coddington Hot Rods By Boyd Stanton, CA	Crane	HMV-260-2-NC 113901	204°	216°	.427	.454	112°	
Ken Fenical Posie's Hummelstown, PA	Crane	HMV-272-2-NC 113941	216°	228°	.454	.480	112°	
Art Chrisman C.A.R.S. Santa Ana, CA	Crane	HIT-280-NC 114201	224°	224°	.460	.460	114°	
Bill Keifer Calif. Customs Roadsters Orange, CA	Crane	272-H10 10005	216°	216°	.454	.454	110°	
Butch Bunn Butch's Rod Shop Dayton, OH	Perfect Circle	229-1730	204°	214°	.420	.443	112°	

SOURCES

Competition Cams
Dept. HR
3406 Democrat Rd.
Memphis, TN 38118
(901) 795-2400

Crane Cams/Cam Dynamics
Dept. HR
530 Fentress Blvd.
Daytona Beach, FL 32014
(904) 258-6174

Crower Cams
Dept. HR
3333 Main St.
Chula Vista, CA 92011
(619) 422-1191

Engle Racing Cams
Dept. HR
1621 12th St.
Santa Monica, CA 90404
(213) 450-0806

Erson Cams
Dept. HR
550 Mallory Way
Carson City, NV 89701
(702) 882-1622

Iskenderian Racing Cams
Dept. HR
16020 S. Broadway
Gardena, CA 90247
(213) 770-0930

Lunati Cams
Dept. HR
P.O. Box 18021
Memphis, TN 38181-0021
(901) 365-0950

Schneider Racing Cams
Dept. HR
1235 Cushman Ave.
San Diego, CA 92110
(619) 297-0227

Continued on page 15

a stick in Time

Dyno? We Don' Need No Stinkin' Dyno!

1A

By Jerry Heasley

1B

1.a & b Isky's bushings require an enlarged hole in the camshaft sprocket and allow repositioning the pin ahead of its zero position, in the direction of rotation. They also make a zero bushing to return the cam to its original position using the enlarged pin hole.

2

2. Degreeing a camshaft is not difficult. The major tools required are a piston stop, degree wheel, dial indicator, and a certain amount of patience.

3. If you've never degreed a cam before, most cam manufacturers produce pamphlets or include the procedure in their catalog. Photocopying this procedure out of your local speed shop's cam catalog would be a quick way to dial yourself into the procedure

3

4. The optimum position for the camshaft will result in the highest cranking compression as read on a simple compression tester.

4

Ever stop to think that when you degree-in a cam, the only thing you're sure of is where it's positioned? You never really know if it's the *right* place for maximum torque and horsepower. With a popsicle compression tester and a few bucks worth of Isky cam bushings, however, you can fine-tune your engine by trial and error, and find the optimum position for the cam.

It's a little-known trick revealed to us by Isky's tech man, T. Willie. According to him, installing various bushings and spinning the engine will produce different compression readings, depending on where the cam is set. The object is to set the cam at the position producing maximum cranking compression pressure. It may not be as effective as running the engine on a Superflow Dyno, but T. Willie's method does produce good results with camshafts having less than 300-degrees duration.

As you know, no two engines are exactly alike, and your particular build may need slightly more or less advance. You might install the cam advanced 2 or 4 degrees as a starting point, but for the serious builder, that's exactly what it is...a start.

To do the compression check, pull all the plugs and leave the timing cover off so you'll have access to the cam sprocket. Isky makes bushings to rotate the cam 4, 6, or 8 degrees, as well as a "zero" bushing to fill the enlarged hole you need to drill in the cam sprocket for any of the bushings you might use.

There are some major considerations involved here, also. Advancing the cam will produce higher and higher readings on a compression tester, but going past 8 degrees may cause any or all of the following: Intake valve contact with the piston; loss of top-end horsepower (the object in having a "short" duration cam is usually to produce more low-end anyway, so this might not be a problem for you); and an increased potential for detonation, due to the higher low-end cylinder pressure.

According to Isky, you could get as much as 20 to 30 additional psi to appear on the tester, but if you need more, you ought to think about changing the compression ratio of the engine. ⑥

$79.95 Cam Test

BY MATTHEW KING

Photos by Matthew King

This article is aimed at anyone who's ever sat in the most important room in the house thumbing through a catalog and blankly wondering which cam to pick for a mild-performance small-block Chevy. We know the drill because we've done it: You skip the tiny grinds and figure one of the middle-of-the-pack cams should do the trick. The problem is which one, when there are several bunched together that all sound good?

To illustrate the dilemma, we flipped through our latest Summit Racing catalog and checked out the company's line of in-house grinds. Skipping the first three weak-suck profiles, we found SUM-K1103, a cam with 214/224 degrees of duration at 0.050-inch lift, intake/exhaust lifts of 0.442/0.465 inch, and a lobe separation angle of 112 degrees. Sounds good. But what about SUM-K1104? That's got 10 degrees more intake duration and a 0.465-inch intake lift; the exhaust profile is the same, so it's a single-pattern cam. Sounds better, but wait! There's also SUM-K1105, a bigger split-pattern 'stick with a hearty 224/234 degrees of duration at 0.050 and 0.465/0.488 lift. That sounds aggressive without being too radical. Since they all cost the same $79.95,

We didn't just stab budget cams into some tricked-out high-dollar motor or a high-mileage junkyard mill—we dialed-in our cam combo the hard way, by building a real-world engine on the cheap and swapping in a trio of cams until we found the right one. By shopping around for the cheapest rebuild kit we could find and keeping machine work to a minimum, we put the long-block together for about $1,000, including parts, machine work, and a set of rebuilt stock heads. Then we topped it off with a used Holley Street Dominator dual-plane manifold and a used Holley 650 double-pumper carb.

why not get a little more bang for the buck? You can see the quagmire we're quickly spiraling into: Some is good but more is better, and before too long, we'll be pulling 9 inches of vacuum and sounding like we're running in Pro Stock Eliminator.

When it comes to cam selection, you can theorize all day long about gear ratios, converters, compression ratios, etc., or you can do what we did: Build an average, mild-performance 350, stab all three cams into it in succession, and run it on a dyno. Since you probably don't have the time or money to do that, we did it for you. And the best part is, you don't even have to get off the throne!

We were suspicious of Northern Auto Parts' advertisement for a complete rebuild kit for $154.95, until we called up and found that the money got us Speed-Pro pistons in any standard overbore; Clevite 77 main, cam, and rod bearings; cast-iron rings; a Melling oil pump; a set of McCord gaskets; a new timing set; freeze plugs; and a Speed-Pro stock replacement cam-and-lifter set. At that price, we were happy to spend $20 more for hypereutectic slugs, $12 to upgrade to Hastings moly rings, and another $6 for a Cloyes double-roller timing set. We also bought a set of Pioneer stock replacement valvesprings for $28, bringing our parts total to $220.95. For $35 more, we could have upgraded to any cam in the Speed-Pro catalog or a cam from Crane's Energizer series.

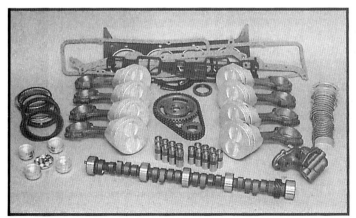

Some guys watch football on New Year's Day; instead, we were at the junkyard pulling an engine because pricing was half off for the holiday. We missed all the big games but scored a complete 350 out of a '72 Nova for $80. We hauled the block and heads to M&R Machine where they were disassembled, cleaned, and Magnaflux-tested for cracks.

After cleaning, M&R bored and honed the two-bolt block 0.030-over and then installed our new cam bearings. We also had M&R recondition the stock rods and hang them on our new pistons.

M&R installed new bronze valve guides, reamed them to size, and then cut new valve seats with a Serdi valve machine, which employs a three-edge cutter to simultaneously produce a three-angle valve job.

Back at the *Car Craft* shop, we re-tapped the head bolt holes and rinsed the block with hot, soapy water before assembling the short-block. We checked ring endgap with a feeler gauge and then used our nifty Power-house tapered piston ring compressor to stuff the pistons in the block. We checked clearances with Plasti-gage, then used lots of assembly lube and torqued the rod bolts to 45 lb-ft.

The small-block's original crank bearing journals were in decent shape, and a quick check with a micrometer confirmed that we could get by with just a polish, which cost only $13.50 rather than about $50 to grind the crank. As a result, we ordered standard-size bearings with our rebuild kit.

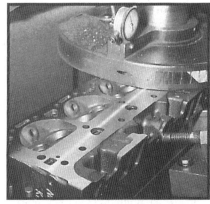

Two 0.002-inch cuts on M&R's surface mill were needed just to remove the warp in the center of each head. A good rule of thumb is that each 0.004-inch cut knocks about 1 cc off a production 76cc chamber head; so, in a bid to increase compression a bit more, we had M&R make three more cuts for a total of 0.010 inch. We didn't cc them, but we guestimated the chambers at 74 cc for the purposes of calculating compression.

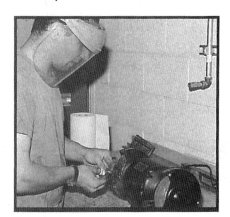

To save money, we reused all the hardware and sheetmetal from the core engine. After soaking them overnight in Chem-Dip, we buzzed the crud off the head bolts with a wire wheel and then chased the threads with a die. We couldn't salvage our pushrods because half of them were bent, so we ordered a new set of stock replacements from Summit for $28.50.

Several of the exhaust valves on our junkyard core's early smog-era 487X-casting heads were deeply sunken, so we had M&R install hardened exhaust seats in addition to doing a valve job and resurfacing the heads. This is where the cost of reconditioning used heads starts to mount—without new seats, the rebuild runs $80 a head; with seats, the cost more than doubled to $180 each.

Used valves were reconditioned by grinding the valve stems, squaring up the tips, and recutting the valve face angle. Then the heads were re-assembled with our new springs, new valve stem seals, and the old retainers and locks.

Cost of a Mule Motor

Core	$80.00
Machine work	598.75
Rebuild kit	220.95
Used manifold	75.00
Used carb	150.00
Headers	79.50
Pushrods	28.50
Intake bolts	9.95
Water pump	21.99
Distributor	24.95
Cap	19.95
Plug wires	39.95
Plugs	7.92
Oil/filter	9.74
Total	$1,367.15

Since we were trying to keep costs to a minimum, we didn't have the block decked. After assembling the short-block, we measured the deck height with a depth gauge and almost choked when the piston turned out to be 0.051 inch in the hole—small blocks usually have a deck height around 0.025-0.030 inch at the worst. Sure enough, a check of the catalog revealed that the Speed-Pro pistons (PN H345P) that came with our rebuild kit are designed to provide a 0.045-inch deck height. This specs out to an 8.34:1 CR in an 0.030-over 350 with 76cc chamber heads, an 0.038-inch-thick head gasket, and 5cc piston re-liefs. We have more deck height, but since we had about 2 cc's knocked off our 76cc chamber heads, our compression works out to a slightly higher 8.37:1 with the 0.041-inch-thick gaskets we used. Yuck.

We didn't use the replacement cam and lifters that came with the rebuild kit because we wanted to try out a few of Summit's line of budget-priced cams, which cost $79.95 with lifters and lube. The first one we stabbed in was the mildest of the three tested—a split-pattern grind with a duration of 214/224 degrees at 0.050-inch tappet lift, 0.442/0.465 intake/exhaust lift, and a 112-degree lobe separation angle. It produced 15 in-Hg of idle vacuum, a flat torque curve, and 288 hp at 5,100 rpm.

We used an Edelbrock two-piece stamped-aluminum timing cover (PN 4242) and a timing cover stud set to facilitate easy on-dyno cam swaps. The inner half of the two-piece unit is installed just like a regular timing cover; the outer piece bolts to it with a gasket in between to prevent leaks. It worked great and saved a ton of time, gaskets, and silicone, but we didn't include it in the cost of the buildup because we intend to swap the original timing cover and bolts back on once we're done.

Before we bolted on the cylinder heads, we used a piston stop and a degree wheel to find TDC on the No. 1 cylinder. Then, without rotating the crank, we installed the balancer and the timing tab and placed a strip of degreed timing tape on the balancer with the TDC mark corresponding to the marks on the timing tab and the balancer. Using this system, we were able to confirm the timing of each cam by mounting a dial indicator on the No. 1 cylinder intake pushrod and checking the relationship of the intake valve opening at 0.050-inch-lift to TDC against the specs on the cam card. All three cams were dead-on.

13

Conclusions

We ran all three cams on Westech Performance Group's SuperFlow dyno with a Holley 650 carb, a Holley Street Dominator dual-plane manifold, a stock HEI ignition, and a set of Hooker 1¾-inch primary headers. The headers are larger than we would probably use for this engine on the street and likely gained us some top-end power at the expense of torque (we bought a set of 1⅝-inch full-length headers from Summit (PNG9001) to use later). All three cams produced peak power with 12 degrees of initial timing (38 degrees total), and, interestingly, all three produced peak horsepower and torque at basically the same rpm points. As you might expect, the smallest cam produced good peak torque, the flattest torque curve, and the best idle vacuum. The middle cam produced 5 more horsepower at the peak with about the same torque curve and a little less vacuum—even so, we'd choose the smaller 214/224 cam over the 224/224 unit.

Although it generated the least idle vacuum, the biggest cam produced the best peak torque and horsepower of all three cams tested: 343.6 lb-ft of torque at 3,900 rpm and 304.3 hp at 5,100 rpm. That's a 15hp gain over the smallest cam with only a small low-rpm torque loss, primarily under 3,500 rpm. As far as we're concerned, the small loss in area under the torque curve would have a marginal effect on driveability and is more than offset by the hefty increase in power at the top end, especially since it produces peak power and torque in the exact same rpm range as the smaller cam. Also note that the 224/234 cam is identical to that used in our El Cheapo car, and we think it runs plenty good enough for daily driving. In this case, we're not afraid to say that bigger really is better.

Here's a neat tip we learned from Westech Performance Group for quick manifold swaps: A blast of Pam cooking spray keeps intake gaskets from sticking.

Our thriftiness during the engine buildup came back to bite us when the water pump that we had found laying on the ground in the junkyard next to the donor car blew off its rear cover during the first dyno pull. A quick trip to NAPA for a $21.99 rebuilt pump put us back in business.

For our engine combo, the single-pattern 224/224 cam was a dog, but the third cam, a dual-pattern grind with 224/234 degrees of duration at 0.050 lift and 0.465-/0.488-inch intake/exhaust lift, found our small-block's sweet spot. After a couple of jetting changes, we made 304 hp at 5,200 rpm and 343.6 lb-ft of torque at 3,900.

Dyno Results

Cam No.1 (PN SUM-K1103): 214/224 at 0.050-inch lift, 0.442-/0.465-inch lift, 112-degree LSA.			Cam No.2 (PN SUM-K1104): 224/224 at 0.050-inch lift, 0.465-/0.465-inch lift, 114-degree LSA.			Cam No.3 (PN SUM-K1105): 224/234 at 0.050-inch lift, 0.465-/0.488-inch lift, 114-degree LSA.		
rpm	lb-ft	hp	rpm	lb-ft	hp	rpm	lb-ft	hp
3,000	322.5	184.2	3,000	317.3	181.3	3,000	311.9	178.2
3,100	323.5	190.9	3,100	319.1	188.3	3,100	321.2	189.6
3,200	325.2	198.2	3,200	320.2	195.1	3,200	324.9	197.9
3,300	332.9	209.2	3,300	327.0	205.5	3,300	328.7	206.5
3,400	337.4	218.4	3,400	335.6	217.2	3,400	329.9	213.6
3,500	338.6	225.7	3,500	332.6	221.6	3,500	335.4	223.5
3,600	339.1	232.5	3,600	334.6	229.4	3,600	336.8	230.9
3,700	338.4	238.4	3,700	335.2	236.1	3,700	338.4	238.4
3,800	343.0	248.2	3,800	335.2	242.5	3,800	342.1	247.5
3,900	**335.6**	249.2	3,900	**339.9**	252.4	3,900	**343.6**	255.2
4,000	333.4	253.9	4,000	336.1	256.0	4,000	338.9	258.1
4,100	332.5	259.5	4,100	336.5	262.7	4,100	341.5	266.6
4,200	333.7	266.8	4,200	334.5	267.5	4,200	336.7	269.2
4,300	330.5	270.6	4,300	329.8	270.0	4,300	337.6	276.4
4,400	328.8	275.4	4,400	327.2	274.1	4,400	335.2	280.8
4,500	324.0	277.6	4,500	325.3	278.7	4,500	331.4	283.9
4,600	316.5	277.2	4,600	322.4	282.3	4,600	326.9	286.3
4,700	317.7	284.3	4,700	317.4	284.0	4,700	324.2	290.1
4,800	310.9	284.1	4,800	312.6	285.7	4,800	324.9	296.9
4,900	307.7	287.1	4,900	310.1	289.3	4,900	319.9	298.5
5,000	301.3	286.9	5,000	304.8	290.2	5,000	317.5	302.3
5,100	297.1	**288.5**	5,100	302.7	**293.9**	5,100	312.5	303.4
5,200	289.7	286.9	5,200	292.4	289.5	5,200	307.3	**304.3**
5,300	283.9	286.5	5,300	287.6	290.3	5,300	292.7	295.3
5,400	277.2	285.0	5,400	276.2	284.0	5,400	280.3	288.2
5,500	268.0	280.7	5,500	268.8	281.5	5,500	272.7	285.5
Average:	318.8	255.6	Average	318.5	255.7	Average	323.6	260.27
Vacuum at 800-rpm idle: 15 in-Hg			Vacuum at 800-rpm idle: 14.2 in-Hg			Vacuum at 800-rpm idle: 12.7 in-Hg		

We played with the jetting a bit for the second cam, which had 10 degrees more intake duration, but we weren't able to gain any power despite moving up two jets sizes in the primaries and secondaries from the stock 67/73 jets to 69/75s. The biggest cam made the best power with 71s in the primaries and 75s in the secondaries. **CC**

SOURCES:

EDELBROCK CORP.
Dept. CC
2700 California St.
Torrance, CA 90503,
310/781-2222
www.edelbrock.com

HOLLEY
Dept. CC
P.O. Box 10360
Bowling Green, NY 42102
502/782-2900
www.holley.com

M&R MACHINE
Dept. CC
811 Airway
Glendale, CA 91201
818/246-4834
www.enginesplus.com

NORTHERN AUTO PARTS WAREHOUSE
Dept. CC
P.O. Box 3147
Sioux City, IA 51102,
800/831-0884
www.naparts.com

POWERHOUSE
Dept. CC
3402 Democrat Rd.
Memphis, TN 38118
800/872-7223
www.powerhouseproducts.com

SUMMIT RACING EQUIPMENT
Dept. CC
P.O. Box 909
Akron, OH 44309
800/230-3030
www.summitracing.com

WESTECH PERFORMANCE GROUP
Dept. CC
11098 Venture Dr., Ste. C
Mira Loma, CA 91752
909/685-4767

Continued from page 9

or retard cam timing with an offset key for the crank sprocket, an offset bushing for the dowel pin in the cam sprocket, or a multiposition chain-and-sprocket set (usually with four degrees advanced and four degrees retarded positions). In any case, you can't tell how much your cam is actually advanced or retarded unless you "degree" it. Today, the generally preferred method of checking (or adjusting) cam timing is to measure (at .050 lift) the opening and closing points of the intake and exhaust in crank degrees before or after the closest top or bottom dead center. For example, the checking specs for the Engle EP25 grind (measured at .050 lifter rise) are:

    Intake Open: 10 BTDC
    Intake Close: 46 ABDC
    Exhaust Open: 50 BBDC
    Exhaust Close: 6 ATDC

For cam checking, TDC is TDC overlap (between the exhaust and intake strokes) and BDC is at the bottom of the intake stroke, 180 crank degrees later. If we add the 10 degrees before TDC when the intake opens, the 180 crank degrees from TDC to BDC, and the 46 degrees after BDC when the intake closes, we get the 236-degree duration (at .050) listed in the chart. We can also see that this cam, set to these specs, would be two degrees advanced. If it were installed straight up, the intake would open eight degrees BTDC and the exhaust would close eight degrees ATDC, the intake would close 48 degrees ABDC, and the exhaust would open 48 degrees BBDC. In the example above, each of these figures is advanced two degrees. See how this works? (This is a single-pattern cam; on a dual-pattern cam the numbers don't come out the same when it is straight up, because the durations of the two lobes differ.) The Engle EP25 is ground two degrees advanced. If you install it by aligning the timing marks, it should reach .050 lift at the points specified above.

One more thing to ponder: If you change the lobe separation angle on a cam, keeping other things equal, where do you install it? Let's say you narrow the lobe centers from 114 to 110 (you can't physically do this, of course—you select a new cam with this lobe separation). If you install it with the intake lobe in the same place, you will be retarding the exhaust four cam degrees, which equals eight crank degrees compared to the first cam. You could also put the exhaust lobe in the original position, which would advance the intake eight degrees. Or, as most cam manufacturers specify, you could split the difference; in this case, narrowing the lobe centers four (cam) degrees would advance the intake four (crank) degrees and retard the exhaust four degrees. Changing lobe centers and cam installation position gives you numerous cam timing variables to play with.

Retarding a cam moves the power range to a higher rpm level; advancing it helps the lower speed ranges. For the street, you don't want to run a cam retarded. Timing-chain stretch is actually a boon for most engines, since the chain will stretch more as rpm increases, allowing the cam to run advanced at low speed, then retard slightly at high speed.

Ron Iskenderian pointed out that you can further advance (about four degrees) a big cam to improve low-speed driveability and bottom-end torque in a street engine, stating, "Advancing a cam has much more of a good effect on low-to midrange than it causes detriment at the top end." Just be sure to recheck valve-to-piston clearance, especially with a big grind, after you advance it, because the intake valve will be opening sooner in relation to piston TDC.

There are many more camshaft basics that we haven't begun to discuss—such as the fact that increasing the rocker arm ratio will increase valve lift and rate of lift without changing duration; or that you can decrease duration on a solid-lifter cam by increasing valve lash, and vice versa. But this is plenty to digest for now. Compare some of this science and theory to the figures in the accompanying cam recommendation charts. Or just pick a cam for a combination like yours and never give it another thought. **HR**

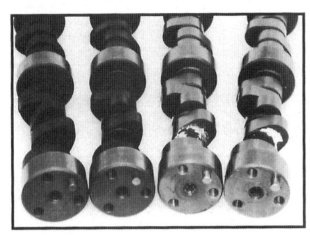

BY MARLAN DAVIS

Photos and graphics by Marlan Davis

Flat-tappet versus roller-tappet? Hydraulic lifter versus solid lifter? Choosing

the best cam for a dual-purpose car can be downright confusing. In theory, given cams of similar duration (at 0.050 tappet-lift), the roller cam should offer more performance; because a roller tappet rolls instead of slides over the cam lobe, it can follow very aggressive lobe profiles with extremely high lifts for a given duration.

A roller cam's opening and closing rates are much faster too. On the other hand, max-performance, professional-level roller profiles are hard on valvetrain components, and the rollers themselves may have long-term driveability problems in a daily driven car. For these reasons, streetable roller cams generally do not take the roller design to its theoretical limits, and while they may still offer improved performance over a flat tappet, the added cost of installing a roller cam and its associated valvetrain components may not always be justified in terms of return on dollars invested.

A similar scenario exists in the hydraulic-versus–solid lifter debate. Because hydraulic lifters pump up at high rpm, theory says that an equivalent solid-lifter cam should make more power over 6,500 rpm because it's able to rev higher before floating the valves; with fewer internal parts, a solid lifter should also be less expensive than a precision hydraulic lifter. However, the unit volume of hydraulic lifter production—including stock applications—is much higher than solid lifters, so in the real world a solid cam

and lifters may cost the same or even more than an equivalent hydraulic cam. Also, solid lifters require periodic adjustment, which can be a hassle.

If you intend to make max power at or below 6,000 rpm, a hydraulic flat-tappet cam is preferred. On the other hand, there's no doubt a solid cam makes the most sense for a car making peak power at or over 7,000 rpm. In terms of 0.050-inch duration, in a typical 350ci small-block, under 240 degrees is clearly flat-tappet territory (unless your car came from the factory already equipped with hydraulic lifters). Over 250 degrees, a roller cam offers a clear performance advantage.

But things get sticky in the transition zones between 6,000-7,000 rpm

and 240-250 degrees at 0.050. Of course, that's precisely the area many hot dual-purpose street cars fall into. With no clear-cut choice, we figured it was time for another *Car Craft* cam comparo.

What We Tested

Four popular Comp Cams camshafts with 0.050-inch durations in the 240-250-degree range were tested on a high-performance small-block Chevy 355ci street engine at Westech Performance. The test profiles included two Magnum cams (a 292H flat-tappet hydraulic cam and a 294S flat-tappet solid cam), an Xtreme Energy hydraulic-roller profile (XR294HR-10), and a Street Roller solid-roller grind (CS 288R-10). All were regular catalog grinds except for the solid roller, which was custom ordered because the current catalog lists no solid rollers in our specified duration range. (See the table for complete specifications.)

The 9.7:1 test engine was based on a GM factory ZZ4 crate engine upgraded with Federal Mogul

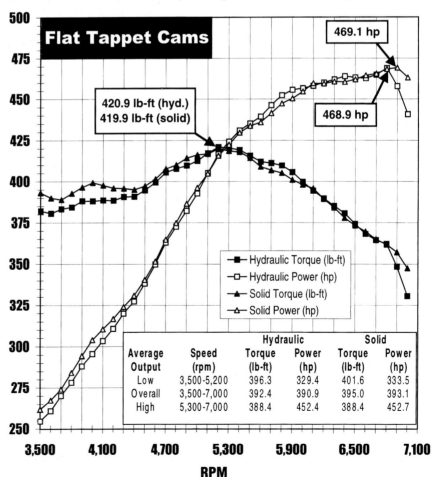

Flat Tappet Cams

420.9 lb-ft (hyd.)
419.9 lb-ft (solid)

469.1 hp

468.9 hp

- ■ Hydraulic Torque (lb-ft)
- □ Hydraulic Power (hp)
- ▲ Solid Torque (lb-ft)
- △ Solid Power (hp)

Average Output	Speed (rpm)	Hydraulic		Solid	
		Torque (lb-ft)	Power (hp)	Torque (lb-ft)	Power (hp)
Low	3,500-5,200	396.3	329.4	401.6	333.5
Overall	3,500-7,000	392.4	390.9	395.0	393.1
High	5,300-7,000	388.4	452.4	388.4	452.7

RPM

The test engine used an Edelbrock Victor Jr. intake with a 2-inch spacer, a Demon 750-cfm double-pumper carb, MSD ignition components, Hooker '55-'57 Chevy headers (1¾-inch primaries with 3-inch collectors), 3-inch duals, and Flowmaster mufflers.

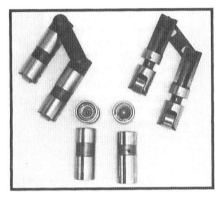

Comp sent us these lifters, clockwise from top left: PN 853-16 hydraulic-roller lifters with permanently attached guidebars; new PN 888-16 lightweight solid roller lifters with detachable guidebars; PN 813-16 "piddle-valve" solid flat lifters, and PN 858-16 High Energy hydraulic flat lifters.

The shape of a roller-cam lobe profile (left) is more square in comparison to the rounder flat-tappet lobe (right). That offers more area under the curve, in theory, improving performance.

lightweight LW2256F forged pistons and Air Flow Research aluminum heads with 2.02-/1.60-inch valves and 190cc intake runners. Among the best-flowing street heads available, the AFR castings produce good power with a milder cam than is normally required for a given combination. On a long-time Westech test mule with over 600 runs on it, leak-down did not exceed 4 percent on any cylinder. All tests were run on Torco 76 92-octane unleaded pump gas using a Demon 750 carb with optimized jetting. The Demon's fuel curve was so stable,

only minimal changes were needed. In all cases, the engine ran best with 36 degrees of ignition advance.

Flat Tappet Cams

Comp's Magnum 292H hydraulic and 294S solid flat-tappet grinds are designed to deliver equivalent performance. To achieve this, the 294S is rated at 2 degrees more advertised duration, 4 degrees more 0.050-inch tappet lift duration, and 0.15-inch more valve lift (with 1.5:1 rockers) than the 292H. We say *rated* because most aftermarket companies' published specs for solid cams don't account for valve lash: When set to Comp's recommended 0.022-inch intake/exhaust (hot) valve-adjustment spec, the actual hot running valve lift was really only 0.503 inch. Similarly, a solid's advertised and 0.050 duration is also about 8-12 degrees less than the published specs.

Despite their zero lash setting, hydraulic lifters do experience some collapse on the top end, so the real-world specs are also slightly less than published, but only by 2-3 degrees and 0.006 inch at most. Therefore, the exact amount of additional lift and duration that must be added to a solid grind to produce results equivalent to an otherwise identical hydraulic depends on the particular design of the respective profiles.

Comparing the two profiles on the dyno validated Comp's claims of more or less functional equivalence (see graph). Both cams produced virtually the same peak torque (420.9 lb-ft for the hydraulic and 419.9 lb-ft for the solid, both at 5,200 rpm) and power (468.9 hp at 6,800 rpm for the hydraulic versus the solid's 469.1 hp at 6,900). Overall, low and high average numbers were more or less identical, with the solid having a slight advantage, especially down low.

Although the tests terminated at 7,000 rpm, a developing trend over 6,800 rpm is clearly apparent: Due to hydraulic lifter pump-up, the power and torque numbers fall off much quicker than with the solid-lifter cam, which maintains output past its 6,900-rpm peak. Cars with optimized gearing typically need to shift 400-600 rpm past the power peak to achieve the best quarter-mile e.t.'s, a task that, in this case, clearly cannot be accomplished with the hydraulic cam and the supplied High Energy lifters. Comp does offer improved performance Pro Magnum hydraulic lifters (PN 858-16 for Chevy V-8s) that may delay pump-up, but they were not evaluated in this test series.

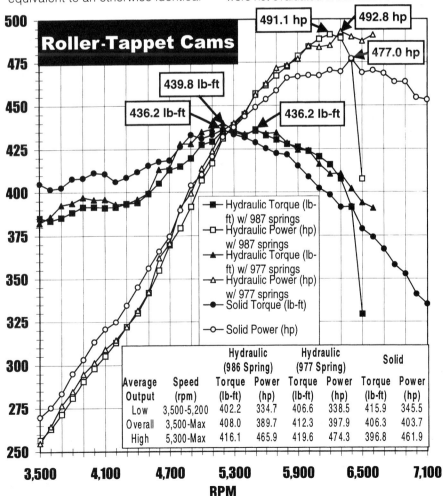

Roller-Tappet Cams

491.1 hp 492.8 hp 477.0 hp

439.8 lb-ft 436.2 lb-ft 436.2 lb-ft

- Hydraulic Torque (lb-ft) w/ 987 springs
- Hydraulic Power (hp) w/ 987 springs
- Hydraulic Torque (lb-ft) w/ 977 springs
- Hydraulic Power (hp) w/ 977 springs
- Solid Torque (lb-ft)
- Solid Power (hp)

Average Output	Speed (rpm)	Hydraulic (986 Spring)		Hydraulic (977 Spring)		Solid	
		Torque (lb-ft)	Power (hp)	Torque (lb-ft)	Power (hp)	Torque (lb-ft)	Power (hp)
Low	3,500-5,200	402.2	334.7	406.6	338.5	415.9	345.5
Overall	3,500-Max	408.0	389.7	412.3	397.9	406.3	403.7
High	5,300-Max	416.1	465.9	419.6	474.3	396.8	461.9

RPM

Hydraulic Roller Cam

The solid-versus-hydraulic roller comparison is less clear-cut. Comp's solid Street Roller cam is a single-pattern design (its intake and exhaust lobes have the same lift and duration). Besides being a dual-pattern grind, the Xtreme Energy hydraulic roller cam also represents the latest technological generation; its intake and exhaust lobes not only have different lift and duration, they also have optimized and discreet profiles and opening and closing rates.

The Xtreme Energy camshaft turned in great peak power numbers. Installed with Comp's recommended No. 987 valvesprings, it churned out 436.2 lb-ft of torque at 5,500 rpm and 491.1 hp at 6,200—but beyond 6,200 rpm, power plummeted into the basement. This points out the major drawback of hydraulic roller lifters: Their great weight in comparison to other lifter designs causes early valve float. One apparent solution is to install stiffer valvesprings. Westech upgraded the 987 springs to the stouter No. 977 springs included with the solid-roller cam. This extended the upper rpm range while pumping up the low-end torque slightly and broadening both the overall torque and power curves. Torque now peaked at 439.8 lb-ft at 5,200 with 492.8 hp at 6,400.

Comp Cams cautions that going with stiffer-than-recommended springs shortens the life expectancy of hydraulic roller lifters, which are currently based on OEM technology that never envisioned sustained high-rpm usage. Running stiff springs with a hydraulic roller can also cause the lifters to bleed down if the vehicle sits overnight; while not detrimental to longevity, the result is momentary lifter clatter in the morning. One possible workaround is to use the manufacturer's standard recommended springs in conjunction with a hydraulic roller rev-kit offered by Air Flow Research.

While the hydraulic-roller clearly outperformed the hydraulic flat-tappet cam downstairs, the solid flat-tappet grind had slightly better low-end torque numbers. Although hydraulic-roller profiles are more aggressive overall than flat-tappet profiles, initial acceleration off the base circle is slightly slower. This can degrade low-end performance. Achieving the same bottom-end performance as an equivalent flat-tappet cam generally requires selecting a hydraulic roller profile with 4-6 degrees less 0.050-inch tappet lift duration.

Solid Roller Cam

Besides being a single-pattern cam based on older technology, the solid

Interference between Comp's hydraulic-roller lifter guidebars and the higher lifter bosses of our test engine's factory roller-cam–style block required using the stock GM roller lifters and hold-down spider that bolts to the late block's lifter bosses. Overall lifter weight was about equal, so performance wasn't affected.

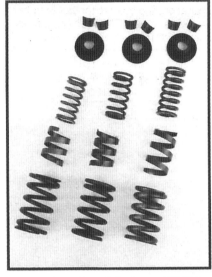

Valvesprings, from left: Comp PN 986, 987, and 977 are all dual-spring-with-damper assemblies but are progressively stiffer. All use the same steel retainer (PN 740-16) and 10-degree locks (PN 611-16). Production heads must be machined to accept them.

roller was also effectively milder than the hydraulic roller due to the previously discussed valve-lash factor, which made it behave like a slightly smaller cam. Nevertheless, as a solid cam, it wanted to rev like there was no tomorrow. Although the solid roller made *only* 477 hp at 6,400 rpm, it was still developing 453.1 hp at 7,100 rpm—the highest rpm tested.

But what's really amazing is this cam's torque production. Although the 436.2–lb-ft, 5,200-rpm peak was a tad less than the hydraulic roller, low-end torque output was clearly superior to any of the other cams tested. Thanks to the fat torque curve, some computer simulations indicate this cam may actually produce better e.t.'s than the higher-horsepower hydraulic roller in a heavy car with an automatic trans.

Why so much torque? Comp Cams'

Billy Godbold explains that a solid cam exhibits "artificial initial acceleration." Although the lash factor delays the cam opening point, when that point is reached, the cam "snaps off the basecircle and reacts faster." The same effect can be seen (albeit to a lesser extent) in the solid flat-tappet profile's slightly superior low-end torque output in comparison to the equivalent hydraulic flat-tappet grind.

Which Do You Choose?

I prefer the solid flat-tappet cam over the hydraulic flat-tappet because it better maintains the powerband upstairs. But if you're just profiling and don't mind short-shifting, the hydraulic delivers about the same performance under the power peak.

The solid roller and solid flat-tappet have the same 0.050 duration; while peak-to-peak numbers show little

Comp Cams Camshaft Specs

Type	Series	Grind Number	Part Number	Valve Lift w/ 1.5:1 Rockers (Int./Exh.)	Valve Lash (Int./Exh.)	Dur. at 0.050" Tappet Lift (Int./Exh.)	Rated Cam Timing at Tappet (hydraulics at 0.006" lift, solids at 0.015" lift)				
							Adv. Dur. (Int./Exh.)	Intake (Opens/Closes)	Exhaust (Opens/Closes)	LDA	Lobe CL (Int./Exh.)
Hyd. flat	Magnum	292H	12-213-3	0.507"/0.507"	Zero	244°/244°	292°/292°	40° BTDC/72° ABDC	80° BBDC/32° ATDC	110°	106°/114°
Solid flat	Magnum	294S	12-224-4	0.525"/0.525"	0.022"/0.022"	248°/248°	294°/294°	41° BTDC/73° ABDC	81° BBDC/33° ATDC	110°	106°/114°
Hyd. roller	Xtreme Energy	XR294HR-10	12-443-8*	0.540"/0.562"	Zero	242°/248°	294°/300°	41° BTDC/73° ABDC	84° BBDC/36° ATDC	110°	106°/114°
Solid roller	Street Roller	CS 288R-10	12-707-8	0.550"/0.550"	0.020"/0.020"	244°/244°	288°/288°	38° BTDC/70° ABDC	78° BBDC/30° ATDC	110°	106°/114°

*Change the 12- prefix to 8- if ordering for an '87-and up factory roller-cam–equipped engine using factory roller lifters, late-type timing chain, and factory thrust-plate..

variation, the solid roller yields better average results. This conforms to expectations that a roller cam offers more "area under the curve." Considering that a solid-roller cam and valvetrain can cost up to three times the price of a flat-tappet cam, the incremental gains in this range from a street-roller solid cam may not justify the added expense. On the other hand, the Xtreme Energy hydraulic roller is worth an extra 20 hp and 15 lb-ft compared to the flat-tappets, and if your car is already equipped with factory hydraulic roller lifters, the expense is reasonable because the original lifters can be reused.

Disregarding price, deciding whether to go with a hydraulic roller or a solid-roller in this performance range is a tough call. If you want a fat torque curve, the advantage lies with the solid-roller. If you want to maximize power, the new-tech Xtreme Energy gets the job done with stiffer springs but at the price of shortened lifter life. This leaves us wondering how an Xtreme Energy solid-roller cam would perform. If the observed trends remain constant, such a grind would improve the top-end performance without sacrificing bottom-end torque. A combo like that would make it easy to get 500 hp with decent heads and induction, mild compression, and a virtually stock bottom-end. Xtreme Energy solid-roller cams weren't available when we ran the test in early 1999 but will be on the market by the time you read this. **CC**

Valvespring Specs								
Part No.	Type	OD	ID	Seat Load (lbs)	Open Load (lbs)	Coil Bind	Rate (lbs/in)	Used with Test Cams
986	Dual with Damper	1.437"	0.695"	120 @ 1.800"	290 @ 1.250"	1.100"	309	292H, 294S
987		1.473"	0.700"	130 @ 1.800"	325 @ 1.250"	1.150"	355	XR294HR-10
977		1.460"	0.700"	160 @ 1.850"	440 @ 1.250"	1.200"	467	XR294HR-10, CS 288R-10

Valve lash on the flat and solid roller lifters was set according to the manufacturer's published recommendations. Comp's Pro Magnum full-roller steel rocker arms were used for durability. At this performance level, Comp's catalog recommends Magnum roller-tip rockers.

This lifter-valley tray from Automotive Specialties (704/786-0187) really came in handy during the cam flog. Roller cams require significantly different pushrod lengths than flat-tappet cams to preserve correct valvetrain geometry.

There's just enough clearance between the tall roller-block lifter bosses to wiggle the solid-roller lifters and their removable guidebars into place without head removal. Comp's new lifter features greatly improved longevity, thanks to a wide oil band and directional groove that feeds extra oil directly to the roller.

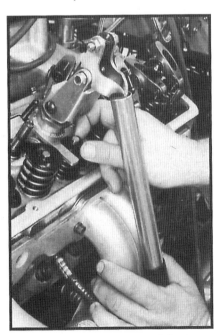

Available from various aftermarket sources including Powerhouse Products (800/872-7223), valvespring micrometers simplify establishing the correct installed height.

Spring swaps were accomplished without removing the heads using a lever-type valvespring compressor and compressed air.

SOURCES

AIR FLOW RESEARCH
Dept. CC
10490 Ilex Ave.
Pacoima, CA 91331
818/890-0616
http://airflowresearch.com

COMPETITION CAMS INC.
Dept. CC
3406 Democrat Rd.
Memphis, TN 38118-1577
800/365-9145
www.compcams.com

WESTECH PERFORMANCE GROUP
Dept. CC
11098 Venture Dr., Ste. C
Mira Loma, CA 91752-1192
909/685-4767

power

Choosing the Right Street Cam: It's All in the Timing

By Dave Emanuel

"**Y**ou've got to remember that it's the total combination that counts." If you read last month's installment you'll remember that engine builder Ralph Thorne of RMS Racing Engines made that statement with respect to selecting and reworking cylinder heads for a street engine. Thorne's point was that for optimum performance, port configuration must be matched to an engine's intake manifold, headers, and cam profile. Keeping the overall combination in mind is even more important when choosing a camshaft. Despite the reams of literature produced by various cam grinders, over-camming remains a problem. According to "The High-Lift Brothers," Herb Kutz and Randy Stacy of Cam Dynamics, "We can't tell you how many cam recommendations we make in a day—it's a bunch—but it's amazing how many guys call up and just want the biggest cam we have. We try to talk them out of it, but some

guys just won't listen. Then, they call us back and ask why the car won't idle below 1200 rpm, why the power brakes don't work, and why the engine doesn't make any power until it gets to 4000 rpm. The answer is simple—they've got *too much camshaft*. But that's not what they want to hear."

That brings up an interesting question. How does an increase in cam timing relate to an engine's power curve? More specifically, as duration is lengthened, what is the payoff, where does it occur, and what does it cost? Obviously, there are many answers, depending upon engine design, displacement, degree of modification, and difference in cam profiles. But to develop a representative answer, we passed a number of Cam Dynamics Energizer grinds through one of RMS Racing Engines' mail order Chevrolet street powerplants and a Super-Flow 901 computerized dyno collected all the pertinent data for subsequent analysis.

The Energizer grinds were selected because they're excellent cams created through state of the art design tech-

Prepared by RMS Racing Engines the 350ci Chevy produced a maximum of 400 horsepower when equipped with a Cam Dynamics 284 Energizer—that represented a 120-hp gain over a stock configuration.

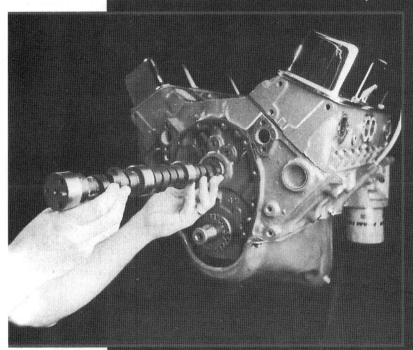

power

niques, and that design is consistent throughout the entire line. Therefore, lift and duration are the only cam-to-cam variables, as ramp design and valve opening velocities are consistent.

The last point is important because of a relatively new term known as "hydraulic intensity." Simply stated, hydraulic intensity is the difference between cam duration at .004-inch lobe lift (the Society of Automotive Engineers' standard for *gross duration*) and .050-inch lobe lift (the industry standard for *net duration*). Current cam designs offer a hydraulic intensity of 50 to 56 degrees compared to 74 to 80 degrees for most older cam profiles. Although hydraulic intensity is of little importance once an engine gets up to speed, it does play a vital role in determining low-speed performance characteristics. As hydraulic intensity is reduced while net duration remains constant, idle characteristics, off-idle response, and low-speed performance improve *without* any reduction in top-end power. Consequently, when testing the effect of camshaft duration, (and attendant lift) hydraulic intensity must be the same for all cams used or the results will be skewed by lobe design differences.

Before studying the accompanying charts, bear in mind that a cylinder head change was performed midway through the tests. This was necessary because net duration of the 272 Energizer was only 216 degrees which would have resulted in excessive cylinder pressure had it been run with an 11:1 compression ratio. The 272 and 278 comparison was performed with heads having 76cc combustion chambers, 1.94-inch intake and 1.50-inch exhaust valves. During the Energizer 278/284 comparison, early model 492 castings with 64cc chambers, 2.02-inch intake and 1.60-inch exhaust valves, were in place. The respective compression ratios were 9.8:1 and 11.3:1.

The most surprising thing about the test results, compared to the cam specifications, is that even across a 12-degree change in duration, a 1½-point drop in compression ratio, and a reduction in valve size, peak torque fell only 28 lbs./ft. (from 400 to 372) while losing *92* horsepower (from 400 to 308)! Think about that for a moment. The cylinder

ENERGIZER 278 vs. 284

278 ENERGIZER

RPM	Corrected Torque (lbs./ft.)	Corrected HP
2750	358	188
3000	371	212
3250	383	237
3500	391	261
3750	398*	284
4000	398	303
4250	391	317
4500	387	332
4750	387	350
5000	380	362
5250	370	370
5500	360	377*
5750	334	366
6000	300	342

284 ENERGIZER

RPM	Corrected Torque (lbs./ft.)	Corrected HP	Power Gain Torque	HP
2750	358	188	0	0
3000	368	210	-3	-2
3250	379	234	-4	-3
3500	395	263	4	-2
3750	401*	286	3	2
4000	398	303	0	0
4250	396	321	5	4
4500	389	333	2	1
4750	385	348	-2	-2
5000	391	372	11	10
5250	383	383	13	13
5500	376	394	16	17
5750	366	400*	32	34
6000	346	396	46	54

* Refers to peak power levels
Test performed with 64cc, 492 heads, with 2.02/1.60-inch valves, 11.3:1 compression, and Holley 300-19 intake.

head change was responsible for a loss of 18 lbs./ft. of torque and 36 horsepower, so the overall reduction in cam timing alone accounted for losing a theoretical 10 lbs./ft. of torque and 56 horsepower. But check out what happened when the RMS Racing Engines-prepared test motor was fitted with a stock cam, intake manifold, and Quadrajet—it produced 371 lbs./ft. of torque but only 280 horsepower—a loss of an additional 28 horsepower but negligible torque.

All this data is wonderful, but in the words of SuperFlow's inimitable Harold Bettes, "What do 'dat mean?" As a first step toward answering that question, consider that compared to a stock con-

PRESSURE TRACES

An engine's compression ratio is another consideration that must be taken into account when choosing a camshaft. The 272 Energizer would have spelled disaster when teamed with an 11:1 compression ratio because of its impact on cylinder pressure. Short duration camshafts are typically designed to operate in conjunction with mechanical compression ratios of 8.0:1 to 9.5:1. As such, intake valve closing is scheduled to occur shortly after bottom dead center. This comparatively early closing event partially compensates for a low mechanical compression ratio by trapping more of the intake charge for the piston to compress, building higher cylinder pressure. But when early intake valve closing is combined with a high mechanical compression ratio, the resulting pressure can easily induce detonation. At the other end of the cylinder pressure spectrum, late intake valve closing (as found in longer duration cams) when teamed with a low-compression ratio, causes extremely low cylinder pressure and a loss of power.

You can't tell a cam by its cover. Externally, the three Energizer cams tested looked identical, but as the horsepower charts demonstrate, there is a big difference in performance.

To save time during cam swaps, a Bo Laws two-piece timing cover was installed. It eliminates the need to drop the oil pan when changing cams. Peterson external wet-sump oil pump is visible at right.

power

figuration, in its as-delivered form, the RMS test engine produced a whopping *120* horsepower increase, but only a *25* lbs./ft. bump in torque. This points out an often-missed point on street engine modifications. The basic engine configuration (bore, stroke, connecting rod length, cylinder head design) establishes a peak torque plateau level; alterations in cam timing, induction and exhaust system efficiency primarily move the position and length of that plateau with respect to engine speed. Second, and to a lesser degree, they either raise or lower torque output, thereby altering the plateau level. And as the plateau is moved up the rpm scale, it also tends to result in an attractive bulge in the upper end of the horsepower figures, while killing the low-rpm torque.

In comparing the performance of the three Energizers, what's most noticeable is that lengthening duration didn't significantly bolster peak torque readings, but it did widen the curve. As demonstrated by the accompanying dyno charts, the torque levels produced by the 284 and 278 Energizers are very close from 2750 to 4750 rpm, but at 6000 rpm, the shorter cam is down 46 lbs./ft., which translates into a drop of 54 hp. Not surprisingly, (with the low-compression heads installed) the 272 and 278 Energizers are closely matched in torque output, but only from 2750 to 3750 rpm. The curves begin drifting apart 1000 rpm sooner than those corresponding to the 278/284 comparison.

What isn't apparent in these charts is the loss in low-speed torque that accompanies each step up in cam duration. But from manifold vacuum readings at idle, it is clear that a duration increase of six degrees does slightly crimp the power curve from idle to 2750 rpm. In essence, whenever a cam change is made, torque is subtracted from one end of the power curve and added to the other. The most desirable situation is one in which the payback exceeds the cost—that is, you give up 15 lbs./ft. of torque at the low end but get back 35 or 40 at the top of the usable rpm band. Or, if you've already installed "too much" cam and are returning to reality, you don't give up anything, but your engine produces an additional 50 to 60 lbs./ft. of torque where you can use it.

Another interesting aspect of these tests is the difference in the torque curves. The 284 Energizer didn't begin

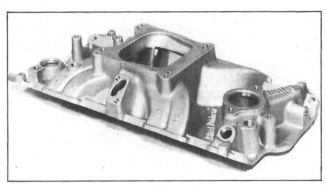

A Holley 300-19 Street Dominator was used throughout the tests so that the intake did not restrict top-end horsepower during tests of the 284 Energizer. However, for street driving, a dual-plane manifold is a much better choice, as it increases midrange torque.

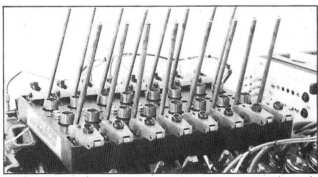

Cam Dynamics' organizer tray made life easier during cam swaps. With a place for everything, and everything in its place, time wasted searching for mislaid parts was eliminated.

Fel-Pro's Printoseal intake manifold gaskets proved to be the hot tip for maximum sealing with minimum fuss. The silicone beads around port openings sealed perfectly and eliminated the need for repeated applications of RTV. The gaskets retained their integrity through the numerous manifold drills.

ENERGIZER 272 vs. 278

272 ENERGIZER

RPM	Corrected Torque (lbs./ft.)	Corrected HP
2750	335	175
3000	350	200
3250	365	226
3500	372*	248
3750	363	259
4000	352	268
4250	358	290
4500	350	300
4750	340	308*
5000	321	305
5250	303	303
5500	284	297
5750	256	280

278 ENERGIZER

RPM	Corrected Torque (lbs./ft.)	Corrected HP	Power Gain Torque	HP
2750	341	179	6	4
3000	357	204	7	4
3250	367	227	2	1
3500	380*	253	8	5
3750	376	268	13	9
4000	372	284	20	16
4250	372	301	14	11
4500	367	314	17	14
4750	361	327	21	19
5000	348	332	27	27
5250	341	341*	38	38
5500	318	333	34	36
5750	283	310	27	30

Test performed with 76cc chambers, 1.94/1.50-inch valve cylinder heads with 9.8:1 compression, and Holley 300-19 intake.

CAMS AT A GLANCE

CAMSHAFT	DURATION (degrees) NET	GROSS	HYDRAULIC INTENSITY (degrees)	LIFT (inches)
284 Energizer	284	228	56	.480
278 Energizer	278	222	56	.467
272 Energizer	272	216	56	.454

power

to seriously outrun the 278 version until after 4750 rpm. However, in the 272/278 comparison, the longer cam begins flexing its muscles 1000 rpm sooner—at 3750 rpm—indicating that with the 272 Energizer, the cam itself was the primary power restrictor—its duration is so short that the valves aren't off their seats long enough to allow maximum flow through the cylinder heads, intake manifold, and headers.

This illustrates the importance of matching a camshaft to other engine components; fitting cylinder heads with larger valves and greater flow capacity would have produced no power gain with the 272 cam because it wasn't even allowing the small valve heads to reach maximum flow capacity. Conversely, installing the 284 Energizer without concurrently switching to freer breathing heads would have been equally non-pro-ductive because the small valves and ports would be too restrictive in the rpm band where the cam is designed to produce maximum power. What's more, the "big cam, small head" mismatch is doubly bad because there's no payback—you give up low-speed power without realizing an increase at high rpm.

When all the technospeak and data is reduced to practical application, they indicate that a 350 cubic inch engine with free flowing cylinder heads and a mechanical compression ratio of 11.0-11.5:1 likes a cam with 228-232 degrees of net duration. According to Thorne, "We have a lot of customers who want a solid, reliable 400 horsepower street engine, so we usually recommend one of our high-compression versions equipped with a 284 Energizer and dual-plane manifold. It's an excellent combination when the engine is linked to a 4-speed gearbox, or a torque converter with a 2500-to-3000 rpm stall speed. It's mild enough to provide good low-speed driveability, yet also delivers a bunch of horsepower.

A 278 Energizer would produce slightly better off-idle response, but would cost 23 horsepower at the top-end. While that isn't a good trade-off for a Camaro, Nova, or Corvette with a manual transmission, the milder cam does make sense if a car is fitted with a stock torque converter and/or high (low numerically) rear end gearing. This is especially true in heavier vehicles.

Top a 350 with low-compression, small valve heads and the 278 Energizer becomes the heavy hitter, supplying a 33 hp advantage over the 272 cam. However, even though the Energizer cams offer excellent idle characteristics for their respective durations, if idle quality is a major concern, the 272 will be the better choice.

Now for the fly in the ointment. Displacement is also part of a total engine combination and the components that work best in a 350 won't provide the same results in a 305. Most cam manufacturers recommend a maximum duration of 216-218 degrees (at .050-inch lift) for street engines displacing 305 inches or less.

That's it for our three-part street engine series. If at first all this information is imposing, go back over the first two parts, digesting the information bit by bit. Then the next time you're in the market for a cam, manifold, or cylinder head swap, you'll know just what to do. Ⓖ

The cam degreeing operation can be a chore, but it is a relatively simple operation with a Cam Dynamics "Tune-A-Cam" kit. All the Energizers checked out on the numbers.

A SuperFlow 901 dyno produces an almost overwhelming amount of data. By monitoring a variety of air and fuel temperatures, flow rates and pressures, a reason can usually be found for aberrations in the power curve.

As in the previous tests, a Holley 650 cfm electronic carburetor was mounted atop the intake manifold. Console control of the fuel mixture allowed easy optimization of the air/fuel mixture.

SOURCES

RMS Racing Engines
Dept. CC
5005 Highway 78
Lilburn, GA 30247
404/979-5942

Bo Laws Automotive
Dept. CC
1015 W. Church Street
Orlando, FL 32805
305/425-9007

Cam Dynamics
Dept. CC
460 Walker Street, Bldg. A-18
Holly Hill, FL 32017
904/258-8845

Fel-Pro Incorporated
Dept. CC
7450 N. McCormick Boulevard
Skokie, IL 60076
312/761-4500

CAM SELECTION BASICS

Camshaft Power Tuning

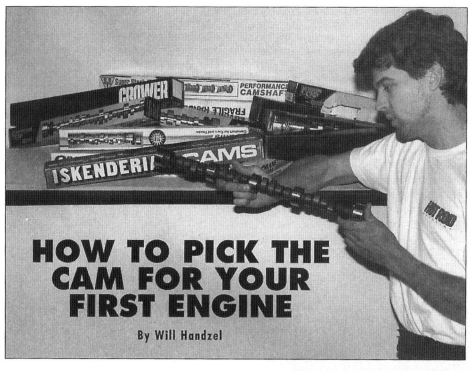

HOW TO PICK THE CAM FOR YOUR FIRST ENGINE

By Will Handzel

To make choosing a cam for your engine less of a guessing game and more of a decision based on knowledge and experience, the basics of camshaft technology have been explained thoroughly in the last few How It Works tech articles. If you are building your first engine or are trying a new engine-parts combination, you are gaining experience as you go, and you may need to rely on a cam company's experience to select the proper camshaft. It is important to know what information the cam company will need so it can give you a good recommendation. You'll probably also have questions to ask of the cam company tech people after they have recommended a cam. These tips will make the purchasing experience much easier and get you the right cam for your application the first time.

WHAT IS NEEDED TO SELECT A CAM?

To get the engine performance you want, you need to provide the proper information to a cam company so it can recommend a camshaft for your engine combination. The most common engine built by the first-time hot rodder is a small-block—whether it's a Chrysler, Ford or GM engine. The engines are in the 300- to 400ci range and have similar traits. Here, we have used the 350ci Chevy, the most common of these engines, as our example. And to make this example a real-world version of a first-timer's engine, we've used as many factory components as possible to keep the cost down (cast crank, stock rods, pistons, valvetrain) and added an aftermarket intake, carb and headers. Custom machine work should be kept to a minimum to keep down the cost and complexity. This engine will cost from $1000 to $3500 to build, depending on how much scrounging you do to get the parts together. It can make between 250 to 300 horsepower at around 5000 rpm and about 350 lbs-ft of torque at 3500 rpm.

The following information should be determined long before you call the cam company.

INFORMATION	EXAMPLE
Engine design	350ci small-block Chevy with perf. cast-iron cylinder heads
Intended rpm range	idle to 5500
Usage	street/strip, rough idle okay
Carburetor	Holley 600-cfm vacuum secondaries (part No. 0-1850)
Intake manifold	Weiand dual plane (part No. 8004)
Exhaust	1⅝-inch headers
Compression ratio	9:1
Weight of vehicle	3500 pounds
Transmission	stock automatic & 2500-stall converter
Rearend gear	3.50:1
Tire height	28 inches

This list makes a rough outline for a common engine combination that will have enough power to be fun and will be durable and inexpensive to build.

Using the above information as an example, we called a few of the top aftermarket camshaft suppliers to get

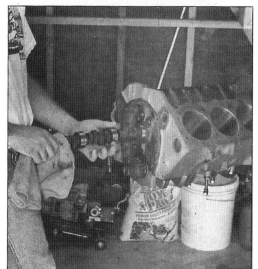

The cam is the brains of the internal combustion engine, so picking the correct camshaft is critical to ending up with the engine you want. The common mistake is to pick a cam that is way too aggressive. These cams are designed for engines that will operate in the high-rpm ranges, but they are often chosen for a street-driven engine because of the rumpity-rump idle quality—at the sacrifice of driveability and torque.

their camshaft recommendations. Their suggestions are listed below in Table 1.

Almost all of the cams recommended will have a stock-type idle with vacuum at idle being near the stock 18 to 22 inches of mercury (in/Hg). Since many hot rodders want their hot rods to sound the part, an idle with more lope to it might be desired. To get a stock-type engine to do this, a cam with more valve overlap—which can be achieved through either more duration or tighter lobe-separation angle—will be needed. Idle quality will decrease with the increase in duration or decrease in lobe-separation angle because the valve overlap causes weird vacuum signals at the carburetor, making the fueling inconsistent at idle. So if you are running a stock automatic transmission and converter and vacuum-assisted equipment (power brakes, for example), a lopey idle might not be what you want.

The reason most want the lopey idle is because race cars usually have a rough idle—and we want our cars to look and sound like race cars. The reason race cars have that rough idle is because the engines used are designed for high-rpm operation. To get the air/fuel mixture in the engine and the exhaust out at high rpm, race cars need a camshaft with as much lobe lift and as many degrees of duration as possible and a narrow lobe-separation angle, which results in valve overlap. A cam like this has extremely poor idle quality—the engine won't run below 2000 rpm—but idle quality doesn't really matter on a race car.

For the low-buck street guy to get a lopey idle and see an increase in power without a drastic decrease in driveability, he needs a cam with a lobe-separation angle of 110 degrees—the same lobe lift as recommended earlier—and duration numbers of about 218 degrees at .050 inch lifter movement. This would be roughly equal to 270 degrees of "advertised" duration. The reason you want to stay away from an increase in lobe lift is because of the changes you'll need to make to a stock engine if the cam has more than approximately .460 inch lift. Any more than that and the valvesprings could begin to suffer coil bind, the retainers may hit the valve-stem seal, or the valve may hit the top of the piston. If you are trying to build a low-dollar engine, making changes to the valvetrain will run up the cost of the engine considerably.

This brings up another critical point regarding camshaft selection. The cam is just one component in the very intricate valvetrain system. Making a drastic change in the camshaft will most likely require changes throughout the valvetrain. As an example, for the cams recommended in Table 1, many of the cam companies recommend new valvesprings, rocker arms and pushrods. (The cams

MANUFACTURER	CAM NAME	PART NO.	FLAT TAPPET LIFTER	ADV DURATION (degrees)	
				int	exh
COMP CAMS	Magnum	12-210-2	hyd	268	268
CRANE	Max Vel.	HMV-272-2	hyd	272	284
CROWER	267-HDP	00240	hyd	267	272
EDELBROCK	Perf Plus	2102	hyd	278	288
ERSON	Hi Flow	110321	hyd	284	284
GM	Perf. pts	24502476	hyd	2	2
ISKY	Super Cam	201262	hyd	262	262
LUNATI	Hi Eff.	06105	hyd	260	260
MANUFACTURER	dur at .050 inch (degrees)		valve lift (w/1.5 rockers) (inches)		
	int	exh		int	exh
COMP CAMS	218	218		.454	.454
CRANE	216	228		.454	.480
CROWER	210	216		.445	.445
EDELBROCK	204	214		.420	.442
ERSON	218	218		.472	.472
GM Perf. pts	212	222		.435	.460
ISKY	208	208		.435	.435
LUNATI	210	210		.441	.441
MANUFACTURER	lobe lift (inches)		lobe sep. (degrees)	recommended installation	
	int	exh			
COMP CAMS	.303	.303	110	cam grnd 4 degrees adv.	
CRANE	.303	.320	112		
CROWER	.297	.297	112	adv. 4 deg.	
EDELBROCK	.280	.295	112	straight up	
ERSON	.314	.314	108	adv. 2-4 deg.	
GM Perf. pts	.290	.307	112.5	install with intake lobe C/L at 109 degrees	
ISKY	.290	.290	108	adv 3 degrees	
LUNATI	.294	.294	110	4 degrees grnd in	

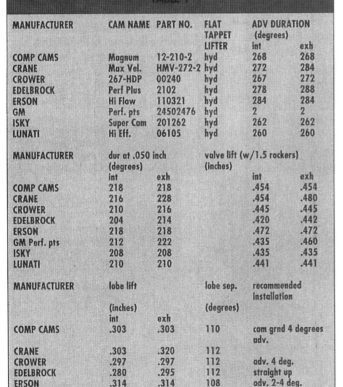

As you can see, there are no exact cam specs for a specific application. Every cam company has its own theories on what lobe profile, duration, lift, lobe-separation angles and installed location are needed to make power from an engine. Understanding why these differences exist will come as you learn more about camshaft technology.

When a high-performance camshaft is selected, always check clearances in the rest of the valvetrain before final assembly of the engine. Using a cam with increased lobe lift or higher ratio rockers can result in valve lift that is greater than the amount the valvespring can compress. This is called valvespring bind (or coil bind) and can be corrected by using different springs or eliminating shims that take away spring height.

When installing a camshaft, many prefer to degree the cam in. This describes the checking procedure that engine builders run through to make sure the camshaft is properly installed in relation to the crank position.

usually come with new lifters, and some come with new timing-chain sets.) They don't recommend these products just to make money off of them. The stock valvesprings often need to be shimmed to obtain the minimum acceptable seat pressure, whereas the new springs will need much less in the way of shims. When you shim a valvespring you take away compressed height, something a stock spring is very close to running out of when you use an aftermarket cam.

There are several problems with using stock rocker arms: They aren't designed for increased-lift cams, they can be worn from usage, and manufacturing variations can result in rockers with different ratios. Most of the aftermarket cam companies have competitively priced rockers that are designed and manufactured for street/strip applications. With these rockers, different pushrods may be required to maintain the proper valvetrain geometry to essentially keep the rocker tip working directly over the center of the valve stem throughout its full range of motion. As you can see, one change can mean making modifications to the entire system to make the whole package work properly.

Building your first engine is very

exciting. Often, it is done on a strict budget with many used parts, and the car that the engine is going into will be driven daily. If you keep in mind the usage the car will see, and also consider future improvements to the drivetrain (possibly going from the 3.50 gear you have to a 4.10, or installing a 3000-stall converter), you can design an engine package that can be easily upgraded in the future. Cam companies can help ensure that your money is well spent if you provide them with enough correct information to make those decisions. Get some of the cam companies' catalogs and read, or perhaps study, the pages on cam basics. The cam companies want you to be an educated buyer so you are a happy customer, and they try to ensure this by putting as much information in the catalog as possible. The more you know, the better the decisions you make with your money will be, which will most likely get you the engine combination you want—a strong-running, durable small-block. **HR**

Sometimes, special offset-ground pin bushings or crank keys are used to advance or retard the cam in relation to the crank. If the cam is advanced four degrees, the valves open and close earlier in relation to crank rotation, but nothing else changes since the cam has not been changed. On a street engine, a cam is often installed advanced four degrees as this helps low-end torque when running a high-performance cam.

SOURCES

Competition Cams, Inc.
Dept. HR07
3406 Democrat Rd.
Memphis, TN 38118
901/795-2400

Crane Cams
Dept. HR07
530 Fentress Blvd.
Daytona Beach, FL 32114-1210
904/252-115

Crower Cams & Equipment Company
Dept. HR07
3333 Main St.
Chula Vista, CA 91911
619/422-1191

Edelbrock Corporation
Dept. HR07
2700 California St.
Torrance, CA 90503
310/781-2222

Erson Cams
Dept. HR07
550 Mallory Way
Carson City, NV 89701
702/882-6600

GM Performance Parts
contact your local
GM Performance Parts dealer

Isky Racing Cams
Dept. HR07
16020 S. Broadway
P.O. Box 30
Gardena, CA 90247-9990
213/770-0930

Lunati Cams
Dept. HR07
P.O. Box 18021
Memphis, TN 38181-0021
901/365-0950

Last month's "How It Works" story gave you the basics of the four-stroke cycle, describing the motion of the intake and exhaust valves in relation to the piston moving up and down in the cylinder. This month we'll examine the parts, collectively known as the "valvetrain," that work with the camshaft to open and close those valves at the right time. Our goal is not to baffle you with cam design philosophy, but to help those of you who have never had an engine apart understand how the

CAMSHAFT AND VALVETRAIN

By David Freiburger

parts function, how cam timing works, and some of the basic terminology. There are many different valvetrain layouts, including overhead cams, multiple valves, and multiple cams. The overwhelming majority of hot rod engines use a single, in-block cam, pushrod-operated overhead valves, and two valves per cylinder, so that's what we'll discuss. For more valvetrain information, check out the "Trial Separation" and "Tech Inspection" stories this month, or the "How To Select a Cam" story in the May '92 issue. Also, cam manufacturers' catalogs are an excellent source of cam tech info!

1 HOW IT WORKS

This is the camshaft, or simply, the cam. From the look of the lobes, which are also called eccentrics, you can see why we sometimes call the cam a bumpstick. In a

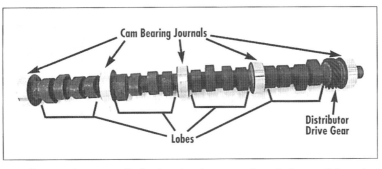

single-cam engine with two valves per cylinder (one intake, one exhaust), there will be twice as many lobes as there are cylinders; this camshaft has 16 lobes, so it's for an eight-cylinder engine. Most camshafts from older V8s will also have a distributor drive gear and an extra eccentric to drive the mechanical fuel pump.

The camshaft slides into the cylinder block from the front, and the round bearing surfaces shown in the previous photo rest on bearings that are pressed into the block, allowing the cam to rotate freely. The cam bearings are not always the same size—often the front bearing has the largest diameter and they get progressively smaller toward the back of the block. On this new Corvette LT1 engine you can see that the cam also drives the water pump.

The camshaft is driven off the crankshaft, usually by a chain called a timing chain. Timing belts and gear drives are also used. In any case, the cam always rotates at half of crank rpm. It takes two full rotations of the crankshaft, and therefore one rotation of the cam, to complete the four-stroke cycle. It is very important that the camshaft be installed in proper relationship to the crankshaft so that the cam opens the valves at the correct time during the piston's stroke. Custom tuning the relationship of the cam timing to the crank timing is what we call degreeing the cam. The timing gears are usually marked with dots that you line up in order to install the cam "straight up," or without degreeing.

With the cam in the block, the lifters, also called tappets or cam followers, can be installed. Lifters are machined

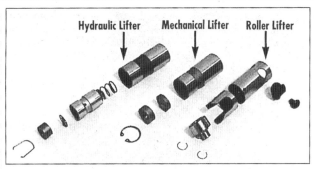

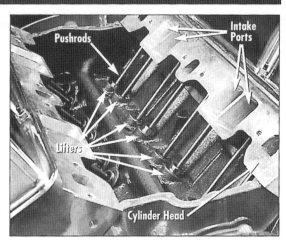

cylindrical pieces of metal that ride on the cam lobes. This photo shows three disassembled lifters. The first (left) is a hydraulic, or "juice" lifter that fills with oil to act as a shock absorber to eliminate clearance in the valve-train—note the plunger and spring. Hydraulic lifters are quiet and don't require a valve-lash clearance. The middle lifter is a mechanical, or "solid" design. These are generally used in high-rpm applications, where hydraulic lifters are not as good, at the cost of increased valvetrain noise and more frequent maintenance due to the necessity of valve lash. The hydraulic and solid lifters shown are the flat-tappet type, but the last lifter is a roller that has a small wheel that contacts the cam lobe. Roller lifters can be either hydraulic or mechanical, and are used in performance applications where a very fast rate of lift is not compatible with a flat-tappet lifter.

In the lifter valley of the engine block there are machined holes called lifter bores. The lifters ride in these bores and touch the cam lobes, which are located just under the lifter bores. Each lifter is free to move up and down in the bore as it follows the contour of the rotating cam lobe. The pushrod then transfers this up-and-down motion to the rocker arm.

Now we progress into the components installed in the cylinder head, the most important of which are the valves. This photo shows some of the valve terminology you'll need to know. The exhaust valve is almost always smaller than the intake valve. How well the valves seal the combustion chamber is very important to engine efficiency. This is accomplished with accurate machining on the valve seat in the cylinder head and on the valve

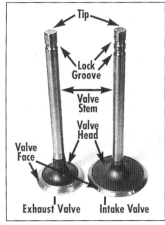

face. This is what is called the valve job. A stock-type valve job sometimes uses a wedge effect between the valve (with a 45-degree angle) and the head (with a 46-degree angle) to ensure a good seal. Hardened valves don't use this interference fit. If you've heard of three-angle or five-angle valve jobs, these are performance modifications to better radius the valve and seat with more angles for improved airflow. Valve seat contact area is also very important in order for the valve to pass heat into the cylinder head. Exhaust valves can reach over 1400 degrees Fahrenheit!

This is the bottom-side, or cylinder-side view of the combustion chamber, which is the side the valves are installed from. The stem of the valve slides through the valve guide, allowing the valve heads to seal the intake and

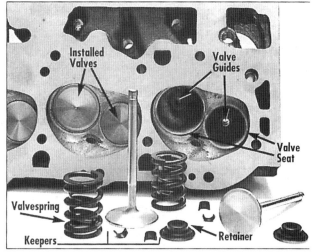

exhaust ports. On the top side of the head, the valvesprings and retainers slide over the valve stems. By compressing the spring with a special tool, you can put keepers in the lock grooves on the valve and release the spring. The keepers are little wedges that hold the assembly together. The springs hold the valve shut and keep the lifters in contact with the cam. Not shown are the valve-stem seals that go around the valve stem to keep oil from leaking down the valve guide and into the cylinder.

STUFF YOU OUGHTA KNOW

Coil Bind: If a high-lift cam is installed with stock valvesprings, or if the wrong valvesprings are used, it's possible to compress the valvesprings so far that the coils stack up and the spring becomes a solid chunk of metal, usually leading to a bent pushrod or broken rocker arm. This can also be caused by too little installed height. At max lift there should be at least .060 inch between the middle spring coils.

Duration: The amount of time in crankshaft degrees that the cam holds a valve off its seat. Duration also dictates the total lift possible due to the rate-of-lift limitations of the lifter.

Installed Height: The distance from the bottom of the valvespring retainer to the valvespring seat surface. Shims are used to make sure that all the springs have the same installed height as the shortest spring on the engine.

Lash: The clearance between the end of the rocker arm and the tip of the valve stem is called lash. With a mechanical cam, a lash of between .010 inch and .030 inch is required to account for the expansion of parts due to heat.

Lift: The maximum distance in inches that the valve is lifted off the seat. Cam lift multiplied by the rocker-arm ratio determines valve lift.

This is the top side of the head with the valves, springs, retainers, and keepers assembled. Look carefully and you can see the keepers around the valve stem. The rocker studs mount the rocker arms, and pushrod guide plates are used in performance applications to keep the pushrods properly lined up. Specially hardened pushrods must be used with guide plates.

This is a small-block Chevy stud-mounted rocker arm and pivot. Note that the rocker arm provides a mechanical advantage, usually between 1.4:1 and 1.7:1, most

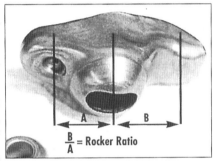

$$\frac{B}{A} = \text{Rocker Ratio}$$

commonly 1.5:1. By doing this, the lift supplied by the cam can be increased at the valve. A cam with a lift of .375 inch at the lobe can be increased to .5625 inch at the valve if you use a 1.5:1 rocker arm. Cam manufacturers advertise lift at the valve and specify what rocker arm was used to attain this number.

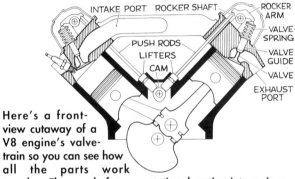

Here's a front-view cutaway of a V8 engine's valvetrain so you can see how all the parts work together. The camshaft turns rotational motion into reciprocating motion that opens and closes the valves at the proper time.

In this photo you see how the pushrod, activated by the lifter on the cam lobe, moves up and down to transfer motion to the rocker arm, which is a lever mounted on a fulcrum. This fulcrum is usually either a stud with a pivot or a single shaft that holds all eight rockers on one cylinder head of a V8 engine. The other end of the rocker arm presses on the end of the valve stem, thereby opening and closing the valve as the rocker moves up and down.

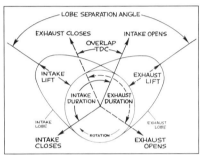

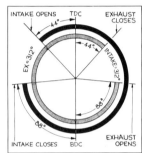

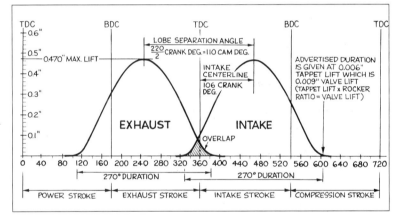

For the sake of simplicity, last month's story on the four-stroke cycle gave the impression that valves open exactly at TDC or BDC. Actually, valves open before you'd expect them to and close after you'd expect them to. Let's make some general observations, beginning with the exhaust stroke. As the piston is on its way down the cylinder from the power stroke, the exhaust valve opens before the piston reaches BDC, allowing residual combustion pressure to begin evacuating the cylinder. Now the piston moves up the cylinder, forcing the rest of the exhaust fumes out. But the intake valve begins to open before the piston reaches TDC and before the exhaust valve closes. This allows the exiting exhaust fumes to create a vacuum that begins to draw the air/fuel mixture into the cylinder before the exhaust valve closes and the piston moving down the cylinder finishes the job. To make things even more confusing, the intake valve remains open even after the piston passes BDC and begins to rise for the compression stroke. The three diagrams above are different ways of expressing the valve opening-and-closing process we've described here. One of the clearest is the graph of the 270 Magnum cam from the Competition Cams catalog. Remember that the degrees given are crankshaft degrees. **HR**

Lobe Separation Angle: The angle between the centerlines of the intake and exhaust lobes. This is ground into the cam and cannot be altered without a new cam. See this month's "Trial Separation" story for more information.

Overlap: The amount of time in crankshaft degrees that the intake and exhaust valves are open simultaneously. Degrees of overlap can be determined by adding the intake opening and exhaust closing timing degrees.

Profile: The combination of lift, duration, and lobe separation angle provided by the camshaft. The profile of the cam lobe is not necessarily the same on both the intake and exhaust lobes.

Rate of Lift: How fast the valve is opened, or how many inches of lift are achieved per degree of crankshaft rotation.

ROLLER CAM HARDWARE

By David Freiburger

When Chet Herbert introduced roller tappet camshafts to racing in 1950, he established an upper echelon of performance hardware that continues to carry that hard-core mystique. The roller tappet design liberates cam lobe specs from the restrictions inflicted by flat tappets. Rollers use a very small tappet-to-lobe contact area that allows a more radical rate of lift per degree of cam rotation. This has traditionally been reserved for racers who combine frightful lift and duration with the abrupt opening and closing rates offered by roller cams. While rollers used to be strictly race track fare, more recent use of hydraulic rollers by both GM and Ford has allowed them to migrate to the street where they can provide less or equal duration than the stock cam, but with far greater lift at all points beyond valve opening. Increasing lift without extending duration boosts torque without affecting the rpm band of the engine. In addition, roller cams reduce tappet-to-cam friction, which is a major source of heat in flat-tappet engines. Street rollers are more feasible today than ever before, but there are some hardware requirements you should know prior to setting your sights on a street roller cam.

VALVETRAIN

Because roller cams offer greater rate of lift and total lift, valve float becomes imminent and stiffer valvesprings are needed. These new valvesprings often have a larger-than-stock diameter that demands cylinder head machining, and the increased spring rate will require heavy-duty screw-in studs. On some engines, special pushrod lengths will be needed to accommodate taller roller lifters or an altered cam lobe base circle, and some roller lifters may require oil galley modifications to the engine block. Neither is the case with Chevy V8 engines. Hydraulic roller cams have inherent rpm limitations that reduce the severity of valvetrain expenditure, but hardened pushrods, pushrod guideplates, and extruded

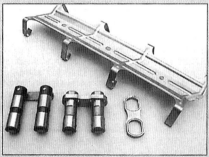

Compare Competition Cams' linked-together retrofit Chevy rollers on the left with the shorter rollers, retainers, and lifter valley tray typical of Fords and GMs.

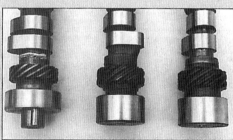

This photo represents different roller cam philosophies: (*from left to right*) an O.E.M.-type one-piece 1050 billet Ford roller; Competition Cams' austempered ductile iron retrofit Chevy roller with integral distributor drive gear; and Crane's 8620 billet Chevy roller with a pressed-on iron distributor drive gear.

These are the three options for fuel-pump pushrods that can be used with billet cams: (*from left to right*) Crane's brass-tipped pushrod and Competition Cams' lightweight ceramic and roller tipped rods. The threaded piece to the right is a locator that screws into the front of the block to keep the roller pushrod lined up. Keep in mind that a stock fuel pump pushrod could cause wear on a steel roller cam.

Chevy's part No. 10456413 is a coated distributor drive gear used in new GM roller cam engines, and the gear used in new Ford small-blocks is a Motorsport part No. M-12390F. These gears should be compatible with aftermarket billet cams, which would solve the hassles of short-lived bronze gears.

aluminum roller rocker arms should be considered mandatory for solid roller cams. Since roller cams don't have taper-ground lobes, a cam thrust button and an appropriate timing chain cover must be used to prevent forward cam walk.

Remember that late-model Ford and GM hydraulic roller cams will not work in older blocks due to taller lifter bore height and lifter retaining trays used in the new engines. Late-model cams also don't have fuel pump lobes. Crane Cams and Competition Cams offer hydraulic roller retrofit kits for big- and small-block Chevys, and Crane has kits for small-block Fords.

DISTRIBUTOR DRIVE GEAR

Standard gray-iron cam blanks can't handle a narrow roller-to-lobe contact area combined with high spring pressures. As a result, most aftermarket roller cams are ground from flame-hardened 8620 steel billet. Copper coating between the lobes prevents the flame hardening from making the cam brittle. Unfortunately, the metallurgical mismatch between a billet camshaft and a stock iron distributor drive gear will destroy the distributor gear within a few thousand miles, and it usually wipes out the cam gear in the process. A steel distributor gear will last longer than an iron distributor gear, but is guaranteed to hash the cam gear if it does fail. The compromise has been to use a soft manganese bronze distributor gear that wears out quickly without damaging the cam gear, and is easier and cheaper to replace than the cam. Today's bronze alloys last much longer than the ones used in the '60s, but the inconvenience still keeps some roller cams off the street. However, recent innovations have solved this problem for Chevy and Ford owners who select hydraulic roller cams.

Crane's line of retrofit Chevy hydraulic rollers have an 8620 steel billet core with a pressed-on iron drive gear so you can use them with your stock iron distributor gear. The Competition Cams retrofit rollers use even newer technology with an austempered ductile iron cam. The austempering process provides hardness control such that the lobes have a higher Rockwell rating than the drive gear, so an iron distributor gear must be used.

The '87-and-newer GM roller engines use a 5160 steel billet cam matched with a Chevy steel distributor gear (part No. 10456413) that has a special coating to protect the cam. The specific material used to coat this gear is not common knowledge, but it is suspected that this gear is compatible with aftermarket steel rollers. There have been no long-term tests to verify this, but this could be the solution to fast-wearing bronze gears. Unfortunately, this gear can't be used with MSD distributors due to their larger .500-inch distributor shaft. MSD distributors come with an uncoated steel gear.

The current O.E.M. Ford roller cams are made of 1050 steel and are compatible with the Ford Motorsport steel distributor gears (part No. M-12390F). This Motorsport gear works well with Crane's 8620 steel cams and Competition Cams' 1050 steel roller cams, but a standard iron gear should be used on austempered ductile iron camshafts.

LONGEVITY MODS

Whether you use an iron, steel, or bronze gear, there are steps you can take to extend the life of a Chevrolet distributor gear. First, use white grease to confirm that the cam is making full contact with the distributor gear teeth. Check this whenever you install a new distributor or intake manifold, or if the heads, intake, or block have been milled. Mismatch problems can be corrected with an oversize gear or shims between the distributor and the intake manifold. Shims and oversize gears are available from MSD.

The next consideration is oiling. Cut a .030-inch by .030-inch groove in the bottom ring of your Chevy distributor, creating an oil source to lube the distributor gear and prolong its life. Scuff the gear with sandpaper or Scotch-Brite to help retain oil on its surface. Be aware that high-volume and/or high-pressure oil pumps cause extra load on the distributor gear.

Regardless of which roller cam you choose, a little forethought and the right parts can reward you with not only a strong street powerplant but miles of hassle-free performance, as well. **HR**

The bronze distributor gear on the left is much softer than the stock iron gear on the right and is designed to sacrifice itself rather than chew up the cam gear.

Roller cams require a cam thrust button to prevent forward cam walk. This is Crane's trick needle bearing cam button and bolt-locking retainer kit.

A Dremel MotoTool or a similar grinder may be used to cut a .030-inch by .030-inch groove in the bottom ring of a Chevy distributor to improve distributor gear oiling.

Solve your roller "campatability" problems with a complete cam package such as this Ford retrofit CamPonent kit from Crane. Everything you need will be included in the kit.

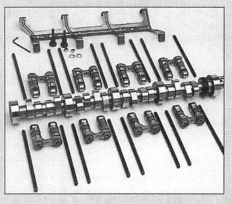

SOURCES

Competition Cams
Dept. HR06
3406 Democrat Rd.
Memphis, TN 38118
901/795-2400

Crane Cams
Dept. HR06
530 Fentress Blvd.
Daytona Beach, FL 32114
904/252-1151

Ford Motorsport Performance Equipment
Dept. HR06
17000 Southfield Rd.
Allen Park, MI 48101
313/337-1356 (tech hotline)

MSD Ignition
Dept. HR06
1490 Henry Brennan Dr.
El Paso, TX 79936
915/857-5200

TECH BOOK

TRIAL SEPARATION

HOW CAMSHAFT LOBE SEPARATION ANGLE CAN IMPROVE POWER

By Dave Emanuel

Sometimes we all need a little change in our lives. The same could be said for that camshaft that pumps the valves open and closed in your street engine. What was once state of the art is now obsolete. The bump and grind has changed, and knowledgeable hot rodders are now taking a closer look at their camshafts in search of more power. Because a street engine must be able to make good power and perform well during the boulevard ballet, compromise is the name of the game.

With respect to camshafts, compromises are required to achieve the optimum tradeoff between low-speed torque and high-rpm horsepower. During the

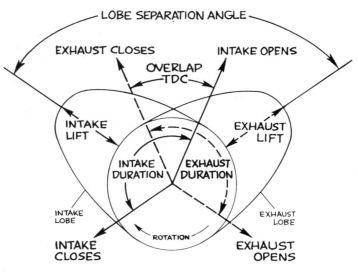

cam selection process, lift and duration specifications are the most commonly used criteria for determining a camshaft's suitability for a particular application. Of course there are compromises—as duration increases, so does the rpm at which peak torque and peak horsepower occur. And as the torque peak climbs the rpm scale, low speed performance and driveability suffer.

At this late date, enough data has been accumulated that most camshaft manufacturers and engine builders can

easily select a cam that is reasonably suited to a particular engine and its intended use. But there's another facet of camshaft design that knowledgeable hot rodders usually dial into the selection equation before making a choice— lobe separation. Also called lobe displacement angle, this term refers to the distance, in *camshaft* degrees, between the centerline of the intake lobe and centerline of the exhaust lobe of the same cylinder. In days of old, overlap was the operative term for referencing the relationship of intake and exhaust lobes. Overlap—the period during which a cylinder's intake and exhaust valves are open at the same time—occurs as a piston approaches and leaves top dead center, and extends from the exhaust stroke of one cycle to the intake stroke of the next.

Although the term overlap is still used occasionally, it has been largely replaced by "lobe separation" as a means of referencing the positional relationship of intake and exhaust lobes.

And for good reason; the lobe separation angle can remain constant when duration is altered, overlap typically does not. So comparing the overlap of Cam "A" to that of Cam "B" may or may not be a true picture of both cams' performance potentials, depending upon the difference in durations. Viewed from a different perspective, two camshafts with the same lobe separation

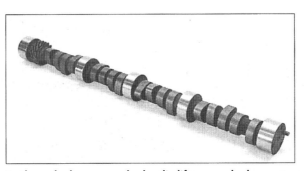

The 355ci small-block that was prepared by Grimes Automotive Machine performed flawlessly during the course of the dyno tests. It produced a maximum of 375 horsepower and 396 lbs-ft of torque with the third pair of test cams. That's impressive performance considering cam duration at .050-inch lift was only 222 degrees.

To the naked eye, one hydraulic-lifter cam looks pretty much like another. However, when installed in an engine, each cam plays a somewhat different tune—even when lift and duration specifications are identical. Tightening lobe separation can produce significant power differences.

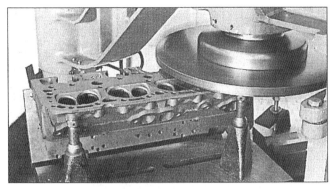

For the two milder pairs of cams, the engine was equipped with stock production 882 cylinder heads. After being surfaced, the heads were treated to nothing more than a three-angle valve job. Fitted with Manley stainless 1.94/1.50-inch intake and exhaust valves, these heads provide adequate airflow capacity for up to about 350 horsepower.

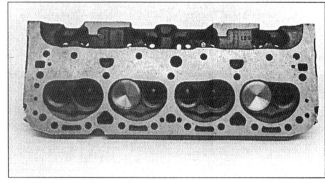

The third pair of cams had over 220 degrees of duration (at .050-inch lift), so larger valves and smaller combustion chambers were required. A pair of 492 castings with 2.02/1.60-inch intake and exhaust valves and 68cc combustion chambers took the place of the 76cc, 882 "smog" heads when these cams were tested.

can have dramatically different overlap specifications, depending upon duration.

When a cam designer wishes to fine tune the power curve produced by a cam, he will frequently alter lobe separation while leaving lift and duration unchanged. As lobe separation is tightened (i.e. 112 degrees to 110 degrees), overlap increases; as separation is widened (i.e. 108 degrees to 112 degrees), overlap decreases.

Consequently, with all other specifications being the same, a cam with 106 degrees of lobe separation will have more overlap than one with 110 degrees. This is frequently seen when comparing similar cams for street and oval track applications. Most engine builders prefer 106 degrees of lobe separation when a camshaft is destined for an oval track engine as opposed to the 110 to 112 degrees of separation that characterize a street cam. Tighter separation typically results in improved mid-range torque, which is highly desirable in short track racing because it propels a car off the corners better. It's for this same reason that drag cars equipped with automatic transmissions typically call for camshafts with tighter lobe separations than their manual-transmission counterparts. The automatic cars typically leave the line with the engine at a lower rpm, hence the need to maximize mid-range torque.

Of course, compromises are involved. Tighter lobe separation results in a rougher idle and loss of idle manifold vacuum, two characteristics that should be minimized (relative to cam duration) to enhance driveability of a street engine. So although it might seem as though some of the milder oval track and drag race cams would be applicable to street engines, they're typically not because of their poor idle and low-speed

Part of the Grimes formula for success is a properly installed Fluidampr. (Note the installation tool and absence of a hammer.) Grimes has found a significant increase in crankshaft life whenever a Fluidampr is installed on a high-performance or race engine.

Although stock rocker arms are more than adequate for mild camshafts such as the ones tested, they're not noted for ratio accuracy. Consequently, Competition Cams Magnum roller rockers were used. Their 1.52:1 ratio guarantees that actual and theoretical valve lift will coincide.

qualities.

All this theory is wonderful, but it needs to be translated into practical applications. To that end, Garry Grimes, from Grimes Automotive Machine, lent his assistance. The test vehicle used for the camshaft comparisons was a 350 Chevy built by the crew at Grimes' shop. The short-block consisted of standard high-performance street engine components—a four-bolt–main block, forged crankshaft, reconditioned stock rods, Manley forged pistons, and Total Seal Gapless rings. For the first two tests, the block was topped with a pair of 882 head castings with Manley stainless 1.94/1.50-inch intake and exhaust valves. The 76cc chambers resulted in a 9.5:1 compression ratio. During the third test, a pair of 492 castings with 68cc chambers, 2.02/1.60-inch intake and exhaust valves was installed. Compression ratio for that combination was 11.0:1. Both pairs of cylinder heads utilized Competition Cams Magnum

rocker arms. The 882 castings were equipped with Champion V12YC spark plugs while the 492 heads had Champion J12YC plugs in place.

The remaining hardware included an Edelbrock Performer aluminum dual-plane intake manifold, Holley 750-cfm carburetor, Stewart Components Stage 1 water pump, a Grimes-prepared HEI distributor, B&B aluminum valve covers, and 1⅝-inch diameter Hedman headers. Considering the amount of dyno thrashing the engine was going to get, Garry elected to install a Fluidampr to ensure optimal engine repeatability and reliability.

After the engine was broken-in on Grimes' dyno, a number of power runs were made with one of the two mildest cams to be tested. Its specifications were: net duration (at .050-inch lift) 205 degrees intake, 214 exhaust; lift .430-inch intake, .450-inch exhaust; lobe separation 112 degrees. Then the cam was swapped for one that was identical

HOW LOBE SEPARATION AFFECTS TORQUE

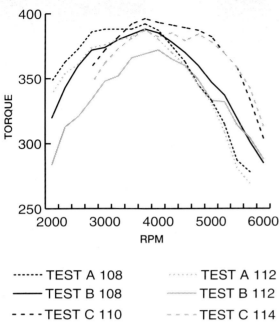

TEST A 108 ------- 　　TEST A 112 ·······
TEST B 108 ——— 　　TEST B 112
TEST C 110 - - - - 　　TEST C 114 — ·· —

It may not be all that glamorous, but for a small-block Chevy, this is one of the most cost effective wet sump systems available—a stock Chevy Z/28 windage tray and oil pan.

except for lobe separation, which was 108 degrees. At first glance, the results appeared to be pretty much as expected; with 108 rather than 112 degrees of lobe separation, the engine produced more mid-range torque. But the cam with tighter lobe separation also produced more top end horsepower. That's exactly opposite of what was expected. Although the difference was only two horsepower at the peak (5000 rpm), above that point, the horsepower advantage of the cam with tighter lobe separation continued to increase. Each cam was tested several times and the data always repeated, so the test data is definitely accurate.

While we were attempting to determine the whys and wherefores of the test results, we moved on to the second pair of cams. (Like all the other cams used in these tests, they were Grimes proprietary grinds.) Specifications for these cams were 218-degree intake, 228-degree exhaust net duration (at .050-inch lift) .460-inch intake and .480-inch exhaust lift. As with the first pair, one cam was ground with 108 degrees of lobe separation, the other with 112 degrees.

This time, the results were much more dramatic. With the 108-degree cam, the engine produced 16 lbs-ft more peak torque and five more peak horsepower. But that only tells part of the story. From 2000 to 2750 rpm the 108-degree cam produced *at least* 30 lbs-ft more torque at every data point; from 3000 to 4000 rpm, the advantage was between 13 and 26 lbs-ft. And even though the cam with tighter lobe sepa-

ration did produce more peak horsepower, the curves crossed at 5750 rpm.

Now the test results from the first pair of cams started to make sense. The duration of those cams was too short to allow the one with wider lobe separation to display its advantage. When rpm moved into the range where wider lobe separation should have been advantageous, the engine couldn't pump enough air through the cylinders to capitalize on it—the valves weren't open long enough. Lengthening duration by 13 degrees eased the airflow deficit enough to allow the power curves to cross at 5750 rpm. Following along the lines of this test, lengthening duration again should result in two horsepower curves that more closely resemble the textbook ideals.

Since the plan was to conduct the tests with legitimate street engine combinations, a cylinder head change was completed prior to testing the next pair of cams. With the 882 heads, compression ratio was 9.5:1, which is suitable for the first two pairs of cams. However, the third pair of cams had a net duration of 222 degrees and .470-inch lift; that's not a particularly good match for 9.5:1 compression ratio because cylinder pressure is at the low end of the scale. Another consideration is that with duration exceeding 220 degrees, stock heads don't offer sufficient airflow capacity to accommodate the camshaft's potential. In place of the 882 "smog" heads, the Grimes Automotive crew installed a pair of 492 iron castings with 68cc combustion chambers, and 2.02/1.60-inch intake and exhaust valves. The heads were ported in the bowl area and finished with a three-

angle valve job.

The third pair of cams was ground with 110 and 114 degrees of lobe separation because those specifications are typical of street cams available with more than 220 degrees of net duration. Most manufacturers feel that with duration in this range, anything less than 110 degrees of lobe separation would trade off too much idle vacuum. Another factor that differentiated the third pair of cams from the previous two was its single-pattern profile. The milder cams were dual pattern grinds with longer exhaust than intake durations. The switch to single pattern cams was made to determine if a change in lobe separation produced dramatically different results when intake and exhaust duration are the same. Judging by the

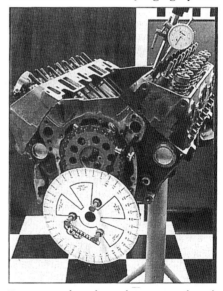

To ensure that the valves opened and closed at the correct time, each cam was degreed-in, using opening and closing points at .050-inch lift. This practice should be part of every camshaft installation.

MANIFOLD VACUUM AT IDLE (NO LOAD)		
CAM DURATION: 205/214		
Lobe Separation:	112	108
rpm	in/Hg	in/Hg
600	16	15
700	17	16
800	18	18
900	19	18.5
1000	20	19
CAM DURATION: 218/228		
600	11.5	11.5
700	13	12.5
800	14	14
900	15	15
1000	16.5	16

test data, it does not.

Results from the third series of tests also met expectations. Again, tighter lobe separation delivered more mid-range power, while wider lobe separation resulted in a higher top-end horsepower reading. This time, the crossover in the horsepower curves occurred at 5250 rpm (below the power peak) and the cam with wider lobe separation continued to enjoy a horsepower advantage up through 6000 rpm.

The results of these tests point to the fact that with respect to lobe separation, less is more. That being the case, it would appear that every cam manufacturer should be grinding street cams with either 108 degrees or 110 degrees of lobe separation. But remember the "c" word—compromise. With the first pair of cams (205 degrees intake duration at .050-inch tappet lift), tighter lobe separation translated to a drop of a full 1 inch of mercury (in/Hg) at idle (see chart). An "acceptable" amount of idle vacuum is a judgment call, so obviously, some manufacturers feel that the power gained by relatively tight lobe separation angles doesn't justify the loss of vacuum. Experience has also shown that wider lobe separations tend to be more forgiving when a camshaft is not properly matched to the engine in which it's installed.

Another aspect of lobe separation's impact on power is that when separation angle is narrowed (with no change in duration) the intake valve closes earlier. In turn, that traps more air in the cylinders at lower engine speeds, resulting in higher cylinder pressure and more mid-range torque. Of course, there are limits to the degree to which intake valve closing points can be moved; if it's too early, cylinder pressure can become excessive or there will be a serious degradation in top-end performance.

What it all boils down to is a matter of determining the optimum compromise for a particular engine. As a general rule (and there are probably a hundred

During the test session, six cams were put through the engine in rapid succession. Every cam performed flawlessly and no lobes went flat—a testimony to the effectiveness of using cam assembly lube in conjunction with proper break-in procedures.

exceptions), whether it's a small-block or big-block, GM, Ford, or Chrysler, a high-performance V8 street engine appears destined to be blessed with the ideal compromise if lobe separation is 108 degrees if net duration is less than 220 degrees. A lobe separation of 110 degrees seems to be ideal when net duration is between 220 and 228 degrees, and 112 degrees is advantageous with net duration above 228 degrees. In essence, with progressively shorter cam duration, tighter lobe separation (within limits) can be tolerated without significant loss of manifold vacuum.

The "ideal" compromises determined by the previous test results are not iron-clad by any means. This isn't a politician's way of weaseling out of making a definitive statement, it's simply an

One of the keys to obtaining maximum performance from any cam is establishing proper valvetrain geometry. Ideally, the tip of the rocker should be exactly centered on the valve tip (as shown here) when the valve is at half its total lift. In the test engine, milling of the block deck surfaces and heads required the use of custom length (.050 inch shorter than stock) pushrods to achieve the desired geometry.

A Holley 750-cfm 4010 model four-barrel and Edelbrock Performer intake manifold are ideally suited to supply the air and fuel needs of a healthy street engine. The dual-plane design accentuates mid-range torque, yet maintains excellent horsepower in the usable rpm range.

acknowledgement that each engine combination may react somewhat differently to a given set of conditions. For example, all things being relatively equal, a 305-cubic-inch engine may not be as happy as a 350 with a cam having the same lobe separation. Although absolute specifications may vary depending on the engine, the *trend* of tighter lobe separation producing more mid-range torque is consistent across the board. Keep that in mind next time you order a camshaft and you'll be a lot closer to the ideal compromise. **HR**

SOURCES

B&B Performance Products
Dept. HR02, 5709 Limestone Rd.
Wilmington, DE 19808; 302/239-5013

Champion Spark Plugs
Dept. HR02, P.O. Box 910
Toledo, OH 43661; 419/535-2442

Competition Cams
Dept. HR02, 3406 Democrat Rd.
Memphis, TN 38118; 901/795-2400

Edelbrock Corp.
Dept. HR02, 2700 California St.
Torrance, CA 90509; 310/781-2222

Fel-Pro, Inc.
Dept. HR02, 7450 N. McCormick Blvd.
Skokie, IL 60076-8103; 708/674-7700

Grimes Automotive Machine
Dept. HR02, 215 Tidwell Dr.
Alpharetta, GA 30201; 404/475-5272

Hedman Manufacturing
Dept. HR02, 9599 W. Jefferson Blvd.
Culver City, CA 90232; 310/839-7581

Holley Carburetor Division
Dept. HR02, 11955 E. Nine Mile Rd.
Warren, MI 48090; 313/497-4000

Stewart Components
Dept. HR02, P.O. Box 5523
High Point, NC 27262; 919/889-8789

Total Seal Gapless Rings
Dept. HR02, 2225 W. Mountain View #6
Phoenix, AZ 85021; 602/678-4977

Vibratech Performance
Dept. HR02, 537 E. Delavan Ave.
Buffalo, NY 14211; 716/895-5404

Pick the item that doesn't fit the set: A) Ronald Reagan, B) three-piece suits, C) Lincoln Towncars, D) right-wing philosophy, or E) street cam profiles. If you picked cam profiles, then you're a rodder who needs to read this story. All the items listed have a common thread: conservatism. While cam selection isn't usually associated with quadra-door road pillows or pinstriped business attire, it should be approached with less flamboyance than rodders generally display. We're not suggesting that three pages can tell you everything about the ideal cam for your application, but we'll give you the information required to make the right decision.

THE SEARCH FOR CAM-A-LOT

Before you buy a cam, you must first determine the intended use: street legal, street/strip, or race only. Once you've figured that out, cam manufacturers will normally ask you a series of questions to determine the right profile for your car. Race applications offer so many variables that a call to your favorite manufacturer becomes necessary. For the street, here's what you'll need to know:

What is your cruise rpm at 60 mph? This is one of the most important considerations because it indicates the operating range that the cam should be optimized for. A cam with a powerband much higher than your cruise rpm creates poor low-rpm response. If your engine combination dictates a cam too large for your cruise rpm, then you're faced with a classic case of compromising one area to fulfill another. But be careful, because over-camming is the most common error made by hot rodders looking for more power.

What is your compression ratio? This is a necessary factor in cam selection because it helps determine the combustion pressure created with a given cam. Since the intake valve is open during the early portion of the compression stroke, a long-duration cam allows more low-rpm pressure to be released as the piston moves up the cylinder. A big cam with a low compression ratio kills combustion pressure and performance. On the other hand, detonation may result if the

compression ratio is too high for a particular cam profile.

If the recommended cam for your compression ratio doesn't match the recommendation for your cruise rpm, the best compromise is to use the cam suggested for your compression ratio. If the diversity between the two cams is great, then you've got a mismatched vehicle combination that should be addressed prior to a cam swap.

What is your transmission, vehicle weight, and gear ratio? These factors determine engine load when accelerating from a stop. A heavy car with stock gears requires a low-rpm cam for acceptable acceleration, whereas a lighter car with lower gears can use a high-rpm cam because it takes less low-end torque to get it moving. Remember that the perfect cam has not yet been designed—low-rpm cams sacrifice high-rpm horsepower and vice versa.

Transmission type has a lot to do with driveability. An auto-

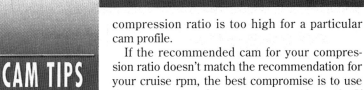

CAM TIPS

BUYING A CAM WITHOUT GETTING THE SHAFT

By David Freiburger

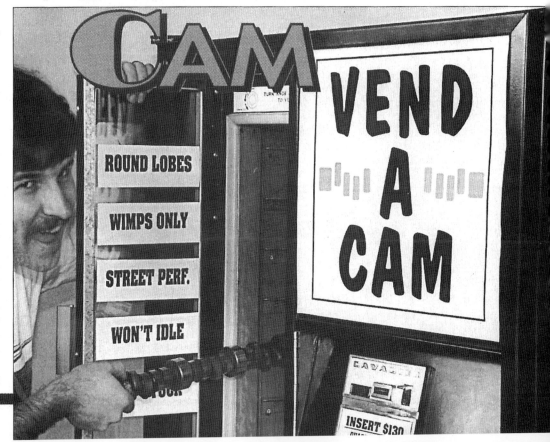

HOW TO SELECT A CAM

ROUND LOBES

WIMPS ONLY

STREET PERF.

WON'T IDLE

VEND A CAM

INSERT $130

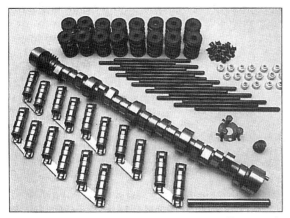

Crane and Competition Cams now offer retrofit hydraulic roller cams. Crane's Cam-Ponent kits include everything you need for a high-performance installation.

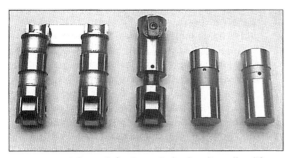

From right to left: Crane's hydraulic roller lifters, Competition Cams' solid roller, solid flat, and hydraulic flat tappets. The Chevy solid lifters retain an oil hole to route oil through the pushrod.

matic can soak as much as 40 lbs.-ft. of torque at idle, so a big cam with a stock torque converter may have difficulty idling. Big cams will require a high stall converter to reduce engine load at idle and to increase the stall rpm at which the vehicle launches. Because of this, manual transmissions are more forgiving to overcammed engines.

What are your intake and exhaust modifications? This determines how fast the engine can move air in and out of the cylinders. A restrictive intake may require a lot of duration to allow the cylinders to fill, and stock exhaust may need more duration to get the fumes out. The catch is that long-duration cams usually work best at higher rpm that's beyond the parameters of a stock engine, so a compromise must be reached.

Is your vehicle computer controlled? Computer-controlled engines have more restrictions in cam design to assure that the computer can handle the changes. Crane's CompuCam 2000 series is designed with this in mind, although some cams may require a new chip to richen the fuel curve.

Beyond these basics, consider smog legality, manifold vacuum, and idle quality. Cam catalogs can supply specific information about applications and cam characteristics. Also, these cams should address the legality question of aftermarket components in emissions-controlled engines.

PROFILIN'

The design elements listed in cam catalogs will help you decide on a specific cam. The elements include lift, adver-

THE DIGITAL COUNTERMAN

Computer programs that are IBM compatible can help when choosing a cam. Contact Crane, Competition Cams, or Wolverine/Blue Racer for more information. You should call a tech service person for race-only recommendations, but the computer can handle your street/strip needs.

We ran a couple of combinations through the programs to give you an idea of a typical street cam and to check for consistency in recommendations. The first was a typical 9:1 350 Chevy with 3.08 gears and a stock Turbo 350 for street performance use in a 3400-pound car. Here are the recommendations we came up with:

Chart A—Mild 350				
Company	Part No.	Lift Intake/Exhaust	Duration at .050	Separation Angle
Crane Cams	HMV-260-2-NC	.427/.454	204/216	112
Competition Cams	12-206-2	.440/.440	212/212	110
Blue Racer	WG1159	.443/.465	214/224	112

For a higher-performance example, we also checked out a 454 with 4.10 gears, 10:1 compression, 2800-stall converter, aftermarket intake, and exhaust in a 3600-pound car. We told the computer we were looking for moderate street/strip performance.

Chart B—Street/Strip 454				
Company	Part No.	Lift Intake/Exhaust	Duration at .050	Separation Angle
Crane Cams	HMV-272-2A-NC	.515/.550	216/228	112
Competition Cams	11-213-3	.550/.550	244/244	110
Blue Racer	WG1081	.510/.510	224/232	114

You'll notice that the recommendations are conservative because the manufacturers know you'll be happier with a cam that's not too big. Crane is the most conservative, but Competition Cams' program sometimes recommends bigger cams based on more detailed input.

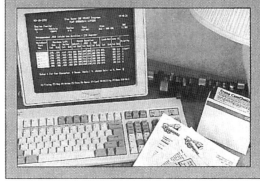

Computer programs from Crane Cams, Competition Cams, and Wolverine/Blue Racer can help with your decision.

tised duration, duration at .050-inch tappet lift, and lobe separation angle. Recommended intake centerline and valve opening and closing timing are included on the spec card that comes with the cam. The profile of the cam lobe is not necessarily the same on both the intake and exhaust lobes. Dual pattern cams usually use extra lift and duration on the exhaust side to compensate for poor exhaust ports, while extra exhaust duration can actually help draw in the intake charge.

Lift is the maximum distance in inches that the valve is lifted off the seat. Increasing lift without changing duration improves torque without affecting the rpm band. The manufacturer will tell you which rocker arm ratio has been used to determine cam lift, and lift can be increased with higher-ratio rockers. When increasing lift, make sure you don't run into valve-to-piston clearance problems.

Duration is the amount of time in crankshaft degrees that a valve is off its seat. Long duration (over 220 degrees at .050-inch tappet lift) gives the engine more time to charge and evacuate the cylinders at high rpm. This improves top-end power at the cost of low-rpm torque. Unfortunately, shorter duration for low-rpm power also dictates the total lift possible due to the rate-of-lift limitations of the lifter.

CALLING ALL CAMS

After you've got an idea about a cam choice, call your favorite manufacturer for a recommendation. Don't trust a buddy's cam recommendation unless his car is exactly like yours and runs the way you want it to.

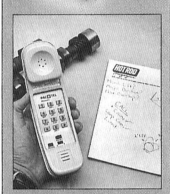

Here are some of the companies that have tech staffs which will provide assistance over the phone.

Competition Cams
Dept. HR
3406 Democrat Rd.
Memphis, TN 38118
(800) 999-0853
(901) 795-2400 (in TN)
[8:00 a.m. to 8:00 p.m. CST (M-F)]

Crane Cams
Dept. HR
530 Fentress Blvd.
Daytona Beach, FL 32114
(904) 258-6174
[8:00 a.m. to 8:00 p.m. EST (M-F)]
(904) 258-8846
[24-hour Dial-A-Cam]

Erson Cams
Dept. HR
555 Mallory Wy.
Carson City, NV 89701
(702) 882-1622
[8:00 a.m. to 5:00 p.m. PST (M-F)]

Lunati Cams and Cranks
Dept. HR
4770 Lamar Ave.
Memphis, TN 38181
(901) 365-0950
[8:00 a.m. to 5:00 p.m. CST (M-F)]

Wolverine/Blue Racer
Dept. HR
4790 Hudson Rd.
Osseo, MI 49266
(800) 248-0134
[8:00 a.m. to 5:30 p.m. EST (M-F)]

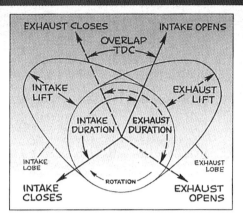

This front-view diagram of a cam's intake and exhaust lobes gives you a better idea of the relationships of the lobes and how their positioning relates to cam timing.

Cam catalogs offer the best cam tech and recommendation information around!

Advertised duration is a generalized term used to define a duration checked at either .004- or .006-inch tappet lift, depending on the manufacturer. **Duration at .050-inch tappet lift** is an industry standard that can be used to compare cams from different manufacturers. Since there's a disparity in duration measurement checking ports, a cam advertised at 272 degrees duration may have less duration at .050-inch tappet lift than a cam from a different manufacturer that's advertised at 270 or 268 duration.

Lobe separation angle is the relationship between the centerlines of the intake and exhaust lobes. This is a fixed relationship that cannot be altered without grinding a new cam. In the '60s we used the term overlap, and lobe separation angle is an indicator of overlap. Overlap is the amount of time in crankshaft degrees that the intake and exhaust valves are

Cam installation can be as scary as cam selection. Crane, Competition cams, and Mopar Performance offer cam installation videos to help you out.

open simultaneously, and it has a large effect on idle quality. A cam with a 108-degree lobe separation angle will have more overlap and a lumpier idle than one with 112 degrees. If you prefer, degrees of overlap can be determined by adding the intake opening and exhaust closing timing numbers, and lobe separation angle can be calculated by adding the intake and exhaust lobe centers and dividing by two.

Lobe separation angle is often confused with lobe centerline. Lobe centerline usually refers to the relationship of the max lift centerline or the intake lobe to top dead center (TDC) or cylinder number one, and is often changed with offset bushings when degreeing the cam. If a cam is designed to be installed on a 110-degree before TDC intake centerline, then a two-degree advance to 108 degrees would increase low-rpm torque. A two-degree retard would put the cam at 112 degrees and increase top-end power.

TAPPET DANCE

Another important consideration in cam selection is lifter type: solid or hydraulic flat tappets and solid or hydraulic roller tappets. For street use, most rodders opt for hydraulic cams due to the simplicity of maintenance and quiet operation. For flat tappet hydraulic cams, bleed-down lifters such as the Crane Hi-Intensity and Rhoades lifters can help reduce low-rpm duration for improved torque with bigger cams, but these should not be used with small cams and high-compression ratios due to possible detonation induced by increased combustion pressure.

Roller hydraulic lifters are popular because they allow greater lift-per-degree of duration, which means more low-end torque and smooth idle. They run great, but at considerably more expense than the old standby flat tappets.

GET ON THE VALVETRAIN

Some extra expense will be incurred by the valvetrain components that are required with your new cam. Any new flat tappet cam needs new lifters. New valvesprings, keepers, and retainers are a good idea—if not mandatory—to prevent damage from valve float. Some cams use smaller-than-stock base circles, so longer pushrods may be needed. Wilder cams require improved rocker arms, shafts or studs, and guideplates. And don't forget the gaskets, cam lube, oil seals, and timing chain. Fortunately, today's cam manufacturers offer complete cam installation kits, such as the Crane Cam-Ponent kits, that include everything you need for the installation. Your cam manufacturer is also the best source for installation tech specifics. **HR**

Camshaft Price Comparo

BY MATTHEW KING

Photos by Matthew King

You've probably decided you need a new bumpstick to tickle your valves.

Great, but before you stab it in, you've got to decide what kind of cam you want, which grind is best, and most important, all the parts required to get that new cam up and running in your engine. To give you an idea of everything that's involved in a cam swap, we called Lunati to get a list of all the parts it recommends to properly install a hydraulic flat-tappet, a mechanical flat-tappet, a hydraulic-roller, and a solid-roller camshaft in a big-block Chevy. We selected cams from Lunati's Special Purpose series that

have similar duration specs, but since the various grinds within each group all cost the same, we've listed specific part numbers only for the purposes of comparing the additional components they require. Then we phoned Jeg's to see how much each cam setup would actually cost at current retail. Depending on the heads you have, some of these setups may require cylinder-head machine work, but we haven't included specific prices because costs vary so much based on what work is done and where you live. However, we did include prices for the extra parts you'll need if a trip to the machine shop is required. As you'll see, the more you want, the more you pay.

Most stock Mark IV production heads will accept single valvesprings with up to a 1.550-inch od. Larger 1.625-inch-od dual springs like the one shown require opening up the valvespring seats and machining the guides down to fit teflon valve-stem seals to clear the diameter of the inner spring and provide adequate retainer-to-guide clearance when the spring is compressed at maximum lobe lift. If you've already upgraded to a set of aftermarket cylinder heads, the good news is that you probably won't need to have any machine work done.

Hydraulic Flat-Tappet

Stabbing in a hydraulic flat-tappet cam is generally the easiest swap because it's what most Mark IV engines came with from the factory. In the best-case scenario, all you need are the cam; an installation kit that includes matched valvesprings, retainers, and locks; and a cam change gasket set. For the purposes of pricing, we spec'd out a cam from Lunati's Special Purpose hydraulic series with 241/241 degrees of duration at 0.050-inch tappet lift and 0.525-/0.525-inch lift (PN 30204), which is about the biggest grind you can run with stock stamped rocker arms.

Hydraulic Flat-Tappet Parts List

Item	Jeg's Part Number	Price
Lunati SP Hydraulic camshaft	638-30204	$139.99
Installation kit	638-65001	181.99
Timing set (optional)	638-93112	25.99
Gasket set	720-4404	20.99
Thrust washer	638-90203	11.99
Cam bolt locking plate	638-90283	2.99
Roller rockers (optional)	638-84174	246.99
Lock nuts (optional)	638-84716	16.99
Rotator spacers (optional)	638-86603	23.99
Total		$357.95
Total with optional parts		$671.91

Hydraulic Roller

Hydraulic roller cams offer the advantages of easy maintenance, long-term durability, and good power with relatively mild specs, and Lunati's tech advisors frequently recommend them for street rods and boats that aren't built for all-out performance. Since most hydraulic-roller grinds are fairly mild in terms of duration, they take the same valvesprings as flat-tappet hydraulic cams, so you probably won't need to have any machine work done to update a Mark IV engine with a hydraulic-roller setup. But roller rockers are usually mandatory because of the roller cam's ability to provide a high ratio of tappet lift to duration. The SP 50250 we spec'd has 242/252 degrees of duration at 0.050 with a whopping 595/612 lift. You will also need a set of ½-inch-shorter retrofit pushrods to make up for the longer hydraulic-roller lifters. The most expensive part of this setup are the lifters, which cost about $375 if you buy them separately.

Hydraulic-Roller Parts List

Item	Jeg's Part Number	Price
Lunati SP hydraulic-roller camshaft	638-50250	$256.99
Cast-iron gear core	N/A	51.00
Installation kit	638-65406	537.99
Gasket set	720-4404	20.99
Thrust washer	638-90203	11.99
Roller cam button	638-90000	9.99
Cam bolt locking plate	638-90283	2.99
Roller rockers	638-84174	246.99
Lock nuts	638-84716	16.99
Retrofit pushrods	638-80160	33.99
Timing set (optional)	638-93112	25.99
Rotator spacers (optional)	638-86603	23.99
Total		$1,189.99
Total with optional parts		$1,239.89

Mechanical Flat-Tappet

High-lift, long-duration mechanical cams make big power, but they can be hideously cruel to valvetrains. Heavy valvetrain components, small-diameter lifters, and canted-valve angles make the big-block Chevy particularly susceptible to cam failure resulting from the high spring pressures needed to keep the valves from floating at high rpm. Roller rocker arms may not be absolutely mandatory for a cam like Lunati's SP 40207 with 300/310 degrees of duration at 0.050 and 540/558 lift, but you'd be a fool not to run them anyway. And one-piece, chrome-moly ⅜-inch pushrods are also pretty much required. All of Lunati's Special Purpose solids require dual valvesprings, so if you're running a set of production cylinder heads with stock umbrella-type valve stem seals, you'll have to have them machined for narrower Teflon seals to clear the inner springs. The guides may also need to be shortened to ensure adequate retainer-to-guide clearance at max lift.

Mechanical Flat-Tappet Parts List

Item	Jeg's Part Number	Price
Lunati SP mechanical camshaft	638-40207	$139.99
Installation kit	638-65050	206.99
Gasket set	720-4404	20.99
Thrust washer	638-90203	11.99
Cam bolt locking plate	638-90283	2.99
Roller rockers	638-84174	246.99
Lock nuts	638-84716	16.99
Pushrods	638-82144	150.00
Timing set (optional)	638-93112	25.99
Rotator spacers (optional)	638-86603	23.99
Machine-work related parts (may not be required with aftermarket heads)		
Teflon valve stem seals	638-78355	20.99
Fel-Pro full gasket set	375-2805	108.99
Total		$796.93
Total with optional parts		$976.89

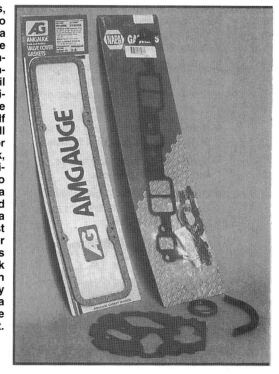

In all cases, you're going to need at least a cam-change gasket set consisting of a timing cover, oil pan, intake manifold, and valve cover gaskets. If you need to pull the heads for machine work, you're also obviously going to need at least a pair of new head gaskets and a set of exhaust manifold or header gaskets to put them back on, at which point you may as well get a complete engine gasket set.

Solid-Roller

The solid-roller camshaft is at the top of the heap in terms of both power potential and cost. Some of this high cost stems from the price of individual components such as lifters and springs, but the main reason a solid-roller is so pricey to install is the sheer brutality it inflicts on the engine's valvetrain. Every component must be up to the task or it won't last for long. Therefore, you need to spend extra money upgrading parts beyond what's necessary even for normal high-performance applications, primarily to handle the tremendous valvespring pressures. Big rollers with lots of lift and duration require stiff dual or even triple springs to keep the valves from floating at high rpm, lightweight titanium retainers with 10-degree locks to keep the stems from pulling out, and thick-wall chrome-moly pushrods to resist deflection. Other highly recommended accessories include aftermarket chrome-moly rocker arm studs (stock studs will snap under the tremendous open spring-pressure load), roller rocker arms, a stud girdle to reduce valvetrain flex, a roller thrust button to keep the cam from walking in the block, and a full-roller timing set, preferably one with a Torrington roller bearing to reduce friction against the block face. As with the hydraulic roller, you will need to get a bronze distributor gear, or better yet, order a cam with a ductile-iron distributor gear. While it's pricey, a roller will usually have greater durability than a very aggressive solid flat-tappet cam, so the price is justified in the long run.

Solid-Roller Parts List

Item	Jeg's Part Number	Price
Lunati SP solid-roller camshaft	638-50204	$256.99
Cast-iron gear core	N/A	51.00
Installation kit	638-65516	607.99
Roller timing set	638-93116	110.99
Gasket set	720-4404	20.99
Roller cam button	638-90000	9.99
Cam bolt locking plate	638-90283	2.99
Roller rockers	638-84174	246.99
Lock nuts	638-84716	16.99
Pushrods	638-82144	150.00
Rocker arm studs	638-86002	47.99
Stud girdle	638-91645	195.00
Rotator spacers (optional)	638-86603	23.99
Machine-work related parts (optional)		
Teflon valve stem seals	638-78355	20.99
Fel-Pro full gasket set	375-2805	108.99
Total		$1,717.91
Total with optional parts		$1,871.88

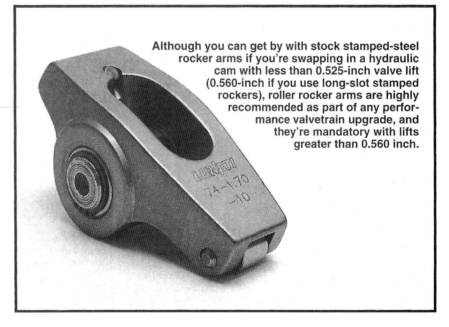

Although you can get by with stock stamped-steel rocker arms if you're swapping in a hydraulic cam with less than 0.525-inch valve lift (0.560-inch if you use long-slot stamped rockers), roller rocker arms are highly recommended as part of any performance valvetrain upgrade, and they're mandatory with lifts greater than 0.560 inch.

The steel billet cores used for most roller camshafts create friction between the steel gear on the end of the distributor and the drive gear on the camshaft, causing one or both to wear out and sending metal throughout the engine. This can be solved by installing a bronze gear on the distributor, but a better solution is to pay extra for a camshaft core that has a ductile-iron distributor drive gear pressed on, like the cam shown; Lunati charges $51 for this service. In the unlikely event you're still running a mechanical fuel pump, a bronze-tipped pump pushrod is also necessary with a billet roller cam.

Depending on how recently your engine has been rebuilt, it's probably smart to install a new timing set. This is always a good idea if the existing chain has more than about 60,000 miles on it. Other parts that aren't absolutely mandatory but are good insurance against premature wear or parts failure are a cam thrust washer that fits between the camshaft sprocket and the block face to reduce friction on the block, and a cam bolt locking plate to prevent the sprocket bolts from loosening.

Another issue with rollers is cam walk. Roller-cam lobes are ground without the tapered profiles that flat-tappet cams have to provide locating thrust that keeps the cam from moving back and forth in the block. To make up for this, you need to install a thrust button between the cam sprocket and the timing cover to keep the cam in place, and may even need to machine the button for proper cam endplay. **CC**

SOURCES

JEG'S HIGH PERFORMANCE
Dept. CC1199
751 E. 11th Ave.
Columbus, OH 43211
800/CALL-JEGS
www.jegs.com

LUNATI CAMS INC.
Dept. CC1199
4770 Lamar Ave.
Memphis, TN 38118
901/365-0950

Source Guide
Cam and Valvetrain

CAM MOTION
Dept. CC1199
2092 Dallas Dr.
Baton Rouge, LA 70806
504/926-6110

CHET HERBERT CAMS
Dept. CC1199
1933 S. Manchester
Anaheim, CA 92802
714/750-1211
www.chetherbert.com

CLOYES GEAR PRODUCTS
Dept. CC1199
615 W. Walnut St.
Paris, AR 72855
501/963-2105

COMP CAMS
Dept. CC1199
3406 Democrat Rd.
Memphis, TN 38118
800/999-0853
901/795-2400
www.compcams.com

CRANE CAMS
Dept. CC1199
530 Fentress Blvd.
Daytona Beach, FL 32114
904/258-6174
www.cranecams.com

CROWER CAMS AND EQUIPMENT
Dept. CC1199
3333 Main St.
Chula Vista, CA 91911
619/422-1191
www.crower.com

**CUSTOM SPEED PARTS/
HARLAND SHARP**
Dept. CC1199
13142 Prospect Rd.
Strongsville, OH 44136
440/238-3260

EDELBROCK CORP.
Dept. CC1199
2700 California St.
Torrance, CA 90503
800/416-8628
www.edelbrock.com

ENGLE CAMS
Dept. CC1199
1621 12th St.
Santa Monica, CA 90404
310/450-0806

**ERSON CAMS/MR. GASKET
PERFORMANCE GROUP**
Dept. CC1199
550 Mallory Way
Carson City, NV 89701
775/882-1622
www.mrgasket.com

FEDERAL-MOGUL
Dept. CC1199
26555 Northwestern Hwy.
Southfield, MI 48034
248/354-9445
www.goracing.com/federalmogul/

FERREA RACING COMPONENTS
Dept. CC1199
2600 NW 55th Ct., Ste. 238
Ft. Lauderdale, FL 33309
888/733-2505
954/733-2505

ISKY RACING CAMS
Dept. CC1199
16020 S. Broadway St.
Gardena, CA 90248
323/770-0930
www.iskycams.com

JESEL
Dept. CC1199
1985 Cedarbridge Ave.
Lakewood, NJ 08701
732/901-1800
www.jesel.com

K-MOTION VALVE SPRINGS
Dept. CC1199
2381 N. 24th St.
Lafayette, IN 47904
800/428-7891
765/742-8494

LUNATI
Dept. CC1199
4770 Lamar Ave.
Memphis, TN 38118
901/365-0950
www.LunatiCams.com

MANLEY
Dept. CC1199
1960 Swarthmore Ave.
Lakewood, NJ 08701
732/905-3366
www.manleyperf.com

MILODON INC.
Dept. CC1199
20716 Plummer St.
Chatsworth, CA 91311
818/407-1211

PETE JACKSON GEAR DRIVES
Dept. CC1199
1207 S. Flower St.
Burbank, CA 91502
323/849-2622

POWERHOUSE PRODUCTS
Dept. CC1199
3402 Democrat Rd.
Memphis, TN 38118
800/USA-RACE
www.powerhouseproducts.com

SCHNEIDER RACING CAMS
Dept. CC1199
1235 Cushman Ave., No. 6
San Diego, CA 92110
619/297-0227

SI VALVES
Dept. CC1199
2175A Agate Ct.
Simi Valley, CA 93065
805/582-0085

T&D MACHINE
Dept. CC1199
4859 Convair Dr.
Carson City, NV 89706
775/884-2292

ULTRADYNE RACING CAMS
Dept. CC1199
8901 First Industrial Dr.
South Haven, MS 38671
800/526-1420
601/349-4447

WHERE TO FIND THE LATEST PERFORMANCE CAMSHAFTS

By Matthew Pearson

Now that you have finished reading the other articles in our special camshaft section (you did read them, didn't you?), you know that the proper camshaft can add performance to your ride. But before you run out and spend your hard-earned dollars in search of the ultimate grind, take the time to figure out which cam is right for you.

To eliminate the guesswork and accompanying headaches, a good starting point is your favorite cam manufacturer. Camshaft technology has become so specialized that companies can make recommendations to match your other engine components for optimum power. Using computer programs and your answers to a few key questions, they can come up with a cam for virtually any application. If your needs are very specialized, some cam companies can even custom-grind cams to your specs.

Now you're asking, "How do I get in touch with my favorite manufacturer?" Well, don't worry, we've taken care of that, too. In an effort to help you in your quest for more power, we have compiled a list of some of the major manufacturers and their newest products. Keep in mind that we have only limited space, so if you don't see the ideal bumpstick for you, feel free to call the companies and ask questions. They'll be happy to assist you.

CUSTOMIZED CAM TECHNIQUES

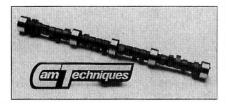

The folks at Cam Techniques say that they can custom-grind camshafts for almost any application, including RV and towing, circle-track racing, road racing and drag racing. They specialize in custom-ground cams and will work closely with the engine builder to supply proper cam timing for your particular combination. They also welcome the challenge of unusual engines or applications. For more information, contact Cam Techniques, Dept. HR07, 105 Cascade Blvd., Milford, CT 06460, 203/878-7104.

70 YEARS AND STILL GRINDING

Camshaft selection for your high-performance street machine or bracket racer can be complicated for a number of reasons. The size of the engine, the type of induction (normal or forced), the gear ratio and transmission type, the engine compression, the type of fuel and the vehicle weight are all factors that Clay Smith Engineering considers when it designs a camshaft. The custom-design process enables the company to properly address all your application specifics. Camshaft kits are available with hydraulic, solid or roller lifters and come complete with springs, chrome-moly retainers and heavy-duty keepers. For more information, contact Clay Smith Engineering, Dept. HR07, 5870 Dale St., Buena Park, CA 90621, 714/523-0530.

DUAL ENERGY CAMS

Specifically designed to optimize high-rpm power for street applications, dual-pattern cams from Competition Cams are available for Ford, Chevy and Chrysler engines. The 265 highlights Competition Cams' latest lobe design technology. Like other Dual Energy cams, the 265 is available in kits that include lifters and timing chains. It is also available as part of a complete performance system. For more information, contact Competition Cams, Dept. HR07, 3406 Democrat Rd., Memphis, TN 38118, 800/999-0853.

COMPUTER-COMPATIBLE CRANES

Crane Cams has two new CompuCam hydraulic roller camshafts for the Dodge Magnum 318 (5.2L) and 360 (5.9L) V8 engines. Not only are they designed to increase torque and horsepower in '92-'93 Magnum V8s, but they are also completely compatible with the stock engine control computer. The CompuCam 2020

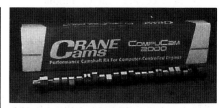

can be used for 318-360 engines that produce low-end and midrange torque for towing and street performance in a stock or mildly modified vehicle. The CompuCam 2030 delivers increased midrange and upper-rpm horsepower and torque with near-stock low-end performance. The 2030 will work with factory valvetrain components and is designed to accept a wide range of engine and powertrain modifications, including supercharging. Both cams are made from billet steel with iron distributor drive gears, which allows you to use the stock Dodge distributor gear. For more information, contact Crane Cams, Inc., Dept. HR07, 530 Fentress Blvd., Daytona Beach, FL 32114, 904/258-6174.

CROWER KITS FOR FORDS AND CHEVYS

The hydraulic roller cam and kit series from Crower is designed to incorporate the reliability of a hydraulic cam with the performance characteristics of a roller. Crower claims that the ability to accelerate the valve quicker than a conventional flat-face hydraulic lifter creates greater area under the lift curve and improved breathing.

According to Crower, the reduced friction also increases fuel economy and alleviates valvetrain noise. Cams and valvetrains are available for Ford applications using stock lifters, and complete kits are available for small-block Chevys. For more information, contact Crower Cams, Dept. HR07, 3333 Main St., Chula Vista, CA 91911-5899, 619/422-1191.

STREET-LEGAL EDELBROCKS

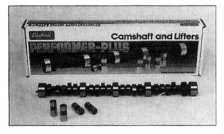

Edelbrock's Performer-Plus camshaft and lifter kits for small-block Chevy V8s are now street legal on pollution-controlled vehicles. Camshaft and lifter kit 2102 for 350ci-and-smaller engines and the 2103 for 400ci engines have been granted Executive Order numbers for use in '57-and-later noncomputer-controlled Chevy small-blocks. Edelbrock's 3702 for '81-and-later 305 and 350 LG-4 and throttle-body injection V8s have also been granted E.O. numbers. The Performer-Plus cams feature more valve lift and duration than stock replacement cams. They are compatible with the original valvetrain components in stock or slightly modified engines. For more information, contact Edelbrock Corp., Dept. HR07, 2700 California St., Torrance, CA 90503, 310/782-2900.

FORD SVO CAMSHAFTS

The M-6250-E303 and M-6250-X303 from Ford Motorsport SVO are hydraulic roller camshafts for '86-'94 small-block V8s. The E303 is designed for use with mass airflow injection systems, GT-40 intake manifolds, headers and improved GT-40 cylinder heads. The E303 can provide potent midrange and strong top-end power through 6000 rpm. It must be used with a five-speed transmission. The X303 is an ultrahigh-performance camshaft. It provides more lift and duration than the E303, but it is not legal for sale or use on pollution-controlled vehicles. Designed for mass airflow injection systems and GT-40 manifolds, headers and cylinder heads, it produces increased torque and horsepower up to 6500 rpm. For more information, contact Ford Motorsport Performance Equipment, Dept. HR07,

44050 N. Groesbeck Hwy., Clinton Township, MI 48036-1108, 313/337-1356.

GM PERFORMANCE PARTS

General Motors Performance Parts Division offers a full line of camshafts for small- and big-block applications. For big-block Chevys, it offers a wide variety of cams from low-maintenance hydraulic lifter grinds to full-race mechanical tappet profiles. The cam and kit applications for small-blocks range from hydraulic roller-tappet types for Corvettes and Camaros to mechanical flat-tappet types for short-track and road-racing 350ci-and-larger V8s. For more information, contact your local General Motors dealer or Cone Chevrolet, Dept. HR07, 600 W. Commonwealth, Fullerton, CA 92632, 714/525-3506.

HI-TECH AND LEGAL

Eleven small-block Chevy performance camshafts from Hi-Tech Engine Components have received Executive  Order numbers from the California Air Resources Board. The cams are now 50-state emissions legal for use in '87-and-older GM 267- to 400ci carbureted, gasoline engines. Hi-Tech has also applied for other E.O. numbers in its ongoing effort to produce a full range of street-legal performance products. For more information, contact Hi-Tech Engine Components, Dept. HR07, P.O. Box 510988, Salt Lake City, UT 84151, 800/453-8250.

LUNATI BRACKET MASTER

The Bracket Master II from Lunati Cams is an economically priced camshaft that combines bottom-end and midrange performance with a broad power range. It can be used for a variety of street/strip applications as well as oval-track racing. The Bracket Master II is available in several profiles of varying aggressiveness for most engine applications. The cam and hydraulic lifter kit—at less than $110—is

one of the most affordable kits on the market. For more information, contact Lunati Cams, Inc., Dept. HR07, P.O. Box 18021, Memphis, TN 38181-0021, 901/365-0950.

CAMSHAFTS BY MOPAR

Mopar Performance camshafts are designed by Chrysler exclusively for Chrysler engines. Mopar offers a full series of profiles from mild to wild, resto to all-out racing. The Purple Shaft cams cover RV applications to bracket-racing designs in hydraulic, mechanical and roller models. All Mopar Performance cams are dyno and track tested by Chrysler engineers. Cam packages are also available with lifters. For more information, contact Mopar Performance, Dept. HR07, P.O. Box 215020, Auburn Hills, MI 48321-5020, 313/853-7290.

SCHNEIDER RACING

The people at Schneider Racing Cams say that they are utilizing the latest advancements in camshaft technology to produce a complete line of performance camshafts. In addition to street-performance variations, Schneider also manufactures full-race cams. Schneider Cams are available for Ford, Chevy and Mopar engines with hydraulic, mechanical or roller lifters. Overhead-cam grinds are also available. For more information, contact Schneider Racing Cams, Dept. HR07, 1235 Cushman Ave., San Diego, CA 92110, 619/297-0227.

SHAVER PERFORMANCE

Shaver has a new line of performance roller cams. Designed to make high-horsepower peaks for  quick acceleration, the Shaver setup is ideal for Sprint Car or late-model applications. All Shaver products are tested for performance and reliability, and the company also features a complete line of lifters and valvetrain components. For more information, contact Shaver, Dept. HR07, 20608 Earl St., Torrance, CA 90503, 310/370-6941. **HR**

CAMSHAFT COMPARO

HAVING A COOL IDLE AND TORQUING IT, TOO!

By Jeff Smith

A long time ago, some hot rodder figured out that in order to be really cool, he had to have a car that not only *looked* fast but *sounded* fast, too. That lopey, drive-in idle burble seems to play a big part in why hot rodders buy a performance camshaft. Those long-duration cams give the engine that lumpy, grumpy, take-no-prisoners choppy idle that sounds like Pro Stockers—only better.

The problem with long-duration camshafts is that for everyday street driving, low-speed throttle response and torque are just nonexistent, as is intake-manifold vacuum. Basically, these cams start to work between 3500 and 4000

These are three of the four hydraulic Competition Cams camshafts we tested, and two of them have exactly the same lift and duration. The only difference was the 110- and 106-degree lobe-separation angles. Despite that slight change, there was a measurable difference between the two. The biggest of the three cams created the least overall power.

These are the Competition Cams components used in the dyno test. The fourth cam was a last-minute addition and isn't shown here. Competition Cams also included a link-belt timing chain, a set of Magnum stainless-steel rocker arms and a new set of lifters for each cam to complete the valvetrain.

rpm. Below that point, throttle response feels more like you put your foot in a bowl of cold oatmeal—it's mushy and not much fun.

But what if we told you how you could have your lumpy idle *and* make great torque and power at the same time? Would you go for it? Follow along as we dive into getting more out of that bumpstick than just style points at the local drive-in.

THE PLAN

We decided to subject a small-block Chevy to a battery of different camshafts to see if we could maximize power throughout a broad rpm range yet produce that characteristic choppy idle quality at the same time. The plan was to start with a popular long-duration cam and then try to pull back the duration while tightening the lobe-separation angle (see sidebar "Trial Separation") to make torque and still produce the characteristic idle lope. Scooter Brothers of Competition Cams agreed to supply the cams and valvetrain pieces we'd need for the test. John Baechtel, formerly of HOT ROD and *Car Craft* magazines, has founded Westech Performance Group, a dynamometer and R&D facility in Mira Loma, California. The facility centers around a brand-new SuperFlow 901 dyno where we performed all the testing. Working with Baechtel was another friend of ours, Louie Hammel, who has a wealth of experience in designing and operating engine dynos.

The test engine was a typical 383, produced by stuffing a 400ci crank into a .030-over 350 short-block with Speed-Pro

flattop pistons, Childs & Albert Dura-Moly rings and bearings and a standard oil pump sitting in a '69 Z/28 oil pan with a windage tray. Rather than a set of trick aluminum heads, we chose a pair of 882 production iron heads fitted with 2.02/1.60-inch valves.

Since we had to install four different cams in two days, we also opted for Competition Cams' two-piece timing-chain cover, which made swapping the cams *much* easier.

Edelbrock supplied a Performer RPM dual-plane intake, and we added a Carburetor Shop 3310 750 vacuum-secondary Holley carb and a set of Hooker 1¾-inch headers.

We decided to start with the biggest cam first and use that as a baseline to evaluate the remaining camshafts in order to optimize the combination while also keeping track of the idle vacuum and rpm. In order to reduce the number of variables in each test, all the cams supplied by Competition Cams were ordered with 106-degree intake centerlines and 110-degree lobe-separation angles with the exception of Test 3, where the lobe-separation angle was moved to 106 degrees.

THE TEST

Test 1 illustrated what happens when you bolt a long-duration cam in an engine that's not equipped to take advantage of that much camshaft. The cam for this test is a popular Competition Cams Magnum 292 hydraulic with 244 degrees of duration at .050-inch tappet lift and .507-inch lift. Even though this is a long-stroke, relatively big-inch engine (Chrysler 383s are "big-blocks"), it barely made over 300 lbs-ft of torque below 2600. Idle quality for this combination was 9 inches of manifold vacuum at 950 rpm, and the engine wouldn't run any slower.

With this long-duration cam, you would expect to make horsepower at the top end, which this cam did. However, at the engine speed range where the cam starts to work, the stock exhaust ports have long since given up. So again, the engine makes less than ideal power: 392 lbs-ft of torque at 3800 rpm and a paltry 339 horsepower at 5200.

TEST RESULTS

The following are the dyno test results from the four camshafts tested in the 383 on Westech's SuperFlow 901 dyno. Each combination was optimized for jetting and timing in order to maximize power. Fuel was 92-octane pump gasoline. All tests were corrected to 29.92 inches of mercury (Hg) at 60 degrees dry air.

Test 1 is the baseline cam with 244 degrees at .050-inch tappet lift. Test 2 is a shorter cam with 219 degrees at .050-inch tappet lift, both with a lobe-separation angle of 110 degrees. Test 3 uses the same cam as Test 2 but with the lobe-separation angle changed to 106 degrees. Test 4 uses the same intake lobe as the two previous cams but adds additional exhaust duration while also moving the lobe-separation angle back to 110 degrees.

The "Diff" line beginning with Test 2 shows the difference in torque (TQ) between the Test 1 baseline and each subsequent test. Notice how the shorter-duration cams improve torque in low and midrange but lose power at the top compared to the long-duration baseline camshaft. Note also that Test 4's dual-pattern cam made better power at the top compared to the single-pattern cams. The "AVG" figure at the bottom is an average of the torque curve. Test 4's torque is an average of 18.7 lbs-ft greater throughout the power curve than Test 1. You'll feel that in the seat of your pants.

	TEST 1		TEST 2			TEST 3			TEST 4		
RPM	TQ	HP	TQ	DIFF	HP	TQ	DIFF	HP	TQ	DIFF	HP
2000	314	119	-	-	-	350	+36	133	354	+40	135
2200	310	130	351	+41	147	342	+32	143	351	+41	147
2400	311	142	363	+52	166	346	+35	158	361	+50	165
2600	328	162	358	+30	177	348	+20	172	358	+30	177
2800	326	174	363	+37	194	369	+43	197	370	+44	197
3000	332	190	374	+42	213	376	+44	215	383	+51	219
3200	357	218	384	+27	234	394	+37	240	398	+41	242
3400	377	244	391*	+14	253	399	+22	259	405	+28	262
3600	387	265	391	+4	268	402*	+15	276	408*	+21	280
3800	392*	283	388	-4	281	397	+5	287	407	+15	295
4000	391	298	380	-11	290	391	0	298	401	+10	306
4200	386	309	370	-16	296	377	-9	301	391	+5	312
4400	379	318	360	-19	301*	369	-10	309	381	+2	319
4600	373	327	343	-30	301	356	-17	312	370	-3	324
4800	360	329	329	-31	300	345	-15	315*	357	-3	326
5000	350	333	315	-35	300	331	-19	315	345	-5	328*
5200	342	339*	295	-47	292	316	-26	313	330	-12	326
5400	330	339	274	-56	282	299	-31	307	310	-20	319
AVG	352.5		354.6			361.5			371.2		

Test 2 showed the effect of a shorter-duration cam (219 degrees at .050-inch duration with .462-inch lift), which pumps the torque up dramatically at low- and midrange engine speeds. This cam used Comp Cams' 275 DEH intake lobe with the same exhaust lobe (usually called a single-pattern camshaft) with a 110-degree lobe-separation angle. Note that at 2400 rpm, the shorter cam pumped the torque by 52 lbs-ft. As you might expect, this shorter cam also gave up a lot of horsepower to the longer-duration cam at the top, losing as much as 56 horsepower at 5400. This cam also improved idle vacuum to 16 inches (which is almost stock) at 950 rpm and idled smoothly at 750 rpm at 13 inches of vacuum.

Test 3 would show us the outcome of tightening the lobe-separation angle. We felt it should have pumped up the torque without losing any more horsepower at the top while also adding that desired lopey idle. Test 3 used the same camshaft as in Test 2 but with the lobe-separation angle tightened

We swapped most of the cams before the engine had a chance to cool down. Here, we've lubed the new cam and are slipping it in place with the aid of a Competition Designed Innovations cam handle that adds some much-needed leverage as the cam is installed.

Each cam was degreed with a Competition Cams degree kit to ensure that each was installed at its proper intake centerline. The cams varied no more than one degree on either side of the specs, which is well within our estimated level of measuring accuracy.

from 110 degrees to 106 degrees and the intake centerline left at 106 degrees. This meant that the exhaust lobe was moved four degrees closer to the intake to increase overlap. The result of this change was a noticeably choppier idle, yet it sounded crisper than the Test 1 camshaft despite an idle vacuum of 16 inches at 950 rpm. This cam didn't generate quite as much torque at the bottom as the previous cam, but it did improve the upper-rpm power slightly, even though it was still down at the top compared to the 244-degree-duration Test 1 cam.

While Test 3 did produce a better combination of overall torque for a street engine compared to the Test 1 cam, we realized during testing that this 383's real limitation was the stock cylinder heads. The stock exhaust port was just not capable of pushing all of the exhaust gas out of the chamber, especially above 4000 rpm where there was less time to do so. It became clear that a dual-pattern camshaft with more duration on the exhaust lobe would help this situation.

Test 4 chose a Comp Cams off-the-shelf DEH 275 dual-pattern camshaft with the same intake lobe as Tests 2 and 3 but with 229 degrees of exhaust duration at .050-inch tappet lift and .482-inch lift versus the intake lobe of 216 degrees and .462-inch lift. The lobe-separation angle went back to its original 110 degrees since the overlap with the longer exhaust duration was similar to the previous 106-degree lobe-separation angle, single-pattern cam.

This test really made the 383 wake up! The power jumped at the lower engine speeds comparable to the two previous cams, but the power improved at the top, too, staying roughly even with the longer-duration Test 1 cam through 5000. Above 5000, the shorter cam started losing power but dropped only 13 horsepower at 5200

"YOU CAN'T TELL A CAM WITHOUT A SPEC CARD..."

When you buy a new aftermarket camshaft, it comes with a timing card specifying lift, duration, lobe-separation angle and intake centerline. The card will also give you specific information to degree the cam. The following is a brief description of each of the four Competition Cams grinds we tested.

CAMSHAFT	DURATION (at .050)	LIFT (in)	LOBE-SEPARATION ANGLE	INTAKE CENTERLINE
TEST 1				
292 H-10	I 244	.507	110	106
	E 244	.507		
TEST 2				
219 H-10	I 219	.461	110	106
	E 219	.461		
TEST 3				
219 H-6	I 219	.461	106	106
	E 219	.461		
TEST 4				
275DEH-10	I 219	.461	110	106
	E 229	.482		

and 20 horses at 5400. Idle quality wasn't quite as choppy with 14 inches of vacuum at 950 rpm, but it still had a noticeable lope. Clearly, for a daily-driven street engine where both cool drive-in idle and good power are important, this last cam is the best compromise of all.

THE EVALUATION

This test was interesting from a number of different standpoints. First, we learned that lobe-separation angle does have an effect on the power curve and should be considered when deciding on your next camshaft. It would have been interesting to evaluate a single-pattern, 219 at .050-inch-tappet-lift-duration cam with a 114-degree lobe-separation angle, but from the testing we've done, it's fairly easy to conclude that the cam would produce a smoother idle with more vacuum and probably would have lost some torque in the midrange,

Edelbrock supplied a Performer RPM dual-plane intake for this test, and Brad Urban from The Carburetor Shop stopped by to help dial in his modified 3310 Holley carburetor.

Each new cam necessitated that we optimize the jetting and timing. The only real change to jetting occurred when we installed the Test 4 cam with its additional exhaust timing. This helped remove residual exhaust gas from the chamber. The engine responded by requiring four-steps-smaller jets for optimal power. The timing remained the same at 36 degrees for all tests using an MSD distributor and 6A module.

All dyno testing was done at John Baechtel's Westech Performance Group on a Superflow 901 computer-controlled dyno. Each run was made at a slow 100 rpm per second acceleration rate with data taken every 100 rpm.

TRIAL SEPARATION

Lobe-separation angle may be a new cam term to some hot rodders. It's related to overlap, which is a term you may have heard before. Lobe-separation angle is the number of crankshaft degrees between the intake and exhaust lobe center-lines. For example, if the exhaust lobe centerline is 114 degrees Before Top Dead Center (BTDC) and the intake lobe centerline is 106 degrees After Top Dead Center (ATDC), adding the two numbers together and dividing by two will produce the lobe-separation angle. In this case, 106 + 114 = 220/2 = 110 degrees.

Lobe-separation angle is a more accurate way to express valve overlap and has become the most popular way to express the relationship between exhaust valve closing and intake valve opening. As the lobe-separation angle gets tighter—from 110 degrees to 106 degrees, for example—this moves the intake and exhaust lobe centerlines closer together, which increases the amount of valve overlap. Conversely, widening the lobe-separation angle, from 110 degrees to 114 degrees, tends to spread the lobe centerlines further apart, which decreases the amount of valve overlap. This can be more clearly seen if you study the accompanying illustration.

Lobe-separation angle is established when grinding the camshaft and cannot be changed except by grinding a new cam. When grinding a new cam, the lobe-separation angle can be changed by moving the intake centerline, the exhaust centerline or both. For our tests, the intake centerline remained the same throughout all four tests to reduce the variables. The lobe-separation angle also

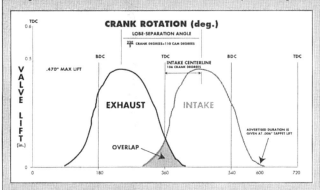

remained the same for all but one of the tests at 110 degrees, with Test 3 having the only cam with a tighter, 106-degree lobe-separation angle.

Lobe-separation angle is often overlooked as a camshaft specification that can be changed to enhance engine performance. Competition Cams grinds virtually all of its performance cams with a 110-degree lobe-separation angle. Most stock factory cams are ground at 114 to 116 degrees. This wider angle tends to smooth out idle roughness by decreasing overlap. The 110-degree separation angle used by Competition Cams and other cam companies typically generates a rougher idle but increases midrange torque.

Generally for street engines, lobe-separation angles of 110 degrees or less tend to generate a rough, lopey idle while increasing torque in the low- and midrange rpm levels. Lobe-separation angles of 112 degrees or more tend to smooth out the idle quality, add intake-manifold vacuum and perhaps increase top-end power since the intake valve is closing later in the cycle.

If you would like to experiment with different lobe-separation angles, Competition Cams (along with Lunati and most other cam companies) offers a service where you can specify a custom-ground cam with a different lobe-separation angle (or perhaps even different intake or exhaust lobes) for no extra charge. In addition, Comp Cams can have that cam at your doorstep within 48 hours through its Cam Express program. Lunati has a similar program that can custom grind a cam in 24 hours.

with perhaps a slight power increase at the higher engine speeds.

We also learned just how important cam selection is to optimizing power for a particular engine combination. For example, if we had merely changed to a good set of aftermarket heads that had a better exhaust port, perhaps the single-pattern, 106-degree lobe-separation Test 3 cam would have outperformed the Test 4 dual-pattern cam. This is possible since overscavenging the chamber with a combination of

While the dyno cell could have easily accommodated a full exhaust system, we chose to run Hooker 1¾-inch headers and matching 3½-inch collectors uncorked. The small holes drilled in the header pipes are for the exhaust gas temperature probes.

The dyno cell at Westech is so big even our wide-angle lens couldn't take it all in—it's big enough to accommodate even the largest truck exhaust system. The ducting in the background is where the air enters the cell. A giant fan at the rear of the cell pulls air through the cell and exhausts it out through the roof.

decent exhaust port flow and additional exhaust cam timing would probably hurt top-end power because the additional overlap would merely pull the fresh air and fuel right out of the exhaust. We have seen this happen on engines with too much cam timing on the exhaust side.

Granted, this story is complex, and there are more variables than we have fingers and toes. Don't expect to be able to digest all this information in one sitting. Even if this is all a little confusing, at least you can see from the power curves that the biggest cam isn't always the best. A smaller cam with tight lobe centers could be the path to a powerful street car that's the envy of the drive-in crowd. And if they ask you how you did it, tell 'em you just let it lope. **HR**

SOURCES

The Carburetor Shop
Dept. HR10
1457 Philadelphia, Unit 24
Ontario, CA 91761
909/947-9722

Competition Cams, Inc.
Dept. HR10
3406 Democrat Rd.
Memphis, TN 38118
901/795-2400
800/999-0853 (Cam Help)

**Competition Designed
Innovations (CDI)**
Dept. HR10
3406 Democrat Rd.
Memphis, TN 38118
800/288-2734

Edelbrock Corporation
Dept. HR10
2700 California St.

Torrance, CA 90503
310/781-2222
310/782-2900 (tech line)

Hooker Headers
Dept. HR10
1024 W. Brooks St.
Ontario, CA 91762
909/983-5871

Lunati Cams
Dept. HR10
P.O. Box 18021
Memphis, TN 38181-0021
901/365-0950

**Westech Performance
Group**
Dept. HR10
11098 Ventura Dr., Ste. C
Mira Loma, CA 91752
909/685-4767

BY MARLAN DAVIS

Photos by Marlan Davis

Cam Lobe Separation Comparo

When it comes to picking a cam, the average car crafter is primarily concerned with gross lift and duration.

He may even "throw in the cam advanced," which can boost low-end power and compensate for timing-chain stretch, but relatively few pay attention to the lobe displacement angle (LDA). Also known as the lobe separation angle, LDA alterations can markedly affect a cam's characteristics, even if overall lift and duration remain unchanged.

What is LDA?

Technically speaking, a cam's LDA equals half the angle in crankshaft degrees defined by the points of maximum exhaust valve lift and maximum intake valve lift. LDA equals the angle between the cam's intake and exhaust lobe centerlines as measured in camshaft degrees, but only if the intake and exhaust lifter bores are oriented at the same angle from vertical in the engine block, as is the case on the small-block Chevy (but not the Chevy Rat motor).

Often, the terms "LDA" and "lobe separation" are mistakenly interchanged with "lobe centerline." The latter is actually the angle in crankshaft degrees between the max lift point of a specific cylinder's intake valve (the "intake centerline") or exhaust valve (the "exhaust centerline"), relative to the piston at TDC during the transition between the exhaust and intake strokes.

Why is LDA Important?

This distinction is important because, although the installer can advance or retard the lobe centerlines (aka "degree" the cam), the displacement angle *between* the centerlines (LDA) is ground into the cam at the time of manufacture and cannot be changed by the end-user. In theory, narrow LDAs tend to increase midrange torque and result in faster-revving engines, while wide LDAs

result in broader powerbands and more peak power—albeit at the price of a somewhat lazier initial response.

LDA combines with a given cam's duration and lift to produce an "overlap triangle." The greater the duration and lift, the more overlap area, LDAs remaining equal. Given the same duration, LDA and overlap are inversely proportional: Increasing the LDA decreases overlap (and vice versa).

How Did We Test?

In what's becoming a *Car Craft* tradition, we decided to test theory against reality. Using the stout 10.8:1 357ci Saturday Night Special small-block Chevy engine detailed in our May '99 issue ("580hp Small-Block Chevy: No Nitrous, No Boost"), Joe Sherman Racing installed three Isky mechanical flat-tappet dual-pattern cams. Except for being ground with three different LDAs—106, 108, and 110 degrees—the cams were otherwise

identical. All were ground "straight-up." In other words, the intake and exhaust centerlines and the LDA are all the same number; the intake and exhaust centerlines occur at the same point in degrees after and before TDC, respectively. The cams were installed 3 degrees advanced from the as-ground position, using Sherman's "quick and dirty" degreeing method (see sidebar and "Cam Spec" chart).

The 106-degree-LDA cam was the same grind used in the May buildup, but additional fine-tuning raised the torque and power curve over that reported in the article. Refinements included optimizing the jetting in the Holley HP–series 950-cfm carb (No. 86 jets now feed all four barrels) from 45 degrees total timing, and a 2-inch spacer plate atop the Edelbrock Super Victor intake manifold.

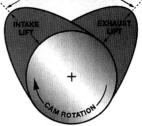

Wide LDA

Narrow LDA

Lobe Displacement Angle (LDA) is ground into the cam at the time of manufacture and cannot be altered by the end-user. In theory, altering the LDA can dramatically affect the engine's torque, power, cranking compression, idle quality, and piston-to-valve clearance.

Isky Test Cam Specs

LDA	Installed Lobe CL (Int./Exh.)	Adv. Timing Dur. (Int./Exh.)	Overlap	Installed Cam Timing @ 0.050in Tappet Lift Dur. (Int./Exh.)	Intake (Opens/Closes)	Exhaust (Opens/Closes)	Valve Lift w/1.5:1 Rockers (Int./Exh.)	Hot Valve Lash (Int./Exh.)
106°	103°/109°		80°		28° BTDC/54° ABDC	62° BBDC/24° ATDC		
108°	105°/102°	290°/294°	76°	262°/266°	26° BTDC/56° ABDC	64° BBDC/22° ATDC	0.580 in/0.585 in	0.014 in/0.016 in
110°	107°/113°		72°		24° BTDC/58° ABDC	66° BBDC/20° ATDC		

What Did We Learn?

The tests, to a large extent, confirmed the theory, but there were some mild surprises. Isky designed this profile to be ground with a 106-degree LDA, and the results bear this out: The 106-degree LDA produced the most peak and average torque, as well as the most average horsepower and the highest cranking compression. The 110-degree cam made the most peak

Angling for Answers

Sherman put his engine under a microscope to give us the lowdown on LDA changes. Besides the usual corrected torque and power numbers, Sherman also kept track of idle quality and vacuum (such as it was with this big a cam), cranking compression, and piston-to-valve clearance. How did reality match theory?

Torque: All cams made peak torque at 5,500 rpm. Sherman says that LDA alterations have little or no effect on the peak torque point, which is primarily determined by camshaft duration. Theory says that narrow LDAs improve midrange torque. The 106-degree LDA cam's 503.9 lb-ft peak torque output was up by 14.6 and 24.1 lb-ft over the 108- and 110-degree cams, respectively. But the 106 cam's overall average torque production advantage was nearly as great throughout the engine's 4,500–7,000–rpm powerband.

Power: Theory says that a wider LDA should make more peak power. The 108- and 110-degree grinds did raise the power peak 500 rpm (from 6,500 to 7,000). However, under 6,750 rpm they were both down in power in comparison to the 106-degree profile. Peak-to-peak, the 110 LDA cam's 583.6 hp was only 3.4 hp greater than the 106's

Cranking compression *decreases* **as LDA increases. On the street, cranking compression numbers are critical for determining an engine's suitability for running on pump gas.**

LDA Test Summary

Isky Test Cams ➡		106° LDA	108° LDA	110° LDA
Peak at Rpm	Torque (Lb-Ft)	503.9 @ 5,500	489.3 @ 5,500	479.3 @ 5,500
	Power (Hp)	580.2 @ 6,500	578.4 @ 7,000	583.6 @ 7,000
Change at Peak	Torque (Lb-Ft)	0.0	−14.6	−24.1
	Power (Hp)	0.0	−1.8	+3.4
Percent Change at Peak*	Torque (Lb-Ft)	0.0%	−2.9%	−4.8%
	Power (Hp)	0.0%	−0.3%	0.6%
Avg. Thru 7,000 Rpm	Torque (Lb-Ft)	476.1	462.8	452.4
	Power (Hp)	525.5	514.2	506.0
Avg. Change Thru 7,000 Rpm	Torque (Lb-Ft)	0.0	−13.3	−23.7
	Power (Hp)	0.0	−11.3	−19.5
Percent Avg. Change Thru 7,000 Rpm*	Torque (Lb-Ft)	0.0%	−2.8%	−5.0%
	Power (Hp)	0.0%	−2.2%	−3.7%
Avg. Cranking Compression (Psi)		180	165	155
Idle Quality (In Hg at Rpm)		4 @ 1,200	5 @ 1,200	6 @ 1,150
Avg. Piston-to-Valve Clearance (In)	Int. (8° ATDC)	0.070	0.090	0.110
	Exh. (8° BTDC)	0.100	0.120	0.140

*Compared to 106° baseline.

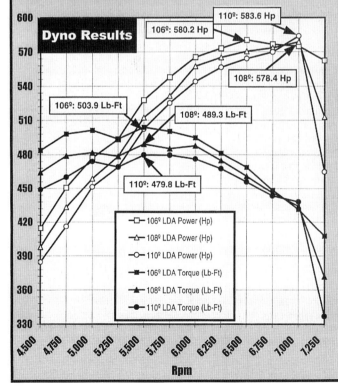

Dyno Results	
110º: 583.6 Hp	
106º: 580.2 Hp	
108º: 578.4 Hp	
106º: 503.9 Lb-Ft	
108º: 489.3 Lb-Ft	
110º: 479.8 Lb-Ft	

—□— 106º LDA Power (Hp)
—△— 108º LDA Power (Hp)
—○— 110º LDA Power (Hp)
—■— 106º LDA Torque (Lb-Ft)
—▲— 108º LDA Torque (Lb-Ft)
—●— 110º LDA Torque (Lb-Ft)

Rpm: 4,500 4,750 5,000 5,250 5,500 5,750 6,000 6,250 6,500 6,750 7,000 7,250

(Y-axis: 330 360 390 420 450 480 510 540 570 600)

580.2 best; the 108-degree cam was actually slightly down, developing only 578.4 hp at its peak. The power curve falls off rapidly over 7,000 rpm in every case, a possible indication of valve float. Moving up to stouter valvesprings might help the wider LDA grinds post better top-end power numbers.

Cranking compression: You'd think that with less overlap, cranking compression numbers should go up with wider LDAs. However, just the opposite is true with this engine: Cranking numbers ranged from a high of 180 psi with the 106-degree cam to a low of 155 psi with the 110-degree grind. Apparently, the narrower LDA cams' earlier intake valve closing built more cylinder pressure. Sherman says that under-180-psi numbers will support 92-octane gas with full advance, 180-200 psi requires careful tailoring of the advance curve, and plus-200-psi pressures mandate high-octane race gas to avoid detonation problems. For racing, if a particular application calls for a wide LDA, the engine-builder could raise the static compression ratio to make up for the loss of cylinder pressure, thereby restoring some of the missing midrange torque.

Idle quality: All three grinds are not suitable for daily street use (nor are they intended to be). Nevertheless, the observed vacuum characteristics indicate a trend that can be applied to milder cams: Wider LDAs build more vacuum. Manifold vacuum at idle ranged from 6 in-hg at 1,150 rpm for the 110-degree grind to only 4 inches(!) at 1,200 rpm for the 106-degree profile.

Assuming otherwise equivalent cams, piston-to-valve clearance decreases as the LDA narrows. That's because with more overlap at TDC, the narrow LDA cam's valves are further off their seats.

Sherman's 357ci Chevy combines a reliable bottom end (including Manley rods and lightweight Sportsman Racing Products pistons) with ported Dart Iron Eagle heads, an Edelbrock Super Victor intake, and a Holley 950-cfm HP-series double-pumper carb atop a 2-inch spacer-plate.

Feeler-Gauge Cam Degreeing

In the real world you won't see any measurable performance difference from 2-degree cam timing phase variations. According to Joe Sherman, on engines like the small-block Chevy where the intake and exhaust lifter bores are in the same plane, it is possible to achieve a plus-or-minus 2-degree level of accuracy without a degree-wheel using only a straightedge and feeler gauges. With the valvetrain properly lashed, rotate the engine to Top Dead Center on the Overlap stroke (both the intake and exhaust valves are open). Place a straight-edge in position across the lifter tops. On a single-pattern cam that's ground "straight up" (neither advanced nor retarded) the straightedge should lay flush against both lifters when the cam is installed in the split-overlap position.

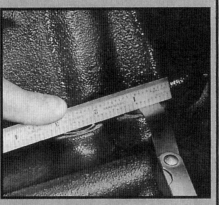

Our test engine's Isky dual-profile cam has 262-degrees intake and 266-degrees exhaust duration (at 0.050-inch tappet lift). The equation tells us that installing the cam 3 degrees advanced requires that the intake lifter be about 0.004-inch higher than the exhaust at TDC/overlap.

- If the exhaust lifter is higher than the intake lifter, the cam is retarded.
- If the intake lifter is higher than the exhaust lifter, the cam is advanced.

Note that many cams—especially street grinds—are ground with advance built in by the manufacturer. Check how much the cam is advanced or retarded by inserting a feeler gauge of the correct thickness between the lower lifter and the straightedge. Every 0.004-0.005-inch of clearance equates to about 1 degree of camshaft duration.

Dual-pattern cams are a little more complicated: You must add in half the duration difference. For example, if the exhaust side has 4 degrees more duration than the intake side at TDC/overlap, the exhaust lifter would be about 0.008-inch higher than the intake lifter if the cam is installed at split-overlap (both intake and exhaust centerlines are the same number).

These relationships can be expressed by the equation:

$$\left(\frac{\text{Int. Dur} - \text{Exh. Dur}}{2}\right) \times 0.004 + (\text{Desired Int. advance or retard} \times 0.004) = \text{lifter offset}$$

- Use a positive number for advance and a negative number for retard.
- A negative result indicates how much higher the exhaust lifter should be in relation to the intake lifter.
- A positive result indicates how much higher the intake lifter should be in relation to the exhaust lifter.

A Jesel beltdrive makes cam swaps and cam phase alterations a cinch. To gain access to the cam, you need only remove the water pump and harmonic damper. Jesel includes a tool to help break loose the bolts holding the cam retaining plate. Be careful— the bolts have left-hand threads!

power and had the best idle vacuum. Piston-to-valve clearance increased as the lobe separation widened. For an in-depth X-ray, see the "Angling for Answers" sidebar.

These tests show that if you're on a budget, the way to make the most horsepower per dollar is to concentrate on building the best torque curve within the operating range in which you desire to run. Since horsepower is a function of torque multiplied by rpm, build for torque and the power will take care of itself; the way you build for torque is to narrow the LDA. On the other hand, daily street drivers must also take idle quality and cranking compression psi into account, and narrow LDA equals increased overlap, which hurts the idle. Time to once again roll out that old cliché: There's no such thing as a free lunch. **CC**

SOURCES
ISKY RACING CAMS
Dept. CC
16020 S. Broadway St.
P.O. Box 30
Gardena, CA 90247-0803
213/770-0930
www.iskycams.com

JESEL VALVETRAIN INNOVATION
Dept. CC
1985 Cedar Bridge Ave.
Lakewood, NJ 08701-6915
732/901-1800
www.jesel.com

JOE SHERMAN RACING ENGINES
Dept. CC
2302 W. 2nd St.
Santa Ana, CA 92703-3548
714/542-0515

By Cole Quinnell

A s with anything in life, the more good choices there are available, the more difficult the decision becomes. For example, there are more than a dozen different aftermarket small-block Chevrolet heads on the market, and cost usually narrows the choice down to two or three. From here, it's fairly easy to choose the best one for your application. However, if we listed all the camshafts available for small-block Chevrolets, it would probably be more pages than this entire issue! The prices are all comparative, and they more or less look the same. So how do you choose a cam? Usually, the decision is made by talking to just about everybody you can get to listen, including friends, speed shop service people, and even the cam manufacturers themselves.

Cam manufacturers are well aware of this situation and have come up with a method of helping you make the right cam selection. Competition Cams, Crane, and Wolverine are three cam manufacturers that have complete computer programs, which take into consideration the variables of your application and make a recommendation based on their experience and knowledge of cam selection. It's kind of like having a cam manufacturer's engineer in your computer who you can talk to anytime you need to make a cam selection!

More than just producing a cam choice from your input, these programs also include utility functions that can help you determine compression ratio, engine rpm at 60 mph, and other useful information for selecting a cam.

We can hear the question already, "Do you need a 1.2 jigawatt computer to run these things?" No. All of these programs are available for IBM compatible computers. If you don't own a personal computer (PC), you can probably gain access to one easily enough. Crane's CamChoice and Wolverine's cam selection programs are available on 5¼- and 3½-inch floppy disks and require computers with 512 K memory or better. The CamQuest program from Competition Cams is available on 5½-inch floppy disks and requires a 1.2 megabyte disk drive. All three programs require a 2.2 or later version of MS-DOS.

Purchasing your next cam should be as easy and painless as possible. With these manufacturers' cam selection programs, attaining your goal of the best cam for your engine is now a little easier.

What you get out of something is directly proportional to what you put into it. In computer terms, that means,"garbage in, garbage out." Cam selection programs require a specific amount of knowledge concerning the vehicle and its intended use. Good examples of this are gear ratio, rear tire size, induction system, exhaust system, vehicle weight, and compression ratio.

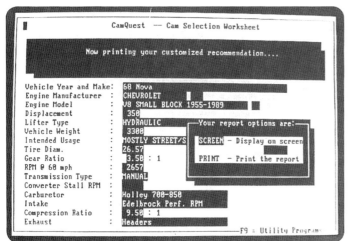

PLEASANT UTILITIES

One of the added bonuses that these cam selection programs offer is the utilities. These utilities are there to help you develop the most accurate information possible for input into the main cam selection programs, but are good enough by themselves to warrant adding to your software collection!

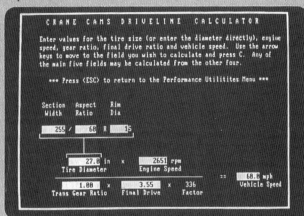

Most of the utilities are simply automotive-related formulas programmed into the computer. The computer asks you to input a specific amount of information and then produces the desired answer. The CamChoice driveline calculator even shows you the formula to help you understand how it derives the final product and allows you to pick the variable.

For example, if you have a tach, but don't know for sure what gear ratio the car has, run the car at 60 mph and note the rpm. Plug these numbers and your tire diameter into

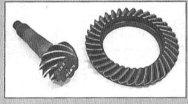

the formula to determine your rear gear ratio. This assumes that your speedometer is accurate of course.

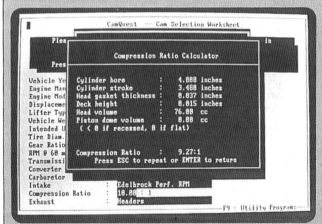

Another utility used to take the guesswork out of engine modifications is a compression ratio calculator included with all three programs we tested. The Wolverine cam selection program also includes options to calculate engine displacement and airflow; valvespring rate and load pressure; approximate drag race brake horsepower; piston velocity and acceleration; atmospheric conditions; and a dynamometer for correcting dyno numbers and making correlations from them. All three programs offer a number of informative and useful utilities, which are extremely valuable.

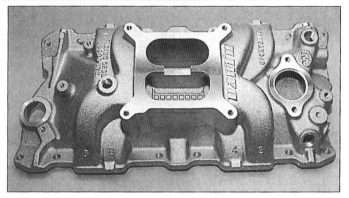

The CamQuest program from Competition Cams asks the most extensive questions before making a recommendation. It even allows for specific name-brand manifolds and knows the powerbands of these manifolds.

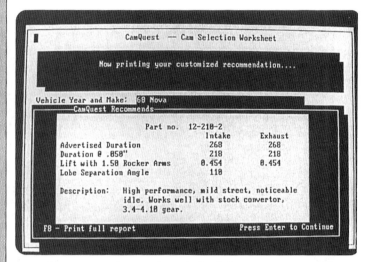

Once the computer has evaluated all of the input information, it will produce a recommendation. For a slightly modified small-block Chevrolet, the CamQuest program suggested Competition Cams' mild 268 performance camshaft. Even though the programs ask for converter stall speed and gear ratio, a suggested converter and gear ratio is included in the cam recommendation.

If you upgrade one component, then you will most likely have to upgrade others. All three cam selection programs suggest valvespring rates and have notes if other valvetrain component upgrades are necessary. Using good quality parts throughout the valvetrain will lead to longevity and minimum maintenance.

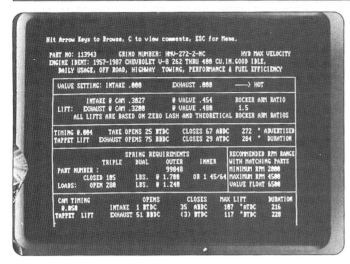

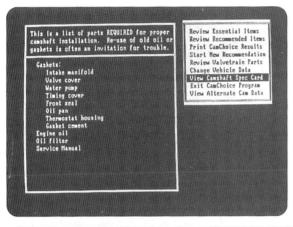

CamChoice from Crane includes an electronic "cam card" in its cam selection program that is identical to the information provided on the actual card included with the cam. The card provides gross and net lift, complete cam timing, and valvespring requirements.

All three programs contain a list of parts required to complete a cam change such as necessary gaskets and a reminder to change the oil and oil filter during the cam swap. The Wolverine program has an alternative list of suggested replacement parts such as radiator hoses, a water pump, and spark plugs to ensure that there are no problems during reassembly or the crucial break-in period.

A very helpful portion of the CamQuest program is an information menu chock-full of commonly asked questions with Competition Cams' answers, concerning camshafts in general and its specific types of cams. The answers to these questions are written in plain English and are easy to understand and correlate to real-life situations. **HR**

SOURCES

Competition Cams
Dept. HR06
3406 Democrat Rd.
Memphis, TN 38118
901/795-2400

Crane Cams
Dept. HR06
530 Fentress Blvd.
Daytona Beach, FL 32114
904/252-1151

Wolverine Gear & Parts Company
Dept. HR06
4790 Hudson Rd.
Osseo, MI 49266
800/248-0134 or 517/523-3611 (in MI)

By Rob Kinnan

The camshaft is one of the most important parts of an engine when it comes to making power, but it's also one of the most confusing parts for a beginner. Advertised versus at-.050 duration, lobe separation, intake centerline, lobe lift…it can throw a newcomer into a major case of tireshake. A 300-page book could be written on the individual design characteristics of a cam and its relationship with all the other parts in an engine, but we have only so many pages each month. Some of the cam stories we've done in the recent past have gotten rather esoteric, involving custom-ground lobes or combination-specific profiles. That's great for someone who's built a few engines, but what about those of you who are just starting to understand how all this works? In the real world, speed shops have the most popular cam grinds in stock, so that's what most beginning engine builders use.

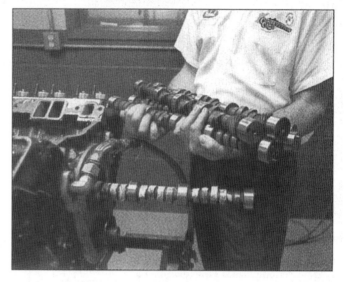

THE GREAT AMERICAN CAM COMPARO

TESTING OFF-THE-SHELF GRINDS FOR STREET PERFORMANCE

We decided to hit the dyno and show what the typical, off-the-shelf grinds do for street performance in a common street engine. Of course, the most common street engine is a mildly warmed-over 350 Chevy, a package just like Racing Head Service's (RHS) High Energy engine. And since RHS is right across the street from Competition Cams, we picked CC's brains and research records to come up with a selection of its most popular cam grinds.

We tested five camshafts in the same engine to show what each cam does, how much power it makes, where it makes it and why you would want one over the others. The test started with a near-stock cam, the Dual Energy 255 hydraulic, and went up in lift and duration in 10-degree increments until we got to the 286 single-pattern cam. In each test, the only parts changed were the cam and lifters. Every other component, including the valvesprings and ignition timing, stayed the same, and in most cases the carb jetting also remained the same as the baseline. Three runs were made with each camshaft, then this data was averaged. The results show that each cam has its advantages and disadvantages compared to the rest. Which one is for you depends on what you want out of your engine and car.

THE ENGINE

We wanted the test engine to be like the typical street engine. That means streetable compression, no expensive cylinder heads, and no high-dollar, trick parts—just a good, solid performer. RHS's 350 High Energy small-block Chevy package is just that. The short-block is completely machined, including honing with torque plates, and assembled with a remachined cast crank, remanufactured rods with new bolts, Silv-O-Lite cast pistons, Sealed Power moly rings and Fel-Pro gaskets. The rotating assembly is balanced.

The cylinder heads are World Products Street Replacement (S/R) iron heads with hardened exhaust seats (for unleaded gas) and 1.94/1.50 stainless-steel valves. These heads are a little better than a set of stock heads at making power, but the biggest benefit is that they are very affordable and feature brand-new castings and parts, not rebuilt stuff. Compression comes in at 8.8:1, and there are several different Competition Cams profiles to choose from. Comp Cams' High Energy hydraulic lifters, pushrods and valvesprings were used throughout our test. The engine comes as a long-block for $1895, but for additional green it can be equipped with an intake, ignition or anything else you want. We specified an Edelbrock Performer intake and a 750-cfm model 3310 Holley four-barrel carburetor, and the dyno headers have 1¾-inch primaries.

We did all the dyno testing on Competition Cams' Superflow 901 dyno. A Performance Distributors HEI was used on the RHS 350 engine and was set at 34 degrees total timing for all the tests.

The tests were run with Comp Cams' High Energy valvesprings and Magnum roller rockers.

Below are specs for the five camshafts we tested on the RHS High Energy 350 dyno mule. The first three are dual-pattern grinds, with roughly 10 degrees more exhaust duration on the exhaust than the intake. Cam number four is a single-pattern hydraulic, and number five is a solid-lifter, single-pattern cam.

TEST 1

The first cam to be tested was the 255 Dual Energy (DE) hydraulic. This cam is similar to a stock grind, with 203 degrees of intake duration and 212 degrees of exhaust duration at .050-lift, intake/exhaust valve lift of .427/.458 and a lobe separation angle of 110 degrees. The Dual Energy cams are dual-pattern, meaning that, in this case, the exhaust has more duration than the intake. A dual-pattern cam is used for several reasons, mostly for increased exhaust scavenging. Since the intake ports typically flow better than the exhaust ports, more exhaust duration means the valve is open longer, compensating for the weaker port flow. Designed for stock-type engines, the 255DE has a very smooth idle and makes most of its power below 5000 rpm, but falls flat on its face after that. This cam made a healthy 389 lbs-ft of torque at only 3000 rpm and 303 horsepower at 5000, but it really nosed over past that, dropping to only 212 at 5500. The vacuum produced at 750 and 1000 rpm was at near-stock levels, illustrating the tame nature of this profile.

TEST 2

The next cam to be tested was the 265DE, which is one step up from the 255. The specs on this cam are 211/221 duration at .050, .442/.465-lift and 110-degree lobe separation angle. This is still considered a mild cam (sometimes called an "RV" cam), but in smaller engines (like a 305 or a 327) it will have a perceptible lope at idle. The idle vacuum is good enough to operate power brakes, and you could run this cam with a stock torque converter without any problems at all. As you can see from the chart, however, it was worth 21 horsepower over the 255 at 5000 rpm, and while the peak torque only increased by 3 lbs-ft, it came 500 rpm higher. Of particular interest is the power made at 5500. Where the 255 was over and done with, the 265 was still making good power.

TEST 3

Jumping ahead another 10 degrees brings us to the 275DE, which pushes the .050-lift duration to 219/229 and

CAM	DURATION (at .050)		LIFT (in.)		LOBE SEP. ANGLE
	int.	exh.	int.	exh.	
Test 1 255DE	203	212	.427	.458	110
Test 2 265DE	211	221	.442	.465	110
Test 3 275DE	219	229	.468	.488	110
Test 4 286H	236	236	.490	.490	110
Test 5 282S	236	236	.495	.495	110

the lift to .468/.488, but still with a 110-degree lobe separation angle. This cam has enough duration and lift that you'll know it's there. The idle has a good lope to it, but with 14.5 inches of vacuum at 750 rpm, it's still docile enough for a daily driver. This cam would also work with a stock converter, but because it loses torque down low to make horsepower up high, it works better with a higher-stall converter. With the 275DE, the 350 kept chugging past the point where the other cams fell off, and made 338 peak horsepower at 5500. We made a few pulls to 6000 with this cam to see if it was indeed peaked out, and it was. Horsepower dropped sig-

To make the five-cam swap a little easier, we installed one of Comp's brand-new belt drives. This way the oil pan doesn't have to be removed to get at the cam—we had the swap down to an hour and a half.

Comp Cam's Robert Pruitt pulled the handle on the Superflow and also took on the arduous task of swapping all these cams in only a day and a half.

nificantly after 5500, but that's also about the rpm limit of the heads. With bigger heads (or if the S/R's were ported), this cam would probably peak at 6000.

TEST 4

For this test we ran out of dual-pattern cams, so we went with the next logical choice in a single-pattern cam: the 286H Magnum hydraulic. This cam has 236-degrees duration and .490-lift on both the intake and exhaust, and a 110-degree lobe separation angle. This cam is on the ragged edge of working with power brakes, but in our experience it *will* produce just enough vacuum to work. The idle is definitely noticeable, to the point where a stock converter will be a bear to live with. A 2500-stall or higher converter is recommended, and the cam will be strangled if the engine doesn't have an aftermarket intake, headers and a good exhaust.

As you can see in the chart, this was almost too much cam for these heads and intake. While it made three horsepower more than the 275, it peaked at 5000 and dropped by seven horsepower at 5500. Normally, a bigger cam will make more power at higher rpm levels, but the 286 ran up against the restrictive heads and dropped off at 5500. Same with the torque. The 286 made more peak torque and at the same rpm, but lost torque higher up when it should have made more. Again, with better heads it would have kept on pulling hard all the way to 6000.

WHICH IS REALLY THE BEST?

While it would seem obvious that the best cam was the 286 hydraulic because it made the most power, that's not necessarily true. In a car with a stock automatic trans, stock converter and a high rearend gear (such as a 3.08:1 or 2.78:1), this cam would probably be a dog, and the car would probably be quicker with the 275 or 265. And with the stock converter, ya better get used to popping the trans in neutral at every stop, because the engine's not going to want to idle in gear. The bigger cam is a better choice only if the car is built for it. A good intake and four-barrel, headers, a 2400-stall or higher converter and some more gear in the rear will be required to let this cam really work. Do you want a daily driver or a street racer?

	TEST 1		TEST 2		TEST 3		TEST 4	
RPM	LBS-FT	HP	LBS-FT	HP	LBS-FT	HP	LBS-FT	HP
2000	358	136	352	134	336	127	314	119
2500	369	175	360	171	348	165	342	162
3000	**389**	222	389	222	379	216	380	217
3500	385	256	**392**	261	**390**	260	**394**	262
4000	372	283	380	289	379	289	381	290
4500	350	300	359	308	364	312	370	317
5000	318	**303**	340	**324**	347	330	358	**341**
5500	212	222	307	322	323	**338**	319	334
VACUUM/RPM								
750:	17.5		16.0		14.5		10.5	
1000:	19.5		18.0		16.5		13.0	

The first two things to look at here are peak horsepower and peak torque. As expected, the biggest cam (the 286H) made the most of both. But looking at both numbers at 2000 rpm and then at 5000 rpm shows what happens to the power curve as the camshaft gets bigger. Increasing duration and lift makes the engine lose power at lower rpm and gain it back, plus some, at higher rpm. From the baseline 255 cam, the 286 picked up 38 horsepower. While peak torque only increased by 5 lbs-ft, the 286 made 40 lbs-ft more at 5000 and a whopping 107 lbs-ft more at 5500! Manifold vacuum also comes down as duration is added. The 286 cam's 10.5 inches at 750 rpm would idle in gear with a stock converter, but not very well. At this point, a higher-stall converter is definitely not just for idle quality, but also to get the engine into its power-band and get the car moving.

TEST 5

For the last test, we wanted to see what happens when comparing a hydraulic-lifter cam to a solid of roughly the same specs. We compared the 286 hydraulic to a 282 Magnum solid. Both are single-pattern cams with 236 degrees of duration at .050-lift, and the 282 solid only has an additional .005-inch of lift, at .495. But while this may look like an apples-to-apples comparison, it's not. Notice that while the .050-lift duration is the same, the advertised duration (282 degrees) of the solid cam is less. Due to the valve lash that is required with a solid lifter, the cam actually ends up being a little smaller (usually comparable to five degrees of duration) than a hydraulic of the same specs. As the dyno chart shows, the solid cam made better power down low and lost power up high, with less peak horsepower. Notice however that the solid cam made more power at 5500 than the

The 286H hydraulic cam and lifters are at top, and the 282 solid is below. While the specs are nearly identical, the solid cam feels "smaller" to the engine because of the lash at the valve. We set lash at .024-inch. One of the neat features of a solid lifter is that you can vary lash to move the power curve around slightly. More lash removes duration and lift, while a tighter setting increases both.

	TEST 4		TEST 5	
RPM	LBS-FT	HP	LBS-FT	HP
2000	314	119	333	127
2500	342	162	352	167
3000	380	217	382	218
3500	**394**	262	**391**	260
4000	381	290	380	289
4500	370	317	364	311
5000	358	**341**	348	332
5500	319	334	320	**335**

VACUUM/RPM		
750:	10.5	13
1000:	13	15

hydraulic at the same rpm, but still less peak horsepower and torque. The vacuum levels also show how much tamer the 282S is, with an additional 2.5 inches of vacuum at 750 rpm.

THE FINAL TEST, WE PROMISE

Pruitt claimed he had done testing with pushrods and actually found a few horsepower simply by replacing stock rods with good aftermarket pushrods. We didn't believe him, so he did the swap, changed nothing else (the 282 solid was in the engine) and made three pulls on the engine. He was right! The stock pushrods were swapped with Comp's Magnum pushrods, which are made from 1010 chrome-moly steel. According to Pruitt, the reason they were worth a few horsepower is due to the fact that, since they're stiffer than stock pushrods, they don't flex under the strain of the valvespring. As the stock pushrod bends, it gets shorter and lessens both duration and lift at the valve. The pushrods were only worth a few horsepower, but every little bit helps! **HR**

	STOCK		MAGNUM	
RPM	LBS-FT	HP	LBS-FT	HP
2000	333	127	331	126
2500	352	167	351	167
3000	382	218	382	218
3500	**391**	260	**395**	263
4000	380	289	381	290
4500	364	311	368	315
5000	348	332	350	333
5500	320	**335**	322	**338**
6000	289	330	294	336

SOURCES

Competition Cams
Dept. HR03
3406 Democrat Rd.
Memphis, TN 38118
901/795-2400

RHS Performance Engines
Dept. HR03
3416 Democrat Rd.
Memphis, TN 38118
901/794-2830

By Jeff Smith

There's more to the world of camshafts than just up-and-down motion. While they still push valves like they did a hundred years ago, the technology of camshaft and valvetrain design has made huge strides in the last 10 years. One size doesn't fit all anymore, and what was the hot cam last year is now old news. Let's take a look at what's new for '95 from one segment of the performance world where it's normal to be eccentric.

CAMSHAFT BUYERS' GUIDE

WHAT'S HOT IN CAMS AND VALVETRAINS

DUAL-PATTERN POWER

Competition Cams has recently unveiled a new Dual Energy line of hydraulic flat-tappet cams for the small- and big-block Chevys and the small-block Ford. These cams offer the latest in computer-designed quick-acceleration ramp designs with dyno-matched longer-duration exhaust lobes for optimal power. These cams make excellent torque and horsepower and are available in 255, 265 and 275 advertised-duration sizes. For more information, contact Competition Cams, Dept. HR03, 3406 Democrat Rd., Memphis, TN 38118, 901/795-2400.

TELEPHONE TECH

Camshafts can be one of the most confusing components in an internal combustion engine. Add to this the

Competition Cams	800/999-0853
Crane Cams	904/258-6174
Crower	619/422-1191
Edelbrock	310/782-2900
Lunati	901/365-0950
Wolverine/Blue Racer	800/248-0134

enormous number of cams available and the selection process can be difficult. Rather than rely on old wives' tales and rumors from uninformed friends, the best way to get accurate information is to call the cam companies themselves. Most of the larger companies now offer telephone lines dedicated to technical assistance. Keep these numbers handy the next time you have a camshaft or valvetrain tech question.

PRESSURE SITUATION

As camshafts evolve with higher and higher rates of valve acceleration, valvesprings are becoming increasingly important, even for street-driven cars. These acceleration rates place a bigger burden on the valvesprings to control the opening and closing

of valves at higher engine speeds. Dime-store stock valvesprings just won't cut it. Lunati now offers H-11 tool-steel valvesprings for both flat-tappet and roller cams that are available in dual- and triple-spring combinations. This steel is also exceptionally durable for long life and helps keep the valvetrain out of valve float. Contact Lunati Cams, Dept. HR03, P.O. Box 18021, Memphis, TN 38181-0021, 901/365-0950.

ROLLER ON

Roller cams used to be reserved for drag race or road race engines only. But now even the factories have picked up on the advantages of roller cams. Crower offers roller lifters in both hydraulic- and solid-roller models for the small- and big-block Chevys that will fit any flat-tappet-style block. For more information on these roller lifters and Crower's complete line of cam and valvetrain components, contact Crower

Cams & Equipment, Dept. HR03, 3333 Main St., Chula Vista, CA 91911, 619/422-1191.

ROCKER ON TOO

A cam will only lift the valve as much as the rocker arm will allow. While rocker ratios will increase lift, high valve lifts combined with high spring pressures will deflect a weak rocker arm. Erson

Cams has developed a new Billet Aluminum Rocker that limits deflection, increasing actual valve lift. The pocket design near the tip reduces weight while increasing lubrication to the tip, and the combination of 7075 T-6 aluminum and the unique profile reduces rocker-tip deflection. Erson currently offers this rocker only for small- and big-block Chevys. Contact Erson Cams, Dept. HR03, 550 Mallory Way, Carson City, NV 89701, 702/882-1622.

TIMING IS EVERYTHING

The most high-tech cam will do you little good if the timing chain and gear

set allow cam timing to wander all over the map. Edelbrock offers a steel timing gear and chain set that not only offers accurate timing and durability, but is also emissions-legal for all non-roller-cam small-block Chevys. When bolting in that new cam, that's a perfect time to add a new timing set as well. For more information on Edelbrock's complete line of cams and valvetrain components, contact Edelbrock Corp., Dept. HR03, 2700 California St., Torrance, CA 90503, 310/781-2222.

MUSCLE CAMS

Restoring the musclecars from the '60s and '70s is still high up on the hot rodding hit parade. For those hard-core resto artists, nothing but an original cam will do for a complete restoration. These cams might have been tough to find at one time, but now Wolverine/Blue Racer has over 65 different applications of hydraulic and

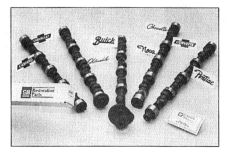

mechanical cams for the popular musclecars. Whether its a Duntov 30-30 mechanical cam for a '68 302 Chevy or a 271-horse 289 Mustang cam, talk to Wolverine/Blue Racer. Plus, these cams come in genuine GM or Ford restoration boxes. For more information, contact Wolverine Blue Racer, Dept. HR03, 4790 Hudson Rd., Osseo, MI, 49266, 800/248-0134.

THE ISKY KIT

There's more to camshaft selection than just picking a cam. You also need to match it with the proper lifters. Isky Racing Cams now offers complete cam-and-lifter selections that make this easy. These kits are available for a number of engines, including the small- and big-block Chevys. For more information, contact Iskenderian Racing Cams, Dept. HR03, 16020 S. Broadway, P.O. Box 30, Gardena, CA 90247-9990, 213/770-0930.

GET ALIGNED

Crane has just introduced a new line of self-aligning roller-tipped rocker arms. These full-needle-bearing rocker arms are designed to replace the "rail"-type stock rocker arms on '88 and later

small-block Chevys. The self-aligning rocker arms do not require pushrod guideplates, and center the rocker with the use of the rails on each side of the roller tip that straddle the valve. These rockers are also a narrow-body style that will fit under the late-model center-bolt valve covers. They cannot be used with a mechanical cam but are available in both 1.5 and 1.6:1 ratios. For more information, contact Crane

Cams, Inc., Dept. HR03, 530 Fentress Blvd., Daytona Beach, FL 32114, 904/258-6174.

SMOG-LEGAL CAMS

It used to be that virtually any modification to your engine was probably illegal from an emissions standpoint. But now, emissions-legal parts have

become hot items. Hi-Tech has now entered the game with a line of 11 C.A.R.B.-exempted camshafts for '87 and older carbureted small-block Chevys. Hi-Tech will also offer a full line of other E.O.'d components in the coming months. For more information, contact Hi-Tech Engine Components, Dept. HR03, P.O. Box 510988, Salt Lake City, UT 84151, 800/453-8250.

ROLL ON

Hydraulic-roller cams are one of the hot products in the camshaft biz these days. Runnin' right up there with the

big dogs is Engle's new hydraulic-roller camshafts and kits for small- and big-block Chevys, as well as the small-block Ford. These cams benefit from what is called an inverse-flank design that keeps the seat timing short yet rapidly accelerates the valves open. This makes for great torque and strong horsepower that isn't possible with a flat-tappet cam. For more details on these hydraulic-roller designs, contact Engle Cams, Dept. HR03, 1621 12th St., Santa Monica, CA 90404, 310/450-0806. **HR**

By The HOT ROD Staff

While swapping an intake or a carburetor is pretty common for the young hot rodder, the first major modification most will make to their engines is swapping in a new camshaft. Often, if the engine is still fresh, the cam can be swapped in without even removing the engine from the car. Here's how.

The first step in this swap is choosing the right cam. It should be carefully selected so that it fits your needs. The 350ci Chevy in this '63 Chevy II is stock other than an aftermarket intake, Holley 600-cfm (part No. 1850) carb and headers and a free-flowing exhaust. The owner called Lunati, and the tech guys there recommended a High Efficiency cam for $90.94 (part No. 06108) to complement this combination. This single-pattern cam has 218 degrees of duration at 0.050-inch lift on the intake and exhaust valves, 0.457-inch valve lift and a lobe separation angle of 112 degrees. A cam kit with lifters, springs, retainers and locks was also ordered for $184.16.

Along with the basics, we've collected some tricks for removing the stock cam and installing an aftermarket cam on a small-block Chevy with as little hassle as possible.

BUMPSTICK BOOGIE
SWAP IN A CAM FOR SOME POWER

Start by draining the water out of the engine and removing the radiator and shroud. On most cars, the grille will also have to be removed to slide the cam in. Remove the belt drives, water pump, harmonic balancer and anything else on the front of the engine. Make sure you tag and bag all the components so everything gets back on the car in its proper place.

Next, remove the distributor, intake (with the carb on it) and valve covers. Then remove all the rocker nuts, rockers, pushrods and lifters. Place all the components in marked ziplock bags, then place all the bags in one box. Now comes the tricky part. On the small-block, the timing chain cover interlocks with the oil pan along its bottom edge, which makes removing and installing the cover without removing the oil pan very difficult. To get the cover off, the oil pan will need to be loosened and pulled off the block at least ¼ inch. Be careful not to bend the cover when removing it so it will seal tightly when reinstalled.

Remove the bolts for the timing chain gear on the cam, install a cam removal tool on the front of the cam (we used the spare tire hold-down bolt) to prevent damaging the cam bearings when sliding the cam out, and remove the stock cam.

Generously apply assembly lube to all the lobes, oil pump eccentric and distributor gear. Wipe fresh engine oil on the bearing surfaces and slide the cam into the engine. Install the timing chain, lining up the assembly dots on the gears. Use thread lock on the bolts and torque them to the proper specs (25 ft-lbs on a small-block Chevrolet) to keep the bolts from backing out later.

Since this cam has more than 0.420-inch max valve lift, the stock valvesprings needed to be replaced to avoid valvespring bind. Lunati single-coil valvesprings (part No. 73943) were installed with Lunati retainers (part No. 75704) and locks (part No. 77003) by sliding a nylon rope into the cylinder through the spark plug hole with the piston at TDC, which holds the valves up while replacing the valvesprings. Leave the factory oil slinger on to prevent excessive oil consumption and install new O-rings on the valve stem.

PARTS YOU NEED BUT PROBABLY WOULDN'T HAVE THOUGHT OF

engine assembly manual (for torque specs, and so on)
rocker nuts (if yours are worn)
engine assembly gasket set (minus head and oil pan gaskets)
cam assembly lube
rtv silicone
contact cement (to hold gaskets in place)
thread lock
valvespring compressor
harmonic balancer puller/installer
cam removal tool
nylon rope
engine oil
valve seals

Clean everything before reassembly. To install the timing chain cover with the oil pan on the engine, clip the ends off the timing chain cover, as shown, install the rubber seal in the cover with contact cement to make sure it stays in the cover, add a dab of silicone at the ends of the rubber seal and install. This is also a good time to install a new front hub seal as well. A good tip when sliding the cover on is to use two punches in the lower bolt holes as guides to slide the cover in and down onto the dowels on the block.

Before dropping the Lunati hydraulic lifters (part No. 71817) in the engine we dabbed assembly lube on the bottom and coated the sides and top with engine oil. The pushrods, rockers, rocker balls and nuts were then installed and the valve lash set. Hydraulic lifters operate with zero lash, so to set the lash the engine is rotated until the exhaust valve begins to open. The intake valve is adjusted to zero lash by tightening the rocker nut while spinning the

pushrod with your fingers. When resistance to spinning the pushrod is felt (before the plunger on the lifter is depressed), turn the adjusting nut a half-turn more—the intake is now set to zero lash. The engine is rotated until the intake valve almost closes fully, then the rocker nut on the exhaust is adjusted the same way. This procedure is repeated on every cylinder.

Use new gaskets when installing the intake with silicone on the front and rear mating surfaces of the block and intake. The original distributor was a points ignition unit that we plan on replacing with a new MSD billet HEI. Installing the distributor gear on the right cam tooth is critical, so try this tip from the pros at Fast Times Motor Works in Morton Grove, Illinois (708/966-FAST). Bring the No. 1 cylinder to around 12 degrees BTDC on the compression stroke (use a timing tab to determine this), install the distributor and hook up the No. 1 plug wire to a spark plug, which is grounded but not installed in the cylinder head. With the ignition on, slowly rotate the distributor and see if a spark jumps the gap on the plug. If it does, you've got the distributor in the right place. If not, check the rotor placement and try again.

Bolt on all the accessories and the radiator, add water to the cooling system, and finish all those tasks that need to be done to run the engine. With the ignition off, use the starter to turn over the engine until you get oil pressure. Turn the ignition on and attempt to fire the engine. If it backfires and won't start, you most likely have the distributor off a tooth, the plug wires are mixed up, or something else is wrong. Stop trying to start the engine and find the problem, or you might wear a cam lobe flat cranking the engine at low rpm. Once the engine fires, vary the engine rpm slowly between 2000 to 2500 rpm for 20 minutes, making certain the oil pressure and water temperature are good and no leaks are found on the engine. **HR**

SOURCES

Lunati Cams, Inc.
Dept. HR03
P.O. Box 18021
4770 Lamar Ave.
Memphis, TN 38181-0021
901/365-0950

MSD Ignition
Dept. HR03
1490 Henry Brennan Dr.
El Paso, TX 79936
915/857-5200

CAMSHAFT TECH

HOW TO AVOID THE BUMPSTICK BLUES

By Rob Kinnan

BEASTIE BUMPSTICK CO.

"Where bigger is always better"

#B4-ULOOS
Gross Valve Lift:
Duration, Advertised:
Duration, at .050-Lift:
Lobe Seperation:

Truly Gross
Horrendous
Completely disgusting
You don't want to know

CHOOSING THE RIGHT CAM

Find the flaw in the following combination: a '67 Impala running a 327 small-block with stock heads, 8.5:1 compression, a 305-degree-duration cam, a two-barrel carb, stock exhaust manifolds, a Powerglide automatic, a stock converter and 2.73:1 rear gears.

If you identified the camshaft as the component that doesn't fit with the rest, give yourself a gold star. If you didn't figure it out or did but still aren't sure exactly why the cam is wrong, you need to read the following.

A car that idles rough, stalls in gear, is a bear to drive in traffic and gets abysmal gas mileage is still cool if it rocks when you floor the loud pedal. An engine that suffers these driveability headaches and still gets blown away by a Chevette is the worst possible hot rodding experience. Trust us, we've been there. The most prevalent reason for engines that don't run as they should is an improper camshaft for the engine and vehicle combination. And that's understandable, because choosing a cam is one of the hardest, most confusing parts of building an engine. The counter guy at the local speed shop/quick lube/food mart isn't the best source of information, so knowing the approximate cam specs for your combination is vital to

an enjoyable machine, be it full race or full cruise.

The problem is that there are many things to consider when choosing a cam, and it involves much more than just the other engine parts. The entire vehicle and the sum of its parts are just as important. Below is an outline of what all those specs and numbers mean in the camshaft catalog and a general explanation of how they affect performance, followed by a rundown of the areas that must be addressed at cam selection time. This information is guaranteed to make your next cam choice almost painless, if not completely enjoyable. We'll concentrate on the spectrum covering pure street cars to fairly quick bracket racers/sorta street cars. Race cars (or anything that runs quicker than, say, 11.00 in the quarter-mile) is a whole other ball of wax.

UNDERSTANDING CAMSHAFT SPECIFICATIONS

There are many numbers and terms used when describing a camshaft's design that must be understood when choosing a cam. It's good to know exactly how each of these specs affects the engine's performance, but one of the most important is duration, so pay special attention to that one. Also, look at the recommendations given by the cam companies for our six sample vehicles at the end of this article. Compare how the specs change from one example to the other, then refer back to the paragraphs just below to see why one has more duration or lift than the other.

LIFT: The cam's basic function is to open the valves. Lift refers to how far the valve is opened (or lifted) off its seat. A street performance cam will usually have between .450- and .550-inch lift. More lift can increase power, and increased lift without changing duration increases power without affecting the point of peak power on the rpm band. The rocker arms have a direct effect on lift because they don't have a 1:1 lever ratio. A cam that has .318 inch of lobe lift (that's how far it lifts the lifter) will open the valve .477 inch with 1.5:1 rocker arms (.318 x 1.5 = .477) and .508 inch with 1.6:1 rockers. Generally, a stock engine will tolerate .500-inch lift before the valves hit the pistons or the valvesprings hit coil bind, but any time lift is increased, these clearances should be checked.

DURATION: Duration is how long the cam holds the valves open. It's expressed in degrees of crankshaft rotation (remember, the cam rotates at half the speed of the crank). A 280-degree-duration cam holds the valves open longer than a 260-degree-duration cam. Holding the valves open longer allows more air and fuel into the engine and also allows more to get out through the exhaust. Longer duration (higher number) improves top-end power but almost always sacrifices low-end torque. Lower duration improves low-end torque and makes the car idle better, but it limits top-end power, and you can get only so much valve lift with a short duration cam due to the rate-of-lift limitations of the lifter. Roller cams, which we'll discuss below, have the advantage of allowing high rates of lift with relatively short duration.

The confusing thing about duration is the difference between "advertised" and "at .050-lift" duration. At .050-lift duration is measured from the point where the cam moves the lifter up .050 inch until .050 inch before the lifter is all the way back down. Most cam manufacturers differ in where they start and finish measuring for advertised duration. Some start at .004-inch lift, some at .008-inch and some measure it somewhere in between. That's why the .050-lift numbers are the best to go by. A 280 cam (advertised duration) from one

manufacturer could actually have less at –.050 duration than a 278 cam from another, due to the different points at which the companies measure advertised duration.

LOBE SEPARATION ANGLE: This is the relationship between the centerlines of the intake and exhaust lobes. A 110-degree lobe separation angle means that the peak opening points of the intake and exhaust lobes are 110 degrees apart. This is ground into the cam and can't be changed without changing cams. Lobe separation angle is another way of expressing overlap, which is the term formerly used by cam manufacturers. Overlap is the amount of time that both valves are open in the same cylinder. When both valves are open at the same time, cylinder pressure drops. A cam with 106 degrees of lobe separation angle will have more overlap and a rougher idle than one with 112 degrees, but it'll usually make more midrange power.

DUAL-PATTERN CAMS: A dual-pattern cam is one that has different duration and/or lift specs for the intake and exhaust. Usually, the exhaust lobes have more duration and lift than the intakes. Depending on the engine, this can be beneficial for engines with poor exhaust-port flow or otherwise-restricted exhaust systems. You'll notice in the cam recommendations below that Crane, Crower and (in a few cases) Lunati prefer dual-pattern cams over single-pattern for the examples we provided. Whenever you see a figure like 280/292, that's a dual-pattern cam with 280 degrees duration on the intake lobes and 292 degrees on the exhaust.

TYPE OF LIFTER: A hydraulic-lifter cam is the best choice if the car is to be a daily driver, because it doesn't

need periodic lash adjustments. A solid-lifter cam is beneficial in high-rpm applications (6500 rpm and higher), but it requires a lash adjustment every few months. Hydraulic and solid, nonroller cams are also called "flat-tappet" cams. A roller cam is normally associated with hard-core race engines, but several companies make street rollers that are docile enough for a daily driver, yet still make serious power. Most roller lifters aren't of the hydraulic type, so they require adjustment just like a solid lifter. Hydraulic rollers are becoming much more common but haven't found much of a following in high-performance circles yet, except in late-model computer-controlled cars. Either type of roller cam and lifter is considerably more expensive than a flat tappet. Also, you can't mix and match cams and

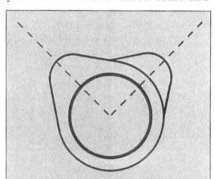

This illustration shows what we mean by lobe separation angle: the angle between the intake and exhaust lobes. Notice that the lobe ramps overlap a bit. While the exhaust valve is closing, the intake is already opening. That's overlap. The narrower this angle (the lower the number), the more time both valves are open in the cylinder and therefore the more overlap.

More than just the engine parts must be considered when choosing a cam. With a high-stall converter and lower (higher numerically) rearend gears, the engine will perform better with a bigger cam than if the car has a stock converter and highway gears. The same combination applies to vehicle weight. A heavy car is harder to get moving than a light car, so it needs more torque down low and usually less duration.

lifters. Because they're ground differently, a solid-lifter cam must use solid lifters and a hydraulic cam must use hydraulic lifters.

WHAT DO YOU WANT THE CAR TO DO?

We'd all like to have a 10-second car with a great stereo, air conditioning, 30-mpg fuel economy and 1.2g handling capability, but reality says that isn't going to happen unless your surname is "The Magnificent." In the real world a street car is built for either ultimate straight-line quickness, driveability with some performance, or a combination of both, which ultimately means a compromise of both. Do you want the car to run 10s or get you to work every day? How about low 13s in a hassle-free daily driver? Does the car have an automatic or manual transmission? How rough an idle can you put up with?

These are by far the most important considerations not just for cam choice but for building the entire car, and they should be taken into account before bolting any part onto the car or engine, be it a camshaft or tires. If the engine or car combination is not matched, no cam in the world will totally fix the

problem. Once you've decided how you want the car to behave, you must build the entire engine and drivetrain to fit.

Everything about the car combination and intended function must be decided upon before choosing the cam. Once this is determined, the following important details must be taken into account to get exactly the right camshaft: the engine's compression ratio, the basic power range of the heads/intake manifold/carb/headers combination, the car's weight, the transmission type (and/or torque converter stall speed), the rear gear ratio and the rear tire size. If you know the actual flow numbers for the cylinder heads, you'll be way ahead of the game.

Because there's an almost infinite number of combinations of all these parameters, it would take forever to explain the intricacies of how these parts all work together with the camshaft, so we've come up with six sample vehicles and called five of the major cam companies for recommendations on what cam they would choose for each vehicle. Compare the cam specs with how radical each car is, and you'll get a good idea of what's needed from the cam. The combinations pre-

sented are very typical of many street cars. If yours is close to one of them, choosing one of the cams recommended will guarantee happiness.

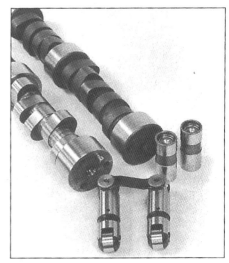

If you can afford it and don't mind occasionally pulling the valve covers and lashing the valves, a roller cam will offer greatly increased performance because its rate of lift is much faster than a flat-tappet cam. Notice the shape of the roller cam's lobes (*left*) compared to that of the hydraulic cam's. The fatter lobe accelerates the lifter and opens the valve much faster.

How important is it to regularly check the valve lash? The lobe of this solid-roller cam went away because the lifter needed rebuilding, causing the lash on this particular lobe to increase too much. Checking the lash would have detected this problem before it manifested itself this way.

TECH LINES & CATALOG INFO

Almost every cam manufacturer has technical experts to answer any question you may have about camshafts. If you know the details of your car and engine combination, the experts at these companies can dial you right into the perfect cam. Don't be afraid to call, that's why they're there. Just tell 'em HOT ROD sent you. And get a catalog, because most of them also have very detailed information on how to choose a cam, how to dial it in and what special considerations are mandatory for your particular engine.

SPECIAL CONSIDERATIONS

High Compression: Cam companies have long preached the gospel of conservative cam specs for a true street car, meaning that you're always better off to go one step smaller on the cam instead of one step bigger. Most of the time that's true, but there are instances where a street car should run an aggressive cam, and sometimes bigger is indeed better.

Overlap (lots of duration and tight lobe-separation angles) decreases cylinder pressure, especially at low rpm, which allows an engine to run a higher compression ratio and still work on pump gas. High cylinder pressure, which is caused partly by a high compression ratio, is what makes an engine detonate on pump gas. Decreasing the cylinder pressure by adding duration is just like taking compression out of the engine, but mostly only at low rpm. A compression ratio of 11.5:1 running on pump gas is not unheard of when the cam has enough overlap and duration to bleed off the low-speed cylinder pressure.

Computer Controls: If smog-legality is a concern in your area and you've got a late-model, computer-controlled car, your camshaft choices are severely restricted to what the cam manufacturers have certified. There are some good cams out there, but don't expect to stuff in a monster roller and sneak it by the smog cops. Even if you don't care about the smog legality, a factory engine-control computer will only handle so much camshaft before it freaks out. Consult the cam companies for recommendations.

Other Stuff You'll Need: Never reuse old lifters with a new cam, even if they've only been run for five minutes. Lifters and cam lobes develop a unique wear pattern almost immediately that won't be compatible with a new camshaft. Also make sure that the valvesprings match the new cam, the pushrods are all straight and the rocker arms will handle any increased lift or stress the cam provides.

RECOMMENDATIONS FROM THE PROS

We called the pros at Lunati, Competition Cams, Crane Cams, Crower Cams and Isky and asked them to choose the best cam for each of the following six sample vehicles. As you'll see, different experts like to take slightly different approaches, some on the radical side and some more conservative. Check out these recommendations, then re-read the previous section describing how the specs affect performance. A side benefit of some of these cams is legality. Crane, for example, has E.O. numbers that make the cams in Vehicles 1, 2, 3, and 6 legal in 50 states in precomputer cars.

Vehicle 1: 350 Chevy, 9.0:1 compression, high-rise dual-plane intake, 600-cfm carb, automatic trans, stock converter, 3.08:1 gears, 3400-pound vehicle weight. Car is 90-percent street, 10-percent strip.

Cam Co.	Part No.	Lift	Adv.Dur.	.050 Dur.	Lobe Sep.
Comp	12-210-2	.454	268	218	110
Crane	113902	.427/.454	260/272	204/216	112
Crower	00240	.445	267/272	210/216	112
Isky	201264	.450	264	214	108
Lunati	00017	.460	290	224	112

Notes: Notice the differences between advertised duration and .050 duration. Comp rates its cam at 268 and 218, respectively, while Lunati rates its cam at 290 and 224. Lunati's cam has 22 degrees more advertised duration but only 6 degrees more at .050 lift.

Vehicle 2: Same as above, but with 2400-stall converter and 3.55:1 gears.

Cam Co.	Part No.	Lift	Adv. Dur.	.050 Dur.	Lobe Sep.
Comp	12-212-2	.480	280	230	110
Crane	100052	.454	272	216	110
Crower	00241	.456/.458	270/276	214/218	112
Isky	201271	.465	270	221	108
Lunati	00010	.480	292	230	109

Notes: A looser converter and steeper gears allow the car to launch and cruise at a higher rpm, therefore these cams are more aggressive to move the powerband up into a higher range.

Vehicle 3: Same as Vehicle 1, but with four-speed manual transmission and 3.55:1 gears.

Cam Co.	Part No.	Lift	Adv. Dur.	.050 Dur.	Lobe Sep.
Comp	12-212-2	.480	280	230	110
Crane	113942	.454/.480	272/284	216/228	112
Crower	00242	.462/.470	280/286	220/226	112
Isky	201281	.485	280	232	108
Lunati	30111	.465/.489	270/280	220/230	108

Notes: A manual tranny allows even higher launch rpm, so the cam can be a little more aggressive than that recommended for the 2400-stall automatic. Notice that Lunati also closed up the lobe separation angle 1 degree for the four-speed, and a full 4 degrees compared to the tight automatic of Vehicle 1.

Vehicle 4: 350 Chevy, 11:1 compression, single-plane intake, 750 double-pumper, automatic trans, 3000-stall converter, 4.11:1 gears, 3400-pound vehicle weight. Car is 50-percent street, 50-percent strip.

Cam Co.	Part No.	Lift	Adv. Dur.	.050 Dur.	Lobe Sep.
Comp	12-225-4	.555	306	260	110
Crane	110692	.502/.516	294/300	238/244	106
Crower	00244	.497/.504	288/296	234/246	112
Isky	201292	.505	292	244	108
Lunati	30115	.520/.540	290/300	240/250	104

Notes: This engine combination is designed to make peak power at a much higher rpm than the previous example, hence the much more aggressive cams. The higher compression ratio also allows more duration.

Vehicle 5: 454 Chevy, 9.0:1 compression, dual-plane intake, 750-cfm carb, automatic trans, stock converter, 3.55:1 gears, 3500-pound vehicle weight. Car is 90-percent street, 10-percent strip.

Cam Co.	Part No.	Lift	Adv. Dur.	.050 Dur.	Lobe Sep.
Comp	11-205-3	.485	268	218	110
Crane	133942	.515/.510	272/284	216/228	112
Crower	01241	.518/.520	276/278	214/218	112
Isky	396271	.543	270	221	108
Lunati	00020	.501/.527	280/290	214/224	112

Notes: Comparing this example to Vehicle 1 shows the effect that displacement has on cam timing. A bigger engine needs a more aggressive cam to have the same powerband and idle quality as a smaller engine. In other words, a cam with 230 degrees of duration at .050 would idle pretty rough in a 305, but it would be fairly smooth in a 454.

Vehicle 6: 302 Ford, 9.5:1 compression, dual-plane intake, 600-cfm carb, automatic trans, 2400-stall converter, 3.50:1 gears, 3200-pound vehicle weight. Car is 80-percent street, 20-percent strip.

Cam Co.	Part No.	Lift	Adv. Dur.	.050 Dur.	Lobe Sep
Comp	31-414-3	.501	270	224	110
Crane	363942	.484/.512	272/284	216/228	112
Crower	15211	.491/.500	276/281	212/216	112
Isky	381271	.496	270	221	108
Lunati	31007	.508	275	225	104

Notes: Compare the grinds for this 302 with Vehicle 2, the 350 Chevy with a 2400-stall converter. The engine and vehicle combinations are very similar, the only real difference being engine displacement, so most of the recommendations for the 302 are a bit smaller. **HR**

The catalogs from the cam companies are usually very complete and offer much more information than we can pack into this article. Read the catalogs and call the manufacturers for specific recommendations.

SOURCES

Competition Cams
Dept. HR04
3406 Democrat Rd.
Memphis, TN 38118
901/795-2400
800/999-0853 (tech line)

Controlled Induction
Dept. HR04
24650 Leafwood
Murrieta, CA 92562
909/677-2332

Crane Technologies Group
Dept. HR04
530 Fentress Blvd.
Daytona Beach, FL 32114
904/252-1151
904/258-6174 (tech line)

Crower Cams
Dept. HR04
3333 Main St.
Chula Vista, CA 91911-5899
619/422-1191

Isky Racing Cams
Dept. HR04
16020 S. Broadway
Gardena, CA 90247
213/770-0930

Lunati Cams
Dept. HR04
4770 Lamar Ave.
Memphis, TN 38118
901/365-0950

Mr. Gasket Company
Dept. HR04
8700 Brookpark Road
Cleveland, OH 44129
216/398-8300

Performance Trends, Inc.
Dept. HR04
P.O. Box 573
Dearborn Heights, MI 48127
810/473-9230

VP Engineering (Dynomation)
Dept. HR04
2921 Patricia Dr.
Des Moines, IA 50322
515/276-0701

ROLL ON

THE BASICS OF A ROLLER CAM INSTALLATION

CAMSHAFT TECH

Face it: Real engines have roller cams (and we're not talking about factory hydraulic rollers). If you think your flat-tappet mill can make some ponies, then you're in for a real surprise. Cost is definitely a hindrance to pitching the old bumpstick for a roller, but often it's a matter of not knowing what's really needed that keeps people from stepping up to a roller camshaft.

If an engine has a good high-performance combination of intake and

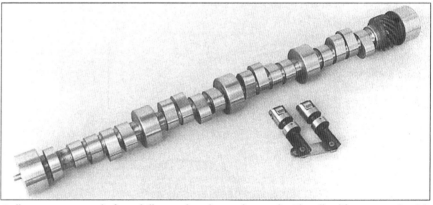

Roller cams are made from billet steel and must be used with roller lifters. You should not use hydraulic-roller lifters on a mechanical-roller cam, or vice versa, because the cam profiles are often different.

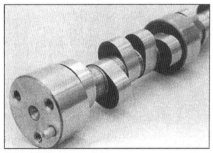

The shape of the lobes on a more radical roller cam is practically rectangular with rounded corners. Because of the limitation posed by a flat tappet, the lobes have much gentler ramps, which open and close the valves gradually rather than snapping them open as a roller cam can. This is a Lunati mechanical-roller cam for a race big-block Chevy. It also has a reduced base circle.

Mike Golding of Crane Cams says that good-quality, needle-bearing-type roller rocker arms are highly recommended when upgrading to a roller camshaft. A roller cam actuates the valves much quicker than a flat-tappet cam and typically requires a valvespring with greater tension. All this adds up to greater stress on the rocker arms. Very mild roller cams, such as stock GM and Ford pieces, can still use stamped-steel rockers, but even GM has gone to a roller rocker on its LT4 engine in '96 Corvettes. Often, adding roller rockers to production cylinder heads requires screw-in studs and clearancing.

The most common problem when installing a roller cam is using valvesprings with too much tension. Roller cams require relatively high open-spring pressures, but many people get carried away and use a spring that could suspend a ½-ton truck. Springs with more tension than required for your cam profile rob power, accelerate valvetrain wear and contribute to breakage. Use springs that match the recommendations by the cam manufacturer, or simply buy their matched spring set for your cam.

On many street grinds, the cam manufacturer can press an iron gear onto its roller cams during the manufacturing process, eliminating the need for a special distributor gear. The street roller cam in the background is fitted with an iron gear. A standard roller cam is in the foreground.

The next consideration is the gear on the distributor. Roller cams are made from billet steel, including the timing gear on most of the cams. This material will become damaged before the gear on the distributor wears out. Since the gear on the cam cannot be replaced, a softer bronze gear should be installed on the distributor, which is meant to be self-sacrificing over a period of time. The more expensive bronze gears are of higher quality and will last much longer than the cheap ones. A bronze-tipped fuel-pump pushrod is also necessary if using a mechanical fuel pump.

JUICE OR SOLID

When choosing a roller cam for the street, you're first faced with the decision of using a hydraulic- or mechanical-roller lifter. The hydraulic-roller lifter is virtually maintenance free once the preload is set properly. These lifters are also quieter than mechanical rollers. They do have some limitations on the amount of duration and lift they can tolerate, much like a hydraulic flat-tappet lifter compared to a solid flat tappet. Mechanical-roller lifters allow you to move the powerband slightly by adjusting the lash, and they boast better valve-timing accuracy. They also cause valvetrain noise and require periodic adjustment. The frequency of such adjustments depends on the driver's right foot. A race-only engine will require regular checks, while a street engine may not ever need to be adjusted once the lash is set properly after engine break-in. Golding does point out that the final lash setting should be made with the engine oil at operating temperature (this is a better indicator of actual engine temperature than coolant temp). He also says that it might be a good idea to run the engine between adjusting the passenger- and driver-side valves.

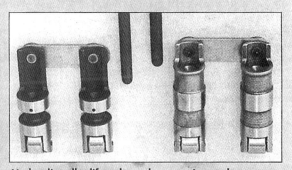

Hydraulic-roller lifters have the same internal parts as a hydraulic flat tappet, plus a roller on the bottom, making them taller than conventional roller lifters. That means that shorter pushrods are required. It's important to check rocker-arm-to-valve-tip contact for proper pushrod length when using a roller cam, because the quick valve velocity can cause problems if this is not correct.

exhaust components, then a roller cam with very similar duration and lift specs to a flat-tappet cam can make more power. That's because a flat-tappet limits the cam profile's rate of lift, so the lobes have a gentle curve and a pointy nose. (See the "Best of How It Works" special section in this issue if you need help with the terminology.) A roller lifter allows it to rise considerably quicker, so the lobe can be much broader, with steep ramps and a wide nose. Even if the lifting action starts and ends at the same point and the maximum lift is the same as a flat-tappet cam, a roller can snap the valves off their seats and bring them to a substantial opening point quickly. This added lift while the valve is opening

and closing means more air and fuel get into the cylinders and more exhaust gets out. And that's the whole premise to making power, except that a roller cam can aid this without increasing duration (relative to the maximum amount of lift), which retains cylinder pressure.

It is true that a roller cam and lifters cost more than a flat-tappet cam and lifter set. But it isn't necessarily true that you have to change much in your engine to run a roller cam. Depending

upon the specific grind you select, you may not have to add more than one or two parts to your engine. You should always ask the salesperson who sold you the cam or the cam company that manufactured it what exactly you should change, but the following information covers most instances. Competition Cams, Crane and Lunati all manufacture a full line of valvetrain components, and they can help you with cam selection and any technical questions you have.

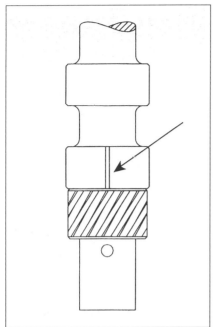

On Chevrolet engines, Crane recommends that a .030-inch-wide and .030-inch-deep groove be machined or filed into the bottom band on the distributor shaft as shown (*arrow*) to provide lubricant to the distributor gears. Place the groove on the distributor so that when timed properly, the groove will face the camshaft. With the distributor in this position, oil will spray both the distributor and the cam gear to significantly reduce gear wear. This trick can improve gear life for any type of camshaft. Ford engines have an oil passage plug that points directly at the distributor gear. A .025-inch hole can be drilled into the plug to lubricate these gears.

INDEPENDENT LIFTERS

Roller lifters do not rotate in their bores as flat tappets have to. In fact, roller lifters cannot rotate, or the roller will not contact the cam lobe in the direction it should. To keep the lifters properly positioned, aftermarket roller lifters are connected with a link bar. The link bar is slotted where it connects to one or both lifters to allow independent up-and-down motion while keeping both lifters from rotating. Competition Cams' Gen II roller lifters perform in a different way. These lifters make use of the bolt-down-lifter retaining boss in late-model GM blocks and replace the link bars with a guide plate. A big advantage is less weight, which means greater rpm potential and less valvetrain stress. The lifters are also tall and require shorter pushrods, which adds valvetrain stability. Other features include a pressure-lubricated wheel to greatly extend bearing and camshaft lobe life, specially heat-treated axle and inner race for the needles for better bearing durability, and the availability of offset pushrod seats. Competition Cams is also working on a similar system for earlier GM products and Ford engines.

The lifters are available with a standard, centered pushrod seat or one that is offset .180 inch and can be rotated 180 degrees to give each lifter either left or right offset. This helps straighten pushrod angles with some aftermarket cylinder heads to improve valvetrain geometry, thus reducing frictional losses and improving durability.

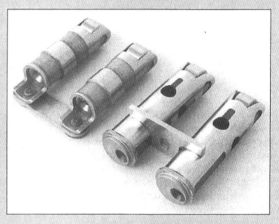

Instead of the conventional link bar used with roller lifters, the new Gen II lifters from Competition Cams utilize a guide plate that bolts to the block between the lifter bores and contacts a machined alignment surface on both lifters to keep them from rotating.

SHAFTED

Looking through the various cam manufacturer catalogs revealed a variety of distributor shaft diameters for a few of the more popular engines. Because this is something you'll need to know before you order a bronze distributor gear, we thought we'd supply a list of common shaft diameters so you can compare yours. Often, the shaft diameter changes above and below the gear, so it's best to remove your current gear and measure the shaft where the gear actually rides.

DISTRIBUTOR MAKE	ENGINE SIZE	SHAFT DIAMETER (IN.)
Chevrolet (most)	262-400, 396-502	.490
Chevrolet (HEI with remote coil)	305, 350, 454	.427
Common aftermarket distributors for Chevrolets	262-400, 396-502	.500
Ford	289, 302, BOSS 302	.466 or .500
Ford	SVO 302, SVO 351, 351W	.530
Ford	351C-400, 351M, BOSS 351, 370, 429, 460	.530
Common aftermarket distributors for Ford	351C-400, 351M, BOSS 351, 370, 429, 460	.500
	352-428 FE	.466 or .500

The old school of roller cam usage believed in restricting oil passages which, among other things, added stress to the oil pump, thus increasing the force on the oil pump driveshaft, the distributor and the cam gears. It's a good idea to use an oil pump driveshaft with a steel sleeve in a Chevrolet engine. A chrome-moly Ford Motorsports shaft should be used in Ford engines. Golding says that oil restrictors aren't recommended with most of Crane's street roller cams, because they usually only lead to insufficient lubrication to the needle bearings. And the valvesprings need all the oil they can get to keep them cool.

Continued on page 74

CAMSHAFT TECH

Cam AND Valvetrain Buyers' Guide

WHERE BIGGER ISN'T ALWAYS BETTER

By Karl Brauer

No other component plays a more crucial role in engine performance than the camshaft. Unfortunately, too many hot rodders choose a cam that's either too big or too small instead of getting the *correct* bumpstick for their needs. By carefully combining the specs of lift, duration, overlap and so on, you can design anything from a massive torque monster to a high-revving screamer. Many of today's cam manufacturers offer cams for specific applications as well as custom grinds for those shade-tree engineers out there. If you don't see exactly what you want in this buyers' guide, call the companies for more information.

ALL REVVED UP

HydraREV is a new system from Air Flow Research that can effectively add up to 1000 rpm to a hydraulic-cam engine's operating range. The system is easy to install and distributes spring pressure without overloading the plunger mechanism to produce a wider peak powerband. HydraREV is currently available for all small-block Chevy configurations. Information: Air Flow Research, Dept. HR04, 10490 Ilex Ave., Pacoima, CA 91331, 818/890-0616.

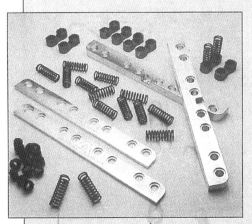

COMPUCAM

Crane Cams now offers CompuCam performance camshaft profiles for late-model computer-controlled Camaros, Corvettes and Firebirds. The new profiles are engineered for increased torque, horsepower and rpm. Information: Crane Cams, Inc., Dept. HR04, 530 Fentress Blvd., Daytona Beach, FL 32114, 904/258-6174.

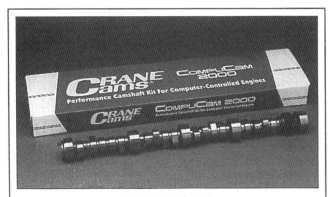

MACHINE-FREE SPRINGS

These new valve-springs from Competition Products require no machining of the seat or guide for installation in small-block Chevys. The springs, part No. 2300, will accept up to .600 lift, are made from state-of-the-art chrome silicon and will work on solid- or high-lift hydraulic camshafts. Information: Competition Products, Dept. HR04, 3200 Medalist Dr., Oshkosh, WI 54901, 414/233-2023.

MOPAR ROLLER

Competition Cams has introduced a new roller lifter for Mopar engines with an .8-inch-diameter wheel to provide additional strength. These roller lifters are available for use in both "LA" and "B" engines as well as Hemis with both high and low pushrod seat placement. Information: Competition Cams, Dept. HR04, 3406 Democrat Rd., Memphis, TN 38118, 800/999-0853.

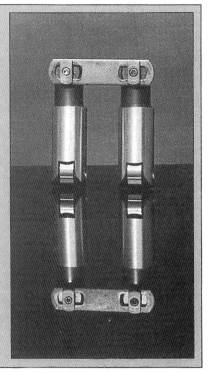

ROLLERIZED ROCKERS

Precision CNC-machined from stainless steel with 1025 heat-treating, these rocker arms from Crower feature oversize needle bearings, sure-lock rocker nuts and steel-tip rollers. Sets are available in all ratios and include one set of Crower sure-lock nuts. Information: Crower Cams, Dept. HR04, 3333 Main St., Chula Vista, CA 91911-5899, 619/422-1191.

TRICK TIMING COVER

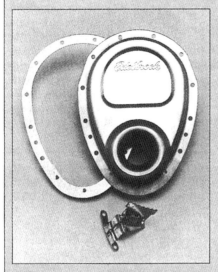

The design of this timing cover from Edelbrock allows quick camshaft removal or cam timing changes without dropping the oil pan or breaking the oil pan seal. The cover is made of light-weight .090-inch aluminum for added strength. The kit includes all the necessary gaskets, bolts and seals. Information: Edelbrock Corp., Dept. HR04, 2700 California St., Torrance, CA 90503, 310/782-2900.

ULTRA-VELOCITY CAM

Engle has developed two new families of cams for small-block GM and Ford V8s. Engle's exclusive Ultra-Velocity and hydraulic-roller profiles quicken valve movement and acceleration of small-block engines, making them ideal for race and street applications. Information: Engle Cams, Dept. HR04, 1621 12th St., Santa Monica, CA 90404, 310/450-0806.

ROLL YOUR MUSTANG

A new hydraulic-roller cam (part No. M-6250-F303) has been released by Ford Motorsports SVO. The cam features high lift (.512), long duration (288) and works great with supercharged 5.0-liter EFI engines. Information: Ford Motorsport SVO, Dept. HR04, 1700 Southfield Rd., Allen Park, MI 48101-2560, 313/845-2274.

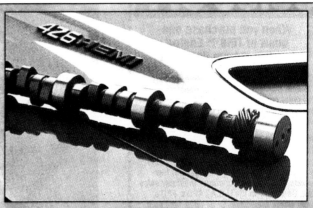

MUSCULAR CAMS

Hi-Tech has a line of more than 125 O.E. camshafts for musclecars. Each cam is ground to the original specifications, so whether you're a purist or someone just looking for the brute horsepower of a bygone era, contact Hi-Tech and ask for its Muscle Car Originals. Information: Hi-Tech Engine Components, Dept. HR04, P.O. Box 510988, Salt Lake City, UT 84151, 800/453-8250.

STRONG PUSH

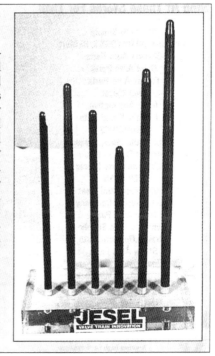

All Jesel push-rods are formed from .080-inch-wall tubing that offers greater stability than conventional .060-inch-wall designs. A variety of diameters and lengths are available, in tapered and nontapered designs. Jesel offers custom pushrods as well. Information: Jesel, Inc., Dept. HR04, Route 34 North, P.O. Box 1407, Wall, NJ 07719, 908/681-5344.

LUNATI TIME

A new timing set from Lunati utilizes a nine-keyway crank gear to advance or retard cam timing by up to 4 degrees. The set also features a true-roller timing chain to provide a high degree of accuracy and durability. Information: Lunati Cams, Dept. HR04, P.O. Box 18021, Memphis, TN 38181-0021, 901/365-0950.

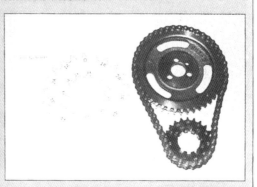

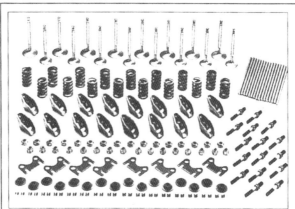

PERFORMANCE PACKAGE

Manley Performance has put together a package of race-proven valvetrain parts that provides a significant increase in power and reliability over O.E.M. components. Available for small-block Chevrolet applications, the kit includes valves, springs, retainers and rocker arms. Information: Manley Performance, Dept. HR04, 1960 Swarthmore Ave., Lakewood, NJ 08701, 908/905-3366.

CAM CORRECT

Speedway Motors' new Cam Correct gives you gear-drive accuracy with a chain. Installed directly on the front of the engine block, the Cam Correct's "shoes" flank the timing chain to reduce chain slack and keep the timing accurate, even with normal chain wear. Information: Speedway Motors, Dept. HR04, P.O. Box 81906, Lincoln, NE 68501-1906, 402/474-4411, ext. 2271.

T&D FOR CHRYSLER'S 360

New for the Chrysler 340/360 is a shaft-roller rocker arm system for W2, W5 or W7 cylinder heads. This system provides the kind of valvetrain stability required in highly modified engines. Reliability is also greatly increased. Information: T&D Machine Products, Dept. HR04, 4859 Convair Dr., Carson City, NV 89706, 702/884-2292.

FORCEPOWER

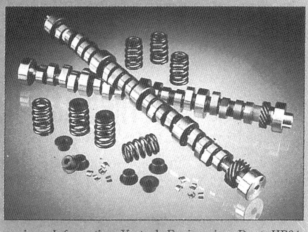

Vortech Engineering introduces the dyno-proven Forcepower Camshaft Kit for 5.0L Ford engines. Development of this camshaft kit came as a result of the need to meet emissions standards while providing additional power for both normally aspirated and forced-induction EFI engines. Information: Vortech Engineering, Dept. HR04, 5351 Bonsai Ave., Moorpark, CA 93021, 805/529-9330.

CAD ROLLER

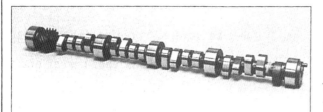

Using state-of-the-art computer-aided design (CAD) technology, TPI Specialties has come up with the ZZ9 hydraulic-roller camshaft. Created specifically for fuel-injected engines, the cam can produce exceptional amounts of power while maintaining surprisingly smooth idle characteristics, according to the company. Information: TPI Specialties, Dept. HR04, 4255 County Rd. 10 East, Chaska, MN 55318, 612/448-6021.

MOPAR MUSCLE

Mopar Performance has an exact issue of the original Mopar musclecar cam for high-performance 383 and 440 four-barrel engines. The kit contains a cam, oil, tappets and instructions. Replacement cams for 440 Six Paks are also available. Information: Mopar Performance, Dept. HR04, 26311 Lawrence Ave., Center Line, MI 48015-1241, 810/497-1225.

ERSON HYDRAULICS

Erson hydraulic-roller cams offer increased power, torque and rpm potential. Erson also offers matched cam kits and pushrods to ensure correct components for specific applications. Information: Erson Cams, Dept. HR04, 550 Mallory Way, Carson City, NV 89701, 702/882-1662. **HR**

Since roller cam lobes have no taper to them (as flat-tappet cams do to cause lifter rotation), the lateral movement of the cam must be limited with a cam button. You need to check cam endplay with the button and the timing cover installed (.005 to .008 inch is acceptable). The cam buttons install in the center of the cam timing gear, and sometimes the gear will need a little clearancing for a proper fit. Use a cam-bolt lock plate (a good idea for any cam) to hold the button in place for easier assembly.

Mike Golding of Crane Cams told us about a few common mistakes to avoid. The first is in selecting the right profile for your application (see "Choosing the Right Cam," also in this section). Golding said that the majority of the problems come in matching the valvesprings to the camshaft. Because of the quick valve-opening action of a roller cam, it generally requires springs with more tension, *but not always*. It's very important to use springs that match the recommendation on the cam card, or buy a matched set from the cam manufacturer. Pay special attention to the "open" rating requirement, as the "closed" rating is often very similar to springs used on flat-tappet cams.

There are a few basic items you'll need to change or add to your engine, but not as many as you might suspect. Look over the accompanying photos and captions to see what you might need, then consider the power possibilities. **HR**

SOURCES

Competition Cams
Dept. HR04
3406 Democrat Rd.
Memphis, TN 38118
901/795-2400

Crane Technologies Group
Dept. HR04
530 Fentress Blvd.
Daytona Beach, FL 32114
904/258-6174

Lunati Cams
Dept. HR04
4770 Lamar Ave.
Memphis, TN 38118
901/365-0950

Camshaft!
Fantasy vs. Reality

BY DOUGLAS R. GLAD

Fantasy: You downloaded a new cam profile into your laptop and the flashing cursor indicates a 200hp increase for your 305. Never mind the ludicrous 320-degree duration and the 0.720 lift. This cam is the max, baby; burbling thunder, smoky burnouts, and the chickadees flocking to your ride like Bee Gees fans.

Reality: You screwed up a Class A ride with bogging, burping, and hesitating because you fumbled the cam selection.

Now we're not going to preach about parts matching and cam profiles—we'd rather act like that high school autoshop teacher who gives you a good dose of theory and lets you hash out the details.

Car Craft has emptied its collective brain (and scraped the already empty brains of co-workers) to bring you all the theories, testing, and dyno-flogging to get the cam boondoggle cleared and cemented into your cranium. We used Chevy engines for simplicity and carved the text into tasty chunks for an easy read.

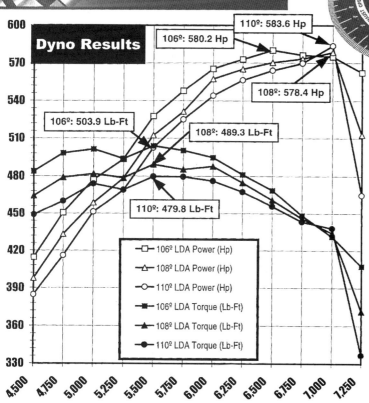

Dyno Results

- □ 106º LDA Power (Hp)
- △ 108º LDA Power (Hp)
- ○ 110º LDA Power (Hp)
- ■ 106º LDA Torque (Lb-Ft)
- ▲ 108º LDA Torque (Lb-Ft)
- ● 110º LDA Torque (Lb-Ft)

110º: 583.6 Hp
106º: 580.2 Hp
108º: 578.4 Hp
106º: 503.9 Lb-Ft
108º: 489.3 Lb-Ft
110º: 479.8 Lb-Ft

Rpm

106 vs. 108 vs. 110
Degrees of Separation

The Fantasy: Cam lobe separation angle affects torque and horsepower.

The Reality: Yup, in our test the smaller 106-degree lobe separation angle produced more torque down low. The 110 produced more peak horsepower, and the 108 was in between.

The Proof: With a 357-inch Chevy we ran identical-spec cams, all degreed straight up with three different lobe separation angles. The 106-degree cam peaked first with 503 lb-ft of torque, followed by the 108 and the 110. The 106 also made the most torque across the rpm range. The 110 made less power and torque than the 106 and the 108 until 6,500 rpm, where it spiked to 583 hp.

Advanced or Retarded?

The Fantasy: Advancing a cam should improve low-speed torque, acting like a short-duration cam. Retarding the cam will have the opposite effect, boosting high-speed horsepower at the cost of torque.

The Reality: Both true.

The Proof: We tried out a 350 Chevy with three different cam-timing settings. The 4-degree advance improved low-speed torque through 4,000 rpm and then began to drop off. Four degrees retarded produced less torque through 4,000 rpm, and running the cam at 0 degrees netted the same torque as the pull at 4 degrees retarded. So as low-speed torque goes, you're better off with the advanced cam.

Horsepower above 4,200 rpm was 365 with the advanced cam; the 0-degree cam and the retarded produced 368. The retarded cam delivered three more horsepower above 4,200.

Torque (lb-ft)

Rpm	4° Adv.	0°	4° Ret.
2,000	333.8	325.0	317.2
2,250	320.9	312.8	297.8
2,500	343.1	338.1	325.0
2,750	389.2	382.6	371.4
3,000	401.6	398.1	391.1
3,250	403.2	400.8	395.1
3,500	406.9	405.3	399.9
3,750	407.4	404.9	399.3
4,000	**408.5**	407.1	402.5
4,250	407.3	**407.6**	**405.3**
4,500	397.0	396.6	396.9
4,750	388.3	387.5	386.6
5,000	383.4	384.1	381.6
5,250	379.9	375.9	375.7
5,500	368.3	370.8	368.8
5,750	352.9	355.4	358.2
6,000	333.2	342.8	343.1
6,250	314.5	321.7	326.7
Avg. thru 4,000	379.4	373.2	369.0
Avg. 4,200-plus	369.4	371.4	371.4
Avg. overall	374.4	373.2	369.0

Power (hp)

Rpm	4° Adv.	0°	4° Ret.
2,000	127.1	123.8	120.8
2,250	137.5	134.0	127.6
2,500	163.3	160.9	154.7
2,750	203.8	200.3	194.5
3,000	229.4	227.4	223.4
3,250	249.5	248.0	244.5
3,500	271.2	270.1	266.5
3,750	290.9	289.1	285.1
4,000	311.1	310.1	306.5
4,250	329.6	329.8	328.0
4,500	340.2	339.8	340.1
4,750	351.2	350.5	349.6
5,000	365.0	365.7	363.3
5,250	379.8	375.8	375.6
5,500	385.7	388.3	386.2
5,750	**386.4**	389.1	**392.2**
6,000	380.7	391.6	392.0
6,250	374.3	382.8	388.8
Avg. thru 4,000	220.4	218.2	213.7
Avg. 4,200-plus	365.9	368.2	368.4
Avg. overall	293.2	293.2	291.1

Big Cams = Big Power

The Fantasy: If a big cam will improve power, a really big cam will produce gobs of power. Big cams are good.

The Reality: True, unless you want to drive on the street. Using a Chevy ZZ4 355-inch small-block, we tested four cams and found that the two smallest ones produced better torque and horsepower in a lower rpm range than the two larger ones. The big Magnum cams pushed the power up to between 6,000 and 7,000 rpm, requiring low gears, stall converters, and other racecar-type apparatus. Don't be stubborn; daily drivers use smaller cams.

The Proof: Cam one is the Competition Cams model 252H. In the olden days this meant the cam had 252 degrees of duration. Now people measure duration at 0.050-inch tappet lift, meaning the cam actually has 206 degrees of useable duration. We will use the big number to make things easier (read 252H=252 duration). The 252H is the smallest cam in the test and made the least amount of power. We'll treat this cam as a baseline or something to throw in a truck. The 398 lb-ft of torque at 3,900 rpm and 347 hp between 2,600 and 5,100 are definitely tow-your-boat numbers.

Cam two is the 268H from Comp Cams; actually *all* the cams are from Comp so we'll stop saying it. This, or one with very similar characteristics, is *the* cam to buy for this engine in a street car. For starters, the cam produced over 400 lb-ft of torque at 4,100 rpm, a good speed for clutch dumping. The 380hp peak was at 5,400, which is where you'll be when the tires stop spinning. If that isn't enough, the motor idles at 800 rpm and produces 16 inches of vacuum to run your auto-

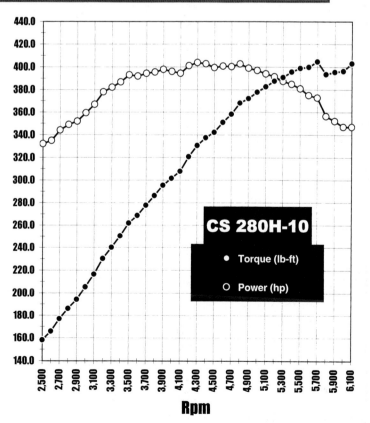

CS 280H-10

● Torque (lb-ft)

○ Power (hp)

Rpm

matic headlight covers. This is as big as you can go with a stock converter.

You're reading this because you think the 280H and 292H were hotter cams. Well, they were, but the 280H is down on torque below 4,300 rpm, which will bog without steep gears, a stall converter, and headers. In fact, Comp Cams (we said it again) recommends these goodies along with some kind of vacuum reservoir to combat the meager 12½ inches at idle. Hard-core guys can live with that, but since the peak horsepower

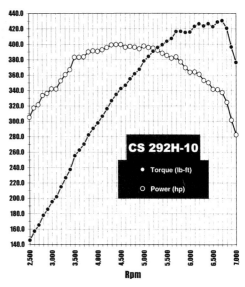

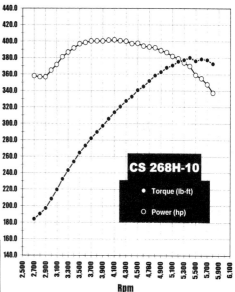

Modern Cam vs. Old Tech Cam

The Fantasy: Newfangled cams with fancy dual-pattern grinds will perform better than old-school cams.

The Reality: True, if you're comparing similar idle characteristics and rpm range.

The Proof: We tested the ancient 327/350 cam with 320 degree of advertised duration and 0.447 inches of valve lift against the Comp Cams Xtreme energy with a split duration of 274/286 intake/exhaust and 0.487/0.490 lift. The 327/350 cam made a peak of 349 hp at 5,400 rpm and 380 lb-ft of torque at 4,100 rpm. The Xtreme energy cam produced 392 hp at 6,100 rpm and 380 lb-ft at 4,400, an increase of 43 hp.

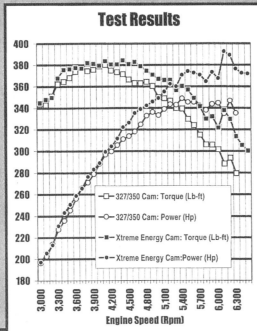

Hydraulic vs. Solid

The Fantasy: Solid-lifter cams produce more power than hydraulic-lifter cams.

The Reality: Yes, but only by a slight margin and the hydraulic cam is better for the street.

The Proof: Using the 292 Hydraulic and the 294 Solid flat-tappet cams, we tested them head to head to see which one made the most power. The cams have different advertised specs to make up for the mechanical lifters' different lash but were rated the same. For example, the hydraulic-lifter cam has an advertised lift of 0.507 and the solid cam is rated at 0.525. When the lash is set at 0.022 on the solid cam, the lift is actually only 0.503. Close enough.

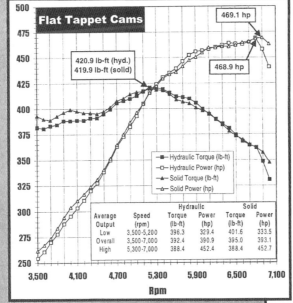

The solid cam produced 469 hp at peak compared to 468 from the hydraulic cam, and the peak torque was 420 and 419 respectively. The two cams were about the same until 6,500, when the hydraulic lifters pumped up and power dropped off. Since the solid cam has to be adjusted periodically and the only real power advantage is around 7,000 rpm, the hydraulic grind is the streetable cam.

moved to 5,700 rpm, that's slightly out of reach for anything with a TPI or TBI setup. The auto-trans guys with stock converters and freeway gears will lose races to the tow truck we talked about earlier.

Heavens to Murgatroid, the 292H Magnum is the cam we all lust after. The reality is the cam will require a 3,000 stall, at least 9.5:1 compression, and a host of other mods that may make the car a chore to drive. The peak horsepower numbers on the 292H were up in the 6,700-rpm stratosphere, really tempting a stock bottom end to blow its lunch. The peak torque was 399 lb-ft, a little lower than the 268H, and occurred at 4,500 rpm. This cam trades torque for horsepower.

Don't get us wrong—this is an awesome piece for your lightweight, four-speed, drag car that doesn't sit in traffic or travel on the freeway, but for a regular street/strip car with reasonable rear gears, the smaller cam is good medicine. **CC**

Doin' The Bump-stick Shuffle

COMPARING A '60s-STYLE GRIND TO THE LOBE LOGIC OF THE '80s

By Joe Pettitt

Camshafts, like most things mechanical, are the practical application of compromise. If you want them to perform in a particular range, you have to trade off performance in another area. Traditionally the trade-off for high-performance cams has been to gain top-end power at the sacrifice of idle quality. The more duration and overlap the cam had (up to a point), the better.

Such was the state of the art in the '60s. Long-duration, substantial-overlap, high-lift cams which gave an engine that distinctive, rough idle had a certain mystique about them. Sure, these radical cams gave a mean staccato idle as the local street hero cruised the parking lot. But how did they perform, really?

Well, in case you weren't around in the '60s to experience firsthand how these combinations ran, we located a '67 Camaro with a fairly typical '60s-style, mild street combination. The engine is a .030-over 327 with a 600 Holley double-pumper flowing through an Edelbrock dual-plane manifold, with a fairly big hydraulic street cam (see chart) and stock cast-iron exhaust manifolds.

This combination had a lumpy idle with little low-end torque. Street driving, even with a 4-speed, was a chore since you had to spin up the engine to get the car moving. Once you got the car rolling and into the mid-to-high rpm, it responded. But in street driving you're doing a lot of stop-'n'-go driving, and the romance of the lumpy idle soon gives way to the harsh reality of driving in traffic: It's not fun; it's work.

At the track it wasn't a killer machine, but it wasn't a total slug either. It turned 15.50s and 15.60 e.t.'s in the mid-to-high-80-mph range. Shift points were high (6000 rpm) to take advantage of the tall cam. To be fair, we note that these times were turned on a low-pressure day, while the second test day was average pressure. (The barometric variance probably increased the e.t. .10 second and reduced mph a few tenths as well.)

After testing the '60s-style grind we installed a Rhoads Variable Valve Timing 222 (VVT222) duration cam and the Rhoads Super Bleed lifters. This cam/lifter combination is designed to shorten the duration at low rpm to improve idle and low-end torque by designing the lifter to "bleed down" at lower rpm, then gain back the duration for good top-end performance.

Looking at the chart we can see that the overall specs of our "Brand X" '60s

After making a few passes at Los Angeles County Raceway to baseline the performance of the '60s-style cam in the test Camaro, Editor Jeff Smith measures the specs (see chart) of the '60s cam. You'll need a degree wheel and dial indicator to do this at home. The test Camaro turned 15.50s and 15.60 e.t.'s with the '60s-style grind.

Be sure to use a high-quality cam lube when installing a new cam and lifters; otherwise, you're sure to damage the cam and the lifters the first time you crank over the engine.

CAM SPEC CHART

'60s STYLE		RHOADS No. S813	
INTAKE			
	Gross Lift (inches)		
.433		.455	
At .050-inch Lift:		At .050-inch Lift:	
Opens: 1 degree BTDC		Opens: 2 degrees BTDC	
Closes: 44 degrees ABDC		Closes: 40 degrees ABDC	
Duration: 225 degrees		Duration: 222 degrees	
EXHAUST			
	Gross Lift (inches)		
.435		.455	
At .050-inch Lift:		At .050-inch Lift:	
Opens: 37 degrees BBDC		Opens: 46 degrees BBDC	
Closes: 8 degrees ATDC		Closes: 4 degrees ATDC	
Duration: 225 degrees		Duration: 230 degrees	
LOBE SEPARATION ANGLE			
112 degrees		112 degrees	
OVERLAP			
9 degrees		6 degrees	

Degreeing the cam is an essential part of the installation sequence. Several aftermarket manufacturers offer piston stops that screw into the spark-plug hole, allowing you to determine Top Dead Center (TDC) of the number-one cylinder with the heads on the block. The procedure is simple: Rotate the crankshaft until the piston lightly hits the stop and note the degree on your degree wheel at this point. Next, reverse the rotation until the piston again hits the stop and note the degree. TDC will be exactly halfway between these two measurements. During the degreeing procedure, Jeff measured the cam specs at .050 inch (see chart).

cam and the Rhoads cam aren't much different. Yet in spite of the similarities (the Rhoads cam is slightly smaller) at .050 inch, we improved the e.t. of the car by .3 second and gained some mph.

What the chart doesn't reveal is the Rhoads asymmetrical lobe design. The opening ramp of the lobes is "fast-acting"; in other words, it's pretty steep and pops the valve open rapidly. The closing

ramp is pretty shallow, allowing the valve to close at a slow rate, which is easier on valve seats.

This asymmetrical grind is intentionally designed to facilitate the bleed-down

DOIN' THE BUMP-STICK SHUFFLE

The test procedure for both cams consisted of going for the best possible e.t.'s. After driving to the track we checked and adjusted the timing (19 degrees initial advance at the crankshaft for a total of 37 degrees), rejetted the carb, let the engine cool down for about 30 minutes, and adjusted the rear tire pressures to 15 psi before staging the car for a run.

The altitude of the track at Los Angeles County Raceway called for rejetting the Holley 600-cfm carb. For the first run, No. 64 primary and No. 74 secondary jets replaced the stock No. 67 primary and No. 76 secondary jets. The No. 28 primary and No. 32 secondary "squirters" were retained.

Car owner Jim Peterson made two passes with the first jetting combination. The first launch was a little soft, which resulted in a 15.63 e.t. at 85.98 mph. After his warm-up pass he came back with a good launch and a 15.35 e.t. at 89.28 mph.

We tried two other jetting combinations. With No. 64 primary and No. 76 secondary jetting the car ran 15.40 at 88.70 mph. With No. 66 primary and No. 77 secondary jetting the car ran a 15.62 at 88.38 mph and a 15.44 at 88.48 mph. The car was slowing down, so we went back to our first jetting combination. After letting the engine cool down, and shifting at a lower rpm, we got our best time of 15.23 at 89.36 mph, an improvement of .3 second and a few mph.

rate of the lifters. At low rpm the slow-closing ramp keeps valvespring pressure on the lifter, forcing oil through a precisely machined groove and reducing the lift and duration of the cam at idle.

The Rhoads Super Bleed lifters used with the VVT222 cam shorten duration by 12 degrees and lift by .035 inch, so at idle the engine reacts as if it has a 200-degree-duration/.420-inch-lift cam with a very short overlap. The idle quality improvement with the Rhoads combination is dramatic. We measured 14.5 inches of vacuum at 800 rpm with the Rhoads versus 11.5 inches with the '60s-style grind. Throttle response off idle turned from rather sluggish to clean and crisp. Getting the car rolling was no problem at all, making street driving fun again.

Above 3500 rpm the Rhoads Super Bleed lifters stay pumped up to deliver

the full amount of lift and duration of the cam, so top-end performance doesn't suffer. In fact, we noticed a slight improvement in mph in our test even though the engine was running through the stock cast-iron exhaust and mufflers. (The addition of a good set of headers and low-restriction exhaust would really help both combinations.)

So, by "tricking" the engine with the variable lifters, Rhoads broadens the torque curve. The engine develops more power sooner and accelerates from a stop quicker. And once the engine reaches 3500 rpm, the lifters stay pumped up to allow the desirable power-producing effects of long duration and overlap.

In our test we really saw the positive effects of the low-end power improvement from the Rhoads combination. The

reduced e.t.'s were the result of harder acceleration in the first section of the track, since we didn't register significant gains in mph. Again, both cams were limited by the exhaust system of the car.

But in view of the solid performance gains registered and the potential locked up in the restricted exhaust, the Rhoads VVT222 with Super Bleed lifters looks like an exceptional combination that'll make your Saturday night special more fun to drive on Monday morning. **HR**

CAM RECOMMENDATIONS
FROM THE EXPERTS

BY THE *CAR CRAFT* STAFF

We figure you don't have time to sit around calling engine experts to get advice on the best camshaft to use in your latest engine. That's why we did it for you. In the next few pages, you'll find specs for what we felt were typical street/strip combos for readers with 350 and 383 small-block Chevys, 360 Mopars, 400 Pontiacs, 351W Fords, and even—are you sitting down?—360 AMCs.

This is the kind of story you can bench-race to death. Just compare our sample engine/vehicle combos with the lump in your driveway; if you have a car that's lighter, has more gear or has a looser converter, or you can live with a more ratty idle, cheat the cam a bit bigger. If the opposite is true, go smaller.

In all, we called 29 engine experts, and it's really interesting to compare their advice for the engines we outlined. Look up their addresses and numbers below, and check out the recommendations on the following pages.

SOURCES

BENNETT RACING
Dept. CC
P.O. Box 593
Haleyville, AL 35565
800/240-RACE
205/486-5520 (tech)

BILL MITCHELL HARDCORE RACING PRODUCTS
Dept. CC
35 Trade Zone Dr.
Ronkonkoma, NY 11779-7343
516/737-0372
www.racersworld.com/bmp

ART BOCKHAUSEN
Dept. CC
1618 W. Coon Lake Rd.
Howell, MI 48843-8961
517/546-5222

JIM BUTLER RACING
Dept. CC
103 Dunn Rd.
Leoma, TN 38468
931/762-4596
E:mail: JBPpontiac@lorettotel.net

CALIFORNIA CLASSIC AMC
Dept. CC
977 Florida St.
Imperial Beach, CA 91932-2213
619/423-0364
www.amcwc.com

COMPETITION CAMS INC.
Dept. CC
3406 Democrat Rd.
Memphis, TN 38118-1577
800/365-9145
www.compcams.com

J. DAVID COOPER
Dept. CC
322 N 16th St. (Loft)
Richmond, IN 47374-3317
765/966-7137
e-mail: wisenheimer@juno.com

CRANE CAMS
Dept. CC
530 Fentress Blvd.
Daytona Beach, FL 32114
904/252-1151

CROWER CAMS AND EQUIPMENT
Dept. CC
3333 Main St.
Chula Vista, CA 91911-5899
619/422-1191, 800/222-2267
www.crower.com

DUTTWEILER ENGINEERING
Dept. CC
1563 Los Angeles Ave.
Ventura, CA 93004-3215
805/659-3648

DVORAK MACHINE
Dept. CC
11109 NE US Hwy. 301
Waldo, FL 32694
352/468-1353
352/468-1050 (fax)

EDELBROCK
Dept. CC
2700 California St.
Torrance, CA 90503
800/FUN-TEAM
310/782-2900 (tech)

ENGLE MFG. CO.
Dept. CC
1621 12th St.
Santa Monica, CA 90404-3790
310/450-0806

FLOWMASTER INC.
Dept. CC
2975 Dutton Ave.
Santa Rosa, CA 95407-7800
800/544-4761

FORD MOTORSPORT SVO
Dept. CC
44050 N. Groesbeck Hwy.
Clinton Township, MI 48036
810/468-1356 (tech)

FORD PERFORMANCE SOLUTIONS
Dept. CC
1004 E. Orangefair Ln.
Anaheim, CA 92801
714/773-9027

H-O RACING
Dept. CC
8780 Bajado Ct.
Rancho Cucamonga, CA 91730
888/703-4477

HUGHES ENGINES
Dept. CC
23334 Wiegand Ln.
Washington, IL 61571-9589
309/745-9558
309/745-5061 (fax)

ISKY RACING CAMS
Dept. CC
16020 S. Broadway St.
P.O. Box 30
Gardena, CA 90247-0803
213/770-0930

DICK LANDY IND.
Dept. CC
19743 Bahama St.
Northridge, CA 91324
818/341-4143
818/341-9564 (fax)

LINGENFELTER PERFORMANCE ENGINEERING
Dept. CC
1557 Winchester Rd.
Decatur, IN 46733-3109
219/724-2552
www.lingenfelter.com

LUNATI CAMS INC.
Dept. CC
P.O. Box 18021
Memphis, TN 38181-0021
901/365-0950
www.dragnbreath.com/LunatiRacing/HomePageFrame.html

MOPAR PERFORMANCE TECHLINE
Dept. CC
P.O. Box 215020
Auburn Hills, MI 48321-5020
248/853-7290

NOWAK & CO.
Dept. CC
249 E. Emerson Ave., Unit F
Orange, CA 92665
714/282-7996

ROCK 'N' ROLL ENGINEERING
Dept. CC
12210 Michigan St., Unit 9
Grand Terrace, CA 92313
909/370-0389

SD PERFORMANCE
Dept. CC
758 N. Batavia, Ste. I
Orange, CA 92868
714/997-3777

JOE SHERMAN RACING ENGINES
Dept. CC
2302 W. 2nd St.
Santa Ana, CA 92703-3548
714/542-0515

ERIC THOMSON PUSHROD POWER/ PUSHRODS FOREVER
Dept. CC
P.O. Box 156
Bonsall, CA 92003-0156
760/742-1113

WARRIOR RACING PRODUCTS
Dept. CC
238 N. Wayne Rd.
Westland, MI 48185
734/728-6600

CAM RECOMMENDATIONS:
400 Pontiac

BY JOHN KIEWICZ

Photo by Marlan Davis

We talked with five Pontiac engine experts and one cam company to prod their craniums for advice and stressed that the engine must be able to be driven on the street, run on pump gas, idle well, generate enough vacuum to operate basic items such as power brakes, and shimmy the 1320 in the high-12-second or low-13-second range. The pros scratched their heads, and each came up with a cam choice as well as additional advice to generate a better final product.

The Combo

Make: Pontiac
Displacement: 406 (400 overbored 0.030 inch)
Compression Ratio: 9.0:1
Cylinder Heads: Pontiac 400 4X or 6X iron heads milled about 0.050 inch to reduce combustion chambers to 92 cc to increase compression
Valve Sizes: 2.11/1.66 (stock)

Intake Manifold: Edelbrock Performer RPM
Carburetor: Rebuilt 750-cfm Quadrajet
Exhaust: 1¾-inch headers with 2½-inch dual exhaust
Transmission: TH400 auto with 2,400-rpm stall
Rear Gears: 3.55:1
Vehicle Weight: 3,600-3,800 pounds without driver
Typical Use: Street/strip

The Expert: Mike Golding at Crane Cams
Cam Manufacturer: Crane Cams
Part No.: H-278-2 (PowerMax)
Type: Hydraulic flat-tappet
Rocker Ratio (In/Ex): 1.5:1/1.5:1
Lift (In/Ex): 0.467/0.494
Advertised Duration (In/Ex): 278/290
Duration at 0.050 (In/Ex): 222/234
Lobe Displacement Angle: 114
Lobe Centerline (In/Ex): 109/119
Notes: The dual-pattern design helps with the restrictive flow on the exhaust port. Use Crane fast-bleed lifters for added vacuum; if you still need more vacuum, install Crane's vacuum reserve canister PN 99590. Use Crane spring and retainer kit PN 28308 at an installed height of 1.57 inches, and upgrade to Crane steel valve retainer locks PN 99097-1 for added strength. No machine work is needed for these springs or locks. Shift rpm should be at about 5,200.

The Expert: Jim Butler at Jim Butler Racing
Cam Manufacturer: Ultradyne
Part No.: Ultradyne 280/288-H10
Type: Hydraulic
Rocker Ratio (In/Ex): 1.5:1/1.5:1
Lift (In/Ex): 0.463/0.484
Advertised Duration (In/Ex): 280/288
Duration @ 0.050-inch lift (In/Ex): 223/231
Lobe Displacement Angle: 110
Lobe Centerline (In/Ex): 104/116
Notes: Install the cam at a 104-degree intake centerline. Use Jim Butler PN 052 valvesprings set at the stock installed height. Shift point should be at 5,500 rpm. Vacuum for the brakes should not be a problem.

The Expert: Bruce Fulper at Rock 'N' Roll Engineering
Cam Manufacturer: Comp Cams
Part No.: Custom grind for Rock 'N' Roll
Type: Hydraulic flat-tappet
Rocker Ratio (In/Ex): 1.65:1/1.65:1
Lift (In/Ex): 0.520/0.520
Advertised Duration (In/Ex): 280/288
Duration at 0.050 (In/Ex): 237/237
Lobe Displacement Angle: 112
Notes: This cam should be used with 1.65:1 rocker arms in place of 1.5:1 units and installed with the intake centerline at 109 degrees. Because engine parts are frequently not within tolerance, Fulper stresses the need for accurate cam degreeing to optimize the setup. This cam could be ground with a tighter lobe displacement angle to generate more power, but it wouldn't be as streetable.

The Expert: Dave Bisschop at SD Performance
Cam Manufacturer: Ultradyne
Part No.: 280/288
Rocker Ratio (In/Ex): 1.5:1/1.5:1
Type: Hydraulic flat-tappet
Lift (In/Ex): 0.463/0.485
Advertised Duration (In/Ex): 280/288
Duration at 0.050 (In/Ex): 223/231
Lobe Displacement Angle: 110
Notes: Install the cam at a 106-degree intake centerline. Use Speed-Pro VS-1606 valvesprings at 1.60-inch installed height, and opt for Crane High-Intensity fast-bleed lifters (PN 99382-16) to help idle quality and boost vacuum. Shift points should be between 5,200 and 5,600 rpm. Head porting and larger 1.77-inch exhaust valves would really help this combo.

The Expert: Ray Hunt at Warrior Racing Products
Cam Manufacturer: Warrior Racing Products
Part No.: 9785744
Type: Hydraulic flat-tappet
Rocker Ratio (In/Ex): 1.5:1/1.5:1
Lift (In/Ex): 0.424/0.424
Advertised Duration (In/Ex): 301/313
Duration at 0.050 (In/Ex): 224/238
Lobe Displacement Angle: 115.5
Notes: Use Warrior PN 950 valvesprings installed at 1.578-inch installed height and upgrade to hardened valve locks (PN 874) and steel spring retainers (PN 872). Upgrading to polylok rocker-arm adjusters allows you to adjust lifters to a true "zero lash." A vacuum reserve canister may be required for power brakes. Shift points should be at 5,700 rpm. Set total spark advance to 34-36 degrees. Upgrading to 1.77-inch exhaust valves is highly recommended.

The Expert: Ken Crocie at H-O Racing
Cam Manufacturer: H-O Racing
Part No.: HC-20D
Type: Hydraulic flat-tappet
Rocker Ratio (In/Ex): 1.5:1/1.5:1
Lift (In/Ex): 0.470/0.486
Advertised Duration (In/Ex): 294/302
Duration at 0.050 (In/Ex): 232/242
Lobe Displacement angle: 112
Notes: Install the cam straight up. Use H-O Racing VS-11 valvesprings with the stock 1.59-inch installed height, and use Rhoads lifters to boost manifold vacuum. You must install polylok rocker-arm adjusters to properly adjust lifter preload. Set total spark advance to 36 degrees with full advance in by 1,500 rpm. Engine shift points should be 6,000 rpm.

360 Mopar

BY DAVID FREIBURGER

Photo by David Freiburger

When duplicating our basic 360 combo, remember that it can be tough to get our goal of 9.0:1-9.5:1 compression without milling the heads or the deck. Even with flat-tops, 360s often have a piston deck height as deep as 0.100 in the hole, causing compression as bad as 7.5:1. If you've simply assembled a 360 without paying attention to milling the heads and deck and calculating true compression, then the cams recommended here may not be optimal due to your reduced cylinder pressure.

The Combo

Make: Mopar
Displacement: 360
Compression Ratio: 9.0:1-9.5:1
Cylinder Heads: Stock early '70s 360
Valve Sizes: 1.88/1.60 (stock)
Intake Manifold: Edelbrock Performer RPM
Carburetor: Holley or Edelbrock 750 cfm
Exhaust: 1¾-inch headers with 2½-inch dual exhaust
Transmission: Auto with 2,400-rpm stall
Rear Gears: 3.55:1
Vehicle Weight: 3,300 pounds less driver
Typical Use: Street/strip

The Expert: Robert Landy at Dick Landy Ind.
Cam Manufacturer: Crane
Part No: 693801
Type: Hydraulic flat-tappet
Rocker Ratio (In/Ex): 1.5:1/1.5:1
Lift (In/Ex): 0.467/0.494
Advertised Duration (In/Ex): 278/290
Duration at 0.050 (In/Ex): 222/234
Lobe Displacement Angle: 114
Notes: Quoting Landy: "Though considerably larger and more powerful than stock, it's relatively mild, generally offers enough vacuum for power brakes, and still works with a stock-type valvetrain and performance single springs such as Mopar Performance's P4120249 or P5249847. We'd suggest MP's 2.02 intake valves, mild porting, and a 700-cfm double-pumper Holley. You could even use a 625-cfm carb with 340-type exhaust manifolds, or use the 750 along with 1¾-inch headers and lower rear gears."

The Expert: Dan Dvorak at Dvorak Machine
Cam Manufacturer: Dvorak custom grind
Part No: N/A
Type: Hydraulic flat-tappet
Rocker Ratio (In/Ex): 1.5:1/1.5:1
Lift (In/Ex): 0.453/0.457
Advertised Duration (In/Ex): N/A
Duration at 0.050 (In/Ex): 218/225
Lobe Displacement Angle: 106
Notes: Dvorak insisted that it's virtually impossible to select a perfect cam with the limited parameters we offered. He prefers to build to each customer's needs. In addition, Dvorak pointed out that the stock stamped-steel rocker arms have a ratio of about 1.42:1, *not* 1.5:1, and that they are way too sloppy on the shaft. Aftermarket, true 1.5:1 adjustable rockers are mandatory, both to adjust lifter preload and to gain 0.030-0.040 lift. Stock head flow drops dead at 0.450 lift, so if you must use stock rockers with less than a 1.5:1 ratio, look for a cam advertised as having lift around 0.480. Dvorak's other concern was proper-length pushrods to prevent excessive lifter preload, which limits effective engine rpm.

The Expert: Dave Hughes at Hughes Engines
Cam Manufacturer: Hughes Real Chrysler Cams
Part No: HE 3038-AL
Type: Hydraulic flat-tappet
Rocker Ratio (In/Ex): 1.5:1/1.5:1
Lift (In/Ex): 0.515/0.535
Advertised Duration (In/Ex): 276/286
Duration at 0.050 (In/Ex): 230/237
Lobe Displacement Angle: 110
Notes: Hughes Real Chrysler cams are specifically designed for the Mopar 0.904-inch lifter foot, which is bigger than Chevy's, thereby allowing more rate of lift per degree of cam rotation than a cam ground with Chevy-type lobes. Hughes reiterated the need for verifying a true compression ratio of 9.5:1, but he's even more interested in achieving a cranking pressure of 165 psi with his cam of choice. He'd like to see a converter with a 2,800 stall instead of our suggested 2,500, and he wants either short 25- to 26-inch tires with 3.55s or a swap to 3.91 gears. He says the powerband will be 2,000-5,900 rpm and shifts should be at 6,200.

The Expert: Larry Shepard at Mopar Performance
Cam Manufacturer: Mopar Performance
Part No: P4452992
Type: Hydraulic flat-tappet
Rocker Ratio (In/Ex): 1.5:1/1.5:1
Lift (In/Ex): 0.474/0.474
Advertised Duration (In/Ex): 280/280
Duration at 0.050 (In/Ex): 238/238
Lobe Displacement Angle: N/A
Notes: Shep advises that 2.02 valves are a worthy upgrade but late-model heads with casting numbers ending in 308 or 576 (available new as Mopar's P4529269) are even better. He also prefers Mopar's M1 intake for a dual-plane but points out that single-planes will make more power. If a Holley is used, Shepard considers a vacuum-secondary *mandatory*. He says 340s can tolerate the same cam if it uses a bit deeper rear-gear or higher-stall converter, but little 318s need more conservative camming.

CAM RECOMMENDATIONS:
350 Chevy

BY MARLAN DAVIS
Photo by John Kiewicz

This one's a mild street performance small-block that must run on 92-octane pump gas and retain sufficient vacuum to operate power brakes and automatic-transmission vacuum modulators. Several of our sources said that if you can afford them, installing 1.6:1-ratio rockers on the intake side helps top-end power; on Chevy production heads, the intake port needs more help on the top end than the exhaust does.

The Combo

Make: Chevy
Displacement: 355 (0.030-over 350)
Compression Ratio: 9.5:1
Cylinder Heads: Factory "492" castings, three-angle valve job
Valve Sizes: 2.02/1.60
Intake Manifold: Edelbrock Performer RPM

Carburetor: Holley 750-cfm vacuum-secondary
Exhaust: 1⅝-inch headers, 2½-inch dual exhaust with mufflers
Transmission: TH350 with 2,500-rpm stall
Rear Gears: 4.10:1
Vehicle Weight: 3,600 pounds less driver
Typical Use: Daily street use, some strip

The Expert: Steve Chryssos at Bill Mitchell
Cam Manufacturer: Comp Cams
Part No.: 12-238-2
Type: Hydraulic flat-tappet
Rocker Ratio (In/Ex): 1.5:1/1.5:1
Lift (In/Ex): 0.462/0.469
Advertised Duration (In/Ex): 262/270
Duration at 0.050 (In/Ex): 218/224
Lobe Displacement Angle: 110
Notes: Recommended installed intake centerline is 108 degrees. Chryssos feels this is a 375hp combo using World Products S/R Torquer heads; if you're stuck with OE heads, go down one cam size. He also points out that "the enthusiast can usually purchase a pair of brand-new 170cc intake-runner cast-iron World Products S/R Torquers for less than the price of re-built OE heads."

The Expert: Comp Cams
Cam Manufacturer: Comp Cams
Part No.: 12-246-3 (Xtreme Energy)
Type: Hydraulic flat-tappet
Rocker Ratio (In/Ex): 1.6:1/1.5:1
Lift (In/Ex): 0.519/0.490
Advertised Duration (In/Ex): 274/286
Duration at 0.050 (In/Ex): 230/236
Lobe Displacement Angle: 110
Notes: The recommended installed intake centerline is 106 degrees. Using Comp Cams PN 812-16 lifters and PN 981-16 springs, the powerband should be 1,800-6,000 rpm with a best shift point of 5,800-5,900. The recommended springs fit in the stock head pocket.

The Expert: Crower Cams
Cam Manufacturer: Crower Cams
Part No.: 00242
Type: Hydraulic flat-tappet
Rocker Ratio (In/Ex): 1.5:1/1.5:1
Lift (In/Ex): 0.462/0.470
Advertised Duration (In/Ex): 280/286
Duration at 0.050 (In/Ex): 220/226
Lobe Displacement Angle: 112
Notes: This is an absolute daily driver with a 2,000- to 5,300-rpm power range, 4,400- to 4,700-rpm power peak, and a 5,500- to 5,800-rpm shift point. Recommended installed intake centerline is 108 degrees.

The Expert: Ken Duttweiler at Duttweiler Performance
Cam Manufacturer: Crane
Part No.: 113821 (Commander)
Type: Hydraulic flat-tappet
Rocker Ratio (In/Ex): 1.6:1/1.5:1
Lift (In/Ex): 0.489/0.473
Advertised Duration (In/Ex): 288/296
Duration at 0.050 (In/Ex): 226/234
Lobe Displacement Angle: 114
Notes: Duttweiler maintains that spreading the lobe displacement angle allows adding more exhaust duration for a given intake duration without affecting driveability and helps piston-to-valve clearance. Using an installed centerline of 107 degrees, Crane PN 99377-16 lifters, and Crane PN 11308-1 valvesprings, the powerband should be 3,000-6,000 rpm.

The Expert: Kevin McClelland at Flowmaster
Cam Manufacturer: Crane
Part Number: 113931 (Max Velocity)
Type: Hydraulic flat-tappet
Rocker Ratio (In/Ex): 1.5:1/1.5:1
Lift (In/Ex): 0.440/0.454
Advertised Duration (In/Ex): 266/272
Duration at 0.050 (In/Ex): 210/216
Lobe Displacement Angle: 114
Notes: Installing the cam 2 degrees retarded (a 109-degree centerline) nets a horsepower gain. Peak power should be 335-340 at 5,500 rpm (shift at 6,000). Fast-bleed lifters are worth 1½ inches Hg (will idle at 15 in gear). Use Crane PN 99377-16 lifters and PN 11308-1 valvesprings.

The Expert: Lunati Cams
Cam Manufacturer: Lunati Cams
Part No.: 07102 (Streetmaster)
Type: Hydraulic flat-tappet
Rocker Ratio (In/Ex): 1.5:1/1.5:1
Lift (In/Ex): 0.507/0.507
Advertised Duration (In/Ex): 285/285
Duration at 0.050 (In/Ex): 235/235
Lobe Displacement Angle: 108
Notes: Lunati was the only company to recommend a single-pattern cam for this application. High-bleed-down lifters (Lunati PN 71817HV) help idle vacuum, and the recommended PN 73943 springs fit the stock spring pockets. Installed intake centerline should be 104 degrees.

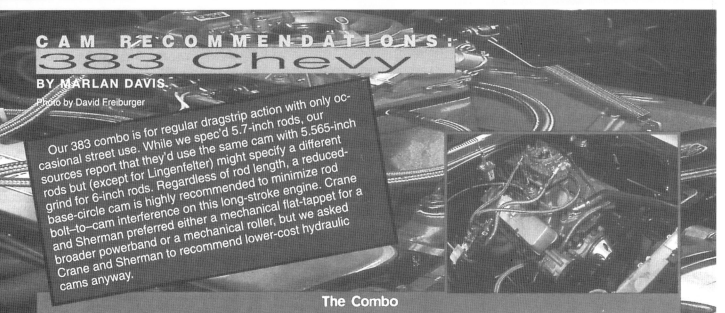

CAM RECOMMENDATIONS:
383 Chevy

BY MARLAN DAVIS

Photo by David Freiburger

Our 383 combo is for regular dragstrip action with only occasional street use. While we spec'd 5.7-inch rods, our sources report that they'd use the same cam with 5.565-inch rods but (except for Lingenfelter) might specify a different grind for 6-inch rods. Regardless of rod length, a reduced-base-circle cam is highly recommended to minimize rod bolt–to–cam interference on this long-stroke engine. Crane and Sherman preferred either a mechanical flat-tappet for a broader powerband or a mechanical roller, but we asked Crane and Sherman to recommend lower-cost hydraulic cams anyway.

The Combo

Make: Chevy

Displacement: 383 (4.030-inch bore, 3.75-inch stroke, 5.7-inch rods)

Compression Ratio: 10.2:1

Cylinder Heads: World Products Sportsman II, pocket-ported

Intake Manifold: Aftermarket single-plane race-type high-rise such as Edelbrock Victor Jr.

Carburetor: Holley 0-4779, 750-cfm double-pumper

Exhaust: 1¾-inch headers, 3-inch dual exhaust with large-capacity aftermarket mufflers

Transmission: TH400 auto with 3,300- to 3,400-rpm stall speed

Rear Gears: 4.56:1

Vehicle Weight: 3,300 pounds less driver (Camaro class)

Typical Use: Regular dragstrip action, weekend street use

The Expert: Steve Chryssochoos at Bill Mitchell

Cam Manufacturer: Comp Cams

Part No.: 12-250-3 (Xtreme Energy)

Type: Hydraulic flat-tappet

Rocker Ratio (In/Ex): 1.5:1/1.5:1

Lift (In/Ex): 0.507/0.510

Advertised Duration (In/Ex): 280/296

Duration at 0.050 (In/Ex): 240/246

Lobe Displacement Angle: 110

Notes: With Comp PN 858-16 lifters and an installed centerline of 108, Chryssochoos guesses this engine will make 475 hp on pump gas—500 with porting. He says the "reverse ramp" lobes best match the heads' fast-burn chambers and 200cc intake runners; go down two cam sizes with OE heads.

The Expert: Crane Cams

Cam Manufacturer: Crane Cams

Part No.: 110691 (Saturday Night Special)

Type: Hydraulic flat-tappet

Rocker Ratio (In/Ex): 1.6:1/1.5:1

Lift (In/Ex): 0.535/0.516

Advertised Duration (In/Ex): 294/300

Duration at 0.050 (In/Ex): 238/244

Lobe Displacement Angle: 106

Notes: Use Crane PN 99377-16 lifters and PN 99838-16 springs and install the cam at a 102-degree intake centerline. The recommended springs will fit the World Products heads without modification. The powerband is 3,200-6,200 rpm, so a 3,500-rpm converter and a 4.56:1 ratio are optimal.

The Expert: Crower Cams

Cam Manufacturer: Crower Cams

Part No.: 00351S (Magnum Street)

Type: Mechanical flat-tappet

Rocker Ratio (In/Ex): 1.6:1/1.5:1

Lift (In/Ex): 0.560/0.546

Advertised Duration (In/Ex): 288/292

Duration at 0.050 (In/Ex): 254/262

Lobe Displacement Angle: 105

Notes: Crower felt that a hydraulic cam just wouldn't cut it for this engine, instead suggesting this solid cam that redlines at 7,200 rpm with a 2,800- to 6,800-rpm powerband. Suggested intake centerline is 101. A reduced base circle is required to clear the rods and is identified by the "S" at the end of the part number.

The Expert: Engle Racing Cams

Cam Manufacturer: Engle Racing Cams

Part No.: 1167

Type: Mechanical roller

Rocker Ratio (In/Ex): 1.6:1/1.5:1

Lift (In/Ex): 0.675/0.633

Advertised Duration (In/Ex): 304/304

Duration at 0.050 (In/Ex): 268/274

Lobe Displacement Angle: 108

Notes: With this cam, the intake opens faster than the exhaust to make more power faster. More street-driven cars can install the intake centerline at 105. More race-oriented applications can use 108 for more top end, but a 4,500-stall converter is recommended. Use Engle 557 lifters and 400 springs.

The Expert: Joe Sherman

Cam Manufacturer: Isky

Part No.: 201292 (292 Mega-Cam)

Type: Hydraulic flat-tappet

Rocker Ratio (In/Ex): 1.5:1/1.5:1

Lift (In/Ex): 0.505/0.505

Advertised Duration (In/Ex): 292/292

Duration at 0.050 (In/Ex): 244/244

Lobe Displacement Angle: 108

Notes: Sherman feels this engine will have a 2,800- to 7,000-rpm powerband, a 6,000-rpm power peak, and a 4,200- to 4,500-rpm torque peak with 8-10 in Hg vacuum at 1,000 rpm. He said to install it at a 104-degree intake centerline and use Isky 202-HY lifters and 6005 valvesprings.

The Expert: John Lingenfelter

Cam Manufacturer: Comp Cams

Part No.: CS 280-2 288-4R12 (Custom for Lingenfelter)

Type: Mechanical roller

Rocker Ratio (In/Ex): 1.6:1/1.6:1

Lift (In/Ex): 0.586/0.586

Advertised Duration (In/Ex): 280/288

Duration at 0.050 (In/Ex): 236/244

Lobe Displacement Angle: 112

Notes: Use full-roller 1.6:1 rockers on both the intake and exhaust, titanium retainers, and one-piece stainless valves of proper length to achieve necessary spring installed height. The lifters are Comp PN 818-16 and the valvesprings are PN 929-16 or 954-16. Lingenfelter considers a 3,300-pound car to be relatively heavy. This calls for fully ported heads, and aluminum Brodix or Dart heads are easier to rework (read: less costly) than iron heads.

CAM RECOMMENDATIONS:
351W Ford

BY MILES COOK

Photo by Scott Killeen

If your blood is blue, this is the page for you. Our Ford mill of choice for the below-noted street machine recipe is the 351W, an engine that came in many Mustangs, Torinos, Fairlanes, and trucks. We ran this typical street/strip combo by five Ford cam makers and/or suppliers and here's what they came up with.

The Combo

Make: Ford
Displacement: 351 (Windsor)
Compression Ratio: 9.5:1
Cylinder Heads: Rebuilt '69-'70 351W cast-iron
Valve Sizes: 1.84/1.54
Intake Manifold: Edelbrock Performer RPM 351W
Carburetor: Holley 0-3310, 750-cfm vacuum secondary
Exhaust: 1⅝-inch headers, 2½-inch dual exhaust
Transmission: Ford C4 auto with 2,400-rpm stall
Rear Gears: 3.50:1
Vehicle Weight: 3,100-3,500 pounds less driver
Typical Use: Mostly street, some strip

The Expert: John Bennett at Bennett Racing
Cam Manufacturer: Lunati
Part No.: 31006, H220
Type: Hydraulic flat-tappet
Rocker Ratio (In/Ex): 1.6:1/1.6:1
Lift (In/Ex): 0.496/0.496
Advertised Duration (In/Ex): 270/270
Duration at 0.050 (In/Ex): 220/220
Lobe Displacement Angle: 110
Notes: There's already 4 degrees advance in the grind, so install it straight up for 4 degrees advance. If you want more duration, Bennett said the Lunati H225 would be good but would need a looser converter, a bit more gear, and less vehicle weight. In general, he felt it's better to be undercammed and have more torque on the street than have no low- and mid-range power combined with a crummy idle and no vacuum.

The Expert: Jim Losee at Edelbrock
Cam Manufacturer: Edelbrock
Part No.: 7182 (Performer RPM)
Type: Hydraulic flat-tappet
Rocker Ratio (In/Ex): 1.6:1/1.6:1
Lift (In/Ex): 0.496/0.520
Advertised Duration (In/Ex): 290/300
Duration at 0.050 (In/Ex): 224/234
Lobe Displacement Angle: 110
Notes: Install the cam straight up with a 3,100- to 3,400-pound car, or advance it 2-4 degrees for a car in the 3,400- to 3,600-pound range. In a lightweight car (3,000-3,200 pounds) consider Edelbrock PN 2182, which has less duration to provide more cylinder fill and pressure and plenty of low- and mid-range power to move a light car. In addition, the Performer RPM cam might be a bit big for stock heads—stepping up to better aftermarket heads makes a huge difference with Ford engines.

The Expert: Troy Bowen at Ford Performance Solutions
Cam Manufacturer: FPS custom grind
Part No.: LX1DP
Type: Hydraulic flat-tappet
Rocker Ratio (In/Ex): 1.6:1/1.6:1
Lift (In/Ex): 0.499/0.510
Advertised Duration (In/Ex): 280/286
Duration at 0.050 (In/Ex): 226/232
Lobe Displacement Angle: 111
Notes: With '69-'70 heads (60cc combustion chambers) install straight up. With '71-newer heads (68-69cc combustion chambers) install 4 degrees advanced. Stock Ford heads don't flow well on the exhaust side, so FPS recommends a split of 6-10 degrees between intake and exhaust. This FPS grind makes good power from 2,400 to 6,200 rpm. For more torque, consider about 6-8 degrees less duration at 0.050.

The Expert: John Vermeersch at Total Performance
Cam Manufacturer: Ford SVO
Part No.: M-6250-A332
Type: Hydraulic flat-tappet
Rocker Ratio (In/Ex): 1.6:1/1.6:1
Lift (In/Ex): 0.472/0.496
Advertised Duration (In/Ex): 290/300
Duration at 0.050 (In/Ex): 214/224
Lobe Displacement Angle: 110
Notes: This cam uses the regular 351W firing order: 1-3-7-2-6-5-4-8. The same grind is also available for 302s (PN M-6250-A312) using the 302 firing order, 1-5-4-2-6-3-7-8.

The Expert: Dan Nowak at Nowak & Co.
Cam Manufacturer: Nowak custom grind
Part No.: AH5 (Street Pro)
Type: Hydraulic flat-tappet
Rocker Ratio (In/Ex): 1.6:1/1.6:1
Lift (In/Ex): 0.510/0.510
Advertised Duration (In/Ex): 284/294
Duration at 0.050 (In/Ex): 224/228
Lobe Displacement Angle: 112
Notes: If you're considering nitrous, stick with lobe separation angles in the 112- to 110-degree range. Naturally aspirated engines will run well with as little as 108. The AH5 grind is available with angles ranging from 106 to 114 degrees.

CAM RECOMMENDATIONS:
360 AMC

BY MARLAN DAVIS
Photo by David Freiburger

The only problem with the AMC 360 is obtaining pistons to provide the desired 9.5:1 compression ratio. By boring a 360 0.045 over to achieve a 4.125 bore—the same as a 400 Chevy small-block's—you can use pistons designed for 18-degree Chevy small-block's—you can use pistons designed for 18-degree Chevy race heads. Their valve reliefs are even in the right place. Most 360 heads have 2.025/1.68 valves. The most desirable heads are the '71 to mid-'73 units with 58cc chambers and stud-mounted rockers that can be made adjustable with aftermarket parts. The '73-present heads have a paired fulcrum–type valvetrain that requires much machining to make them adjustable, and the '70 heads have 49cc chambers.

The Combo

Make: AMC
Displacement: 367.8 (0.045 overbore)
Compression Ratio: 9.5:1
Cylinder Heads: '71 to mid-'73 with 58cc chambers and stud-mounted rockers
Valve Sizes: 2.025/1.68 (stock)
Intake Manifold: Edelbrock Performer AMC
Carburetor: Holley 750 cfm
Exhaust: Ported stock manifolds or 1¾-inch headers with 2½-inch dual exhaust
Transmission: AMC 904 TorqueFlite with 2.78:1 First gear from an '85 318 Chrysler New Yorker A998
Rear Gears: 3.91:1 Chrysler 8¾
Vehicle Weight: 3,250 pounds less driver (Gremlin)
Typical Use: Daily driver capable of low 13s or high 12s

The Expert: Art Bockhausen, National American Motors Drag Race Association cam consultant
Cam Manufacturer: Crane
Part No.: HI-236/3400-12+5, custom grind
Type: Hydraulic flat-tappet
Rocker Ratio (In/Ex): 1.6:1/1.6:1
Lift (In/Ex): 0.544/0.544
Advertised Duration (In/Ex): 286/286
Duration at 0.050 (In/Ex): 236/236
Lobe Displacement Angle: 112
Notes: Install the cam at a 107-degree intake centerline, use Crane lifters PN 99378-16 and springs PN 99838-16. This single-pattern cam is acceptable thanks to the AMC's good exhaust ports. An Edelbrock Torker single-plane, mild porting, a 3,000- to 3,200-rpm converter, and 4.10:1 gears are recommended with this cam.

The Expert: Tony Zamisch of California Classic AMCs and owner of a 216-mph, 695hp Javelin
Cam Manufacturer: Comp Cams
Part No.: 863801 (PowerMax H-278-2)
Type: Hydraulic flat-tappet
Rocker Ratio (In/Ex): 1.6:1/1.6:1
Lift (In/Ex): 0.498/0.527
Advertised Duration (In/Ex): 278/290
Duration at 0.050 (In/Ex): 222/234

Lobe Displacement Angle: 114
Notes: Use Comp Cams PN 99378-16 lifters and PN 99839-16 valvesprings. Install the intake centerline at 109 degrees. Use fast-bleed lifters, Isky adjustable guideplates, aftermarket screw-in studs, heat-treated pushrods, and 5.0L Ford rockers. Zamisch advises even more compression—9.5:1 to 10.75:1—and 4.10 gears.

The Expert: Engle Mfg.
Cam Manufacturer: Engle Mfg.
Part No.: N/A—it's too new
Type: EP-3038 hydraulic flat-tappet
Rocker Ratio (In/Ex): 1.6:1/1.6:1
Lift (In/Ex): 0.548/0.571
Advertised Duration (In/Ex): 276/280
Duration at 0.050 (In/Ex): 230/238
Lobe Displacement Angle: 110
Notes: Use Engle's 622H lifters and 361-007 springs, and set the intake centerline at 108 degrees. This brand-new hot street/strip cam takes full advantage of the large AMC 0.904-inch lifter foot and gives a power range of 2,500-6,000 rpm.

The Expert: Eric Thomson, AMC collector
Cam Manufacturer: Engle Mfg.
Part No.: K-65 series, no. 5065H
Type: Hydraulic flat-tappet

The Expert: J. David Cooper, AMC tech consultant
Cam Manufacturer: Crane
Part No.: 864441 (PowerMax H-288-2)
Type: Hydraulic flat-tappet
Rocker Ratio (In/Ex): 1.6:1/1.7:1
Lift (In/Ex): 0.488/0.527
Advertised Duration (In/Ex): 288/292
Duration at 0.050 (In/Ex): 226/230
Lobe Displacement Angle: 112
Notes: Cooper was the only AMC source who felt that the exhaust port was poor—all the others raved about it. Cooper runs 1.7:1 rockers on the exhaust to increase lift and duration. He says AMCs don't make power over 6,500 rpm, so ported stock iron exhaust manifolds are acceptable.

Rocker Ratio (In/Ex): 1.6:1/1.6:1
Lift (In/Ex): 0.530/0.530
Advertised Duration (In/Ex): 280/280
Duration at 0.050 (In/Ex): 230/230
Lobe Displacement Angle: 110
Notes: Use Engle's 622H lifters and 993 springs, and set the intake centerline at 104 degrees. This cam is designed specifically for the larger-than-Chevy 0.904 lifter diameter for a greater rate of lift. Headers are recommended, and the powerband will be 2,500-6,000.

The Expert: Herman Lewis, AMC Super Stock racer
Cam Manufacturer: Comp Cams
Part No.: Custom grind for Lewis
Type: Hydraulic flat-tappet
Rocker Ratio (In/Ex): 1.7:1/1.5:1
Lift (In/Ex): 0.563/0.497
Advertised Duration (In/Ex): 270/270
Duration at 0.050 (In/Ex): 224/224
Lobe Displacement Angle: 106
Notes: Use 2.080/1.625 valves—install new guides to reduce the stem diameter from ⅜ to the Chevy-style 11⁄32 so you can use cheaper and lighter small-block Chevy valves. Lewis uses 1.7:1/1.5:1 rockers (the exhaust is so good it can use less lift), but this cam provides 0.530 lift with 1.6:1 rockers. **CC**

HOW TO MAKE IT WORK

ENGINE TECH

DEGREEING THE CAMSHAFT

By Jeff Smith

The camshaft is the brain of your engine. It controls when the valves open and close. In a performance engine, the only way to ensure that the camshaft is opening and closing the valves when it should is to "degree" the camshaft. This procedure is fairly complex and requires some special tools, but once you understand how to measure the position of the cam,

it is another way to ensure that the engine is assembled properly. This is also one of the more important steps in blueprinting an engine.

As with most things, there is more than one way to degree a camshaft. In this story, we'll show you the easiest procedure, which is to measure the cam opening and closing points at .050-inch tappet lift. Then it's a simple procedure

to compare these numbers to the published data on the cam card from the cam manufacturer.

We'll detail all the steps required to degree a camshaft in a small-block Chevy, including some tips and suggestions we've learned from the cam manufacturers and professional engine builders. Are you ready to get your degree?

You will need a few specific tools to degree a cam. A degree wheel, a dial indicator and a magnetic base, a lifter, a pointer and piston stop(s) make up the homemade degree-cam tool assortment (A). Many cam manufacturers now offer complete degree-cam kits such as this one from Comp Cams (B). The smaller degree wheels shown here will fit in the tight confines of an engine compartment to allow degreeing the cam in the car. Larger degree wheels tend to be more accurate, but they also cost more.

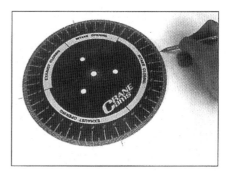

Here's a quick way to check the accuracy of your degree wheel that we learned from Lunati's Dale Browning. Place your degree wheel on a large piece of paper. Mark the four positions of 0, 90, 180 and 270 degrees on the paper. Now rotate the wheel on the top mark to another position, such as 8 degrees After Top Dead Center (ATDC). The other four positions should have the same 8-degree difference. If they don't (and they may not!), your degree wheel is inaccurate. If the error is more than one degree, find a new degree wheel. Errors of less than one degree are acceptable.

We used a flat-tappet hydraulic-lifter cam in a small-block Chevy for our demonstration. The first step is to turn the engine over to Top Dead Center (TDC) on the Number One piston. Rather than use the harmonic balancer bolt to turn the engine, we used this crank nut, available from a number of tool outlets such as Bill Mitchell and Powerhouse. The crank nut requires a very large open-end wrench. We used a large Craftsman adjustable wrench to do the job. Using this crank nut prevents accidentally moving the degree wheel when turning the engine over. It's worth the investment.

With the Number One piston roughly at TDC, mount the degree wheel on the crank with the harmonic balancer bolt, then mount the pointer. We used a length of coat-hanger wire fastened with a bolt as a pointer. Position the pointer to indicate TDC.

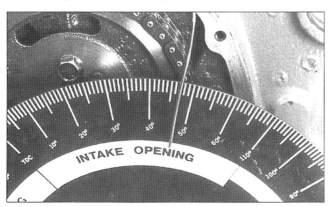

Our engine had the heads removed, so we used this homemade piston stop bolted over the top of cylinder Number One. With the crank bolt snug, back the engine up (counter-clockwise) using the crank nut and install the piston stop. Carefully turn the engine clockwise (using the crank nut) until the piston hits the stop. Write down the reading on the degree wheel on a piece of paper. It should be a number of degrees Before Top Dead Center (BTDC). Rotate the engine counter-clockwise until the piston hits the stop and record the reading. It should be a few degrees ATDC. If the degree wheel is properly positioned at TDC, the degree wheel will have stopped an equal number of degrees on either side of TDC. For example, the readings would indicate 15 degrees BTDC and 15 degrees ATDC.

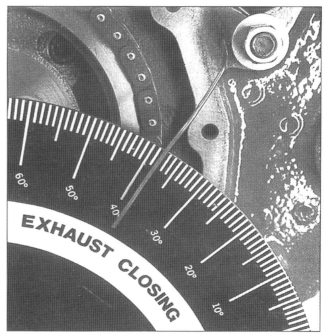

Usually, the two numbers will be different. You can either move the pointer or the degree wheel to obtain true TDC. We've found that moving the degree wheel is easier. In our case, the wheel indicated 47 degrees BTDC and 38 ATDC. Add the two readings together and divide by two (47+38 = 85/2 = 42.5 degrees). Move the degree wheel (with the piston still against the piston stop) to 42.5 degrees and double-check your results. Double- and triple-checking that you have the same number of degrees on both sides of TDC ensures that the degree wheel is positioned properly. If TDC is not accurate, the cam will not be where you think it is.

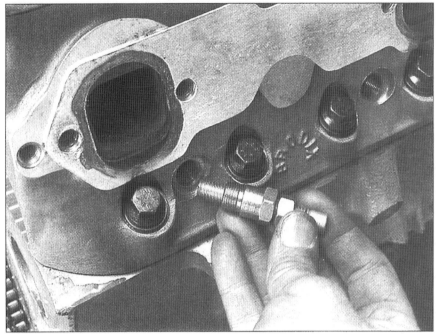

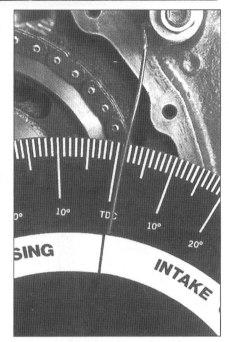

If your engine has the heads installed, you can use this type of thread-in piston stop. The stop threads into the spark plug hole until it contacts the piston. Always turn the engine over by hand when using a piston stop. *Never use the starter motor!* Gently but firmly contact the piston against the stop and record the reading.

With the dial indicator in position, turn the engine clockwise until the lifter begins to rise. Slowly move the crank until you read .050 inch of tappet lift. Record the degree wheel reading and continue to turn the crank past maximum lobe lift. As lobe lift decreases, stop at the .050-inch lobe lift point on the closing side and record the degree wheel reading. Now compare these numbers to the .050-inch intake opening and closing points specified on the manufacturer's camshaft-timing card. If the numbers agree, the cam is positioned "straight up." In our example, the intake at the .050-inch tappet lift opening and closing points occurred at 1 degree BTDC and 40.5 degrees ABDC respectively. This was right on the money for the intake opening and within a degree of the intake closing.

With TDC established, position the dial indicator over the lifter for the Number One intake cam lobe. On the small-block Chevy, this is the second lifter from the front on the driver's side of the engine. The first lifter is Number One exhaust. We used a hydraulic lifter where the pushrod cup has been turned upside down and glued in place *(A)*. The inverted cup has a small hole that positions the dial indicator perfectly. If you do not have a spare lifter, position the dial indicator plunger on the body of the lifter rather than in the cup. Zero the dial indicator on the base circle of the cam and rotate the cam through at least two complete lift cycles to ensure that the lifter always returns to zero. If the indicator does not return to zero, it is binding or producing inaccurate readings *(B)*. It is possible to degree the cam by reading lobe lift from the pushrod, but it's difficult to produce consistent readings.

Continued on page 93

How Big Is **TOO BIG?**

How much cam can you run in a Chevy 350 without becoming unstreetable? To find out, Westech ran four popular Comp Cams flat-tappet hydraulics. Here are the results.

Cam Versus Cam Comparo

By Marlan Davis

Moore's Law: *The mistaken belief that if a little is good, more must be even better.*

The camshaft is one of the most important factors in determining an engine's torque and power bands. Car crafters realize that installing a larger-than-stock cam can yield significant improvements, but all too often they give into temptation and wind up with an overly radical cam that's not really suitable for the rest of the combination. The nut is figuring out how to tread that fine line of maximizing performance while retaining reasonable streetability or overcamming and reducing usable power.

Hoping to get a clue, CAR CRAFT tested four popular Comp Cams hydraulic flat-tappet camshafts in a street high-performance small-block Chevy 355ci engine at Westech Performance. The test profiles included two High Energy grinds (the 252H and 268H) and two Magnum profiles (the 280H and 292H). (Comp designates its cams according to their advertised duration; hence a 252H cam has 252 degrees of advertised duration.) Not only do these cams rank among Comp's top sellers, but each consecutively larger grind shows a consistent 12- to 14-degree increase in duration at 0.050-inch tappet lift—ideal for comparison purposes (see the table for complete cam specs).

The 9.7:1 test engine used Air Flow Research (AFR) aluminum heads with 2.02-/1.60-inch valves and 190cc intake runners. Among the best-flowing street heads available, the AFR castings produce good power with a milder cam than would normally be required for a given combination. To ensure that we were comparing only camshafts, all tests were run with the same intake manifold (an Edelbrock Performer RPM high-rise dual-plane), carburetor (a Holley Pro Series 750-cfm double-pumper), ignition system (an MSD billet distributor triggered by an MSD-6AL box), and exhaust system (Hooker PN 2131 1¾-inch-primaryx3-inch-collector '67-'69 Camaro headers, 3-inch dual exhaust pipes, and 3-inch in-and-out Flowmaster mufflers). Although this setup is close to optimum for a 268H or 280H cam, in the real world a 252H cam would likely perform better with

a standard Performer intake and smaller 1⅝-inch primary-tube headers, while a Victor Jr. intake and 1⅞-inch primary-tube headers could further enhance the 292H cam's performance.

252H High-Energy

Comp Cams says the 252H cam is ideal for 300- to 350ci engines that require good, low-speed torque. The tests more than substantiated this claim, with the engine pumping out a peak 398.2 lb-ft of torque at 3,900 rpm, with over 350 lb-ft from 2,600 through 5,100 rpm. The "small" 252 cam is often overlooked by car crafters in favor of its more radical sisters, yet it was still able to produce nearly 1 hp/ci—347.9 hp at 5,000 rpm, to be precise. The cam idled smoothly at 600 rpm, where it produced 17-18 inches Hg vacuum. With numbers like this, the cam will run in virtually any application, including with computer-controlled engines, overdrive transmissions, and high gear ratios. The cam is even compatible with stock intake and exhaust systems.

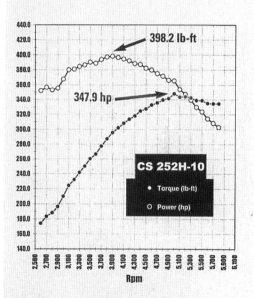

Comp Cams Test Specs								
				Cam Timing @ 0.006" Tappet Lift				
Grind Number	Mfg. Part Number	Valve Lift w/1.5:1 Rockers (Int./Exh.)	Dur. @ 0.050" Tappet Lift (Int./Exh.)	0.006" Dur. (Int./Exh.)	Intake (Opens/ Closes)	Exhaust (Opens/ Closes)	Lobe CL (Int./Exh.)	LDA
High Energy CS 252H-10	12-205-2	0.431"/ 0.431"	206°/ 206°	252°/ 252°	20° BTDC/ 52° ABDC	60° BBDC/ 12° ATDC		
CS 268H-10	12-210-2	0.460"/ 0.460"	218°/ 218°	268°/ 268°	28° BTDC/ 60° ABDC	68° BBDC/ 20° ATDC	106°/ 114°	110°
Magnum CS 280H-10	12-212-2	0.486"/ 0.486"	230°/ 230°	280°/ 280°	34° BTDC/ 66° ABDC	74° BBDC/ 26° ATDC		
CS 292H-10	12-213-3	0.507"/ 0.507"	244°/ 244°	292°/ 292°	40° BTDC/ 72° ABDC	80° BBDC/ 32° ATDC		

280H Magnum

Magnum means "big"—there's no doubt these cams are intended for serious street machines. The entire torque and power curves are skewed noticeably higher: In our tests, the 280H produced less torque than the 268H through 4,300 rpm and less power through 4,100 rpm. Likewise, the 280H's 403.8-lb-ft and 404.7hp peaks occurred at a higher 4,300 and 5,700 rpm, respectively. Over 400 lb-ft were produced between 4,200 and 4,800 rpm, and over 350 lb-ft between 2,900 and 5,900 rpm. The engine exceeded 1 hp/ci between 4,600 and 6,100 rpm. The engine idled at a noticeably choppy 850 rpm, producing 12.5 inches of vacuum. At this point, a vacuum reserve canister may be needed to properly operate power accessories. An aftermarket 2,500-stall converter, steeper gears, headers, and a high-rise dual-plane intake are mandatory.

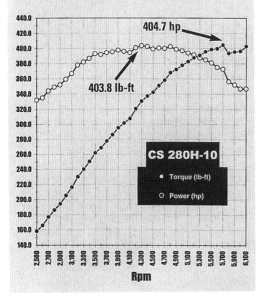

As specified by the manufacturer, each cam was installed on 106-degrees intake centerline. Comp's infinitely adjustable timing belt and a degreed harmonic damper made dialing in each cam a snap.

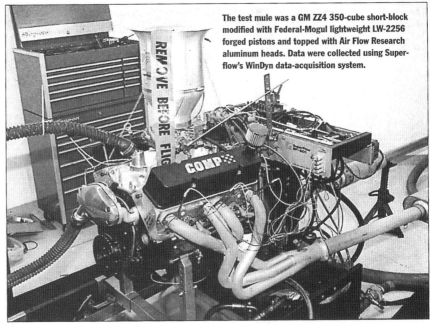

The test mule was a GM ZZ4 350-cube short-block modified with Federal-Mogul lightweight LW-2256 forged pistons and topped with Air Flow Research aluminum heads. Data were collected using Superflow's WinDyn data-acquisition system.

Carburetor jetting and engine timing were optimized for each camshaft. All tests were run on 92-octane unleaded pump-gas. As expected, each progressively larger cam raised the torque and horsepower peaks higher in the rpm range (for complete details on each cam tested, see the accompanying graphs and sidebars). Going from the 252H to the 268H improved both torque and power, with little or no trade-off on the bottom end. The 280H produced more torque and power upstairs, but at the cost of reduced bottom-end performance. The 292H actually made less peak torque than either the 268H or 280H cams, trading off lb-ft for drastically increased top-end horsepower.

We also recorded the minimum smooth-idle rpm and—because most of today's cars have power brakes and air conditioning—the manifold vacuum at idle. Overall, the 252H and 268H cams had acceptable idle quality and vacuum production, the 280H was marginal, and the 292 was totally unacceptable for a daily driven street car.

So how big is too big? Daily driven street cars rarely exceed 5,000 rpm, so you should select a cam that optimizes the curve below this point. Looking at all the numbers, the 268H is the best all-around cam for our Chevy 350, but the 252H is no slouch either. Use the 280H on emissions-exempt cars with stick-shift trannies or high-stall converters. Leave the 292H and bigger cams for dual-purpose weekend warriors with more heavily modified engines.

All this confirms the conventional

268H High Energy

Perhaps Comp's most versatile cam, the top-selling 268H works well in both small- and big-block engines. This thumper produced torque and power peaks of 401.6 lb-ft at 4,100 rpm and 380.2 hp at 5,400 rpm, respectively. Of all the cams tested, the 268H produced the smoothest, best-rounded torque curve—indicating the cam is perfectly matched to the other engine components. The engine made at least 400 lb-ft between 3,700 and 4,300 rpm, and over 350 lb-ft between 2,700 and 5,600 rpm. Its torque output exceeded the 252H at every recorded rpm increment, except between 3,000 and 3,500 rpm. With the 268H, the engine exceeded the "magic" (for a street engine) 1hp/ci level between 4,700 and 5,800 rpm. Producing a slight lope, the cam idled smoothly at a still-acceptable 800 rpm, where it made 16 inches of vacuum—enough to easily run vacuum-dependent accessories. Computerized engines may need a custom chip, however.

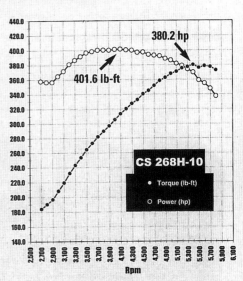

A new set of Comp hydraulic lifters was installed with each cam tested.

Comp's Hi-Tech 1.50:1-ratio, stainless steel roller rockers (PN 1104-16) were adjusted to "zero" lash plus a half turn with the help of this trick Powerhouse Products E-Z Valve Lash Wrench. Comp's PN 981-16 valvesprings proved satisfactory with all four cams.

wisdom that on an average 350ci engine, 280 degrees of advertised duration (230 degrees at 0.050 inch) is the crossover point where you trade off daily driveability for top-end power increases. However, cam "bigness" also depends on the engine's total displacement. For example, on a 454 the 280H cam would behave more like a 268H; but in a 283, you'd probably want the 252H instead of a 268H. Still in a quandary? Remember that Comp also "splits the difference" with its available 260H, 270H, and 286H grinds! Don't become a victim of Moore's Law; if in doubt, go with the smaller cam—you'll be much happier. **CC**

Continued from page 90

From our experience, most cams come within a degree of their timing cards, but you still need to check just to make sure. Often, it may become necessary to move the cam in relation to the crank. One of the most popular ways to do this is with a multikeyway crankshaft gear. These gears usually come with three slots cut in the gear representing 4 degrees advanced, straight up, or 4 degrees retarded. You can see two of the keyway slots in the crank gear in the photo. A second option is to use the offset bushings shown in the upper part of the photo. The bushings are usually cut in 1-, 2-, 3- and 4-degree offsets. The bushings can be placed in the gear to either retard or advance the cam timing. Always recheck the cam timing after making a change to ensure that the cam is positioned properly. Advancing a cam means opening and closing the valves sooner than specified, and retarding the cam means opening and closing the valves later than specified. Advancing a cam usually improves low-speed power, and retarding the cam often improves top-end power while sacrificing low-speed torque. **HR**

292H Magnum

This is the point where you begin to trade off torque for horsepower—not just shift the curves higher. Not only did maximum torque move up to a dual-peak 4,400 and 4,500 rpm, but

at 399.5 lb-ft, the engine's highest torque reading was actually lower than the 268H's and 280H's peaks. On the other end, the engine made a stout 430.5 hp at 6,700 rpm, a gain of over 25 hp over the 280H. It also made more than 400 hp between 5,500 and 6,800 rpm, and more than 1 hp/ci between 4,700 and 7,000. The choppy idle wavered between 850 and 900 rpm, with vacuum output a dismal 8-9 inches. Not really suitable for a daily driven car, this cam requires at least a 3,000-stall converter and no less than 9.5:1 compression. According to Westech, a high-rise single-plane intake like a Victor Jr. could add another 20 hp to this cam's top-end power output.

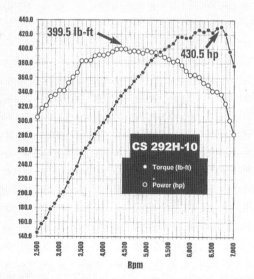

399.5 lb-ft

430.5 hp

CS 292H-10
● Torque (lb-ft)
○ Power (hp)

Rpm

Sources

Competition Cams Inc.
Dept. CC
3406 Democrat Rd.
Memphis, TN 38118
800/365-9145

Westech Performance Group
Dept. CC
11098 Venture Dr., Ste. C
Mira Loma, CA 91752
909/685-4767

SOURCES

Crane Cams
Dept. HR10
530 Fentress Blvd.
Daytona Beach, FL 32114
904/252-1151
904/258-6174 (tech line)

Competition Cams
Dept. HR10
3406 Democrat Rd.
Memphis, TN 38118
901/795-2400
800/999-0853 (cam help)

Lunati Cams
Dept. HR10
4770 Lamar Ave.
Memphis, TN 38181
901/365-0950

Install a ROLLER CAM

Tips for the '87-and-Up Chevys

By David Freiburger

Photos by David Freiburger

We thought it would be a no-brainer how-to. We had all the parts we needed from Lunati. It was just a small-block Chevy cam swap. How tough could it be?

Simple—provided you know the ins and outs of basic cam swapping; the special needs of a cam with roller lifters instead of flat tappets; and the variable we forgot about—the cam-related differences between an older small-block and the newer ones. One-piece rear seals were phased in during 1986, and hydraulic cams came in 1987. However, some of the roller-cam-related block features can also be found on some '86 blocks.

The engine we worked on for this story was a GM Performance Parts PN 12355345 crate 350. This basic 300hp long-block is available from any Chevy dealer and is of the '87-and-up design except for the inclusion of a flat-tappet cam. The engine had served 30,000 miles in a '66 Chevelle, and we wanted to step up the performance. The cam that comes in the crate 350 has 0.435-/0.460-inch lift (using 1.5:1 rockers) and a 212-/222-degree duration at 0.050-inch tappet lift. The new Lunati grind we chose had 0.489-/0.503-inch lift, a duration of 215/218 degrees at 0.050-inch tappet lift, and a lobe displacement angle of 115 degrees. Lunati also provided the related valvetrain components and the tech help to get it all working.

Read on to see what we learned. This is not a step-by-step cam swap, but an overview of roller cam installations in general and, more importantly, the cam-related differences between the '85-and-older and the '86-and-newer blocks.

We noted the first difference between the '86-and-up engines and the older small-blocks when we unbolted the timing-chain cover: The design of the oil-pan gasket is a bit different. This turned out to be a benefit, since we were able to very carefully remove the timing cover without mangling the oil-pan seal, which mates to the cover along its bottom edge. We reassembled it successfully too. With older-design engines, you have to either glop silicone all over the ends of the oil-pan seal or change the entire oil-pan gasket to prevent leaks.

The 30,000 miles had taken their toll on the stock timing chain, but we always replace the timing set when installing a cam anyway. We also noted that this engine used the old-style timing set (and therefore the old cam nose design) even though it was an '86-and-up–type block. That's because the GM Performance 300-horse crate engine comes with a flat-tappet cam. Production '87-and-up engines use a hydraulic roller cam in conjunction with a two-bolt thrust plate mounted to the block behind the cam gear; on this flat-tappet version, the thrust plate is not used.

Lunati makes cams designed for use with the stock '87-and-up thrust plate, and using one would have made this swap much easier. Instead, we used Lunati's pre-'87–type cam. When the double-roller cam gear was installed, we discovered that it hit the block. This is common on small-blocks of all years, and it may require you to clearance the block as shown; we used a cartridge roll from Standard Abrasives and removed metal until we had a 0.030-inch clearance as measured with a blade-type feeler gauge. On some applications, a shim or Torrington bearing can be used to prevent wear between the cam gear and the engine block. If the '87-and-up thrust plate is used, some cam gears may need to be machined for clearance.

We installed the cam simply by aligning the dots on the upper and lower timing gears and not by degreeing. Once the timing set was installed, we had to add a thrust button. A flat-tappet cam has a slight bevel ground into the lobes that prevents the shaft from having too much endplay as the engine is running; a roller cam does not have this, so there must be a way to control endplay. The stock '87-and-up thrust plate accomplishes that, but the older-style cams require a thrust button, as shown.

The thrust button touches the inside of the timing-chain cover to keep the cam endplay from exceeding Lunati's recommended 0.015 inch. However, we've found that the button often presses too much into the timing cover, denting it and pushing the cam too hard rearward. To achieve the proper endplay, you can buy shorter thrust buttons, machine some material off the back of the button (easy to do if you order an aluminum button), or put a dent in the timing cover (which is a bad idea). You can carefully wiggle the cam fore and aft using a screwdriver through a lifter bore to check the endplay, which is usually set by feel and not with a dial indicator. Once the endplay is appropriate, retain the cam button with this three-bolt plate. In theory, you should also use a timing cover specially designed for a thrust button.

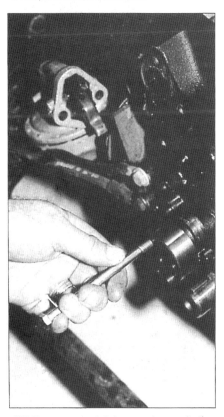

With the cam gear and chain removed, we used a 5/16-18x6 bolt as a handle to slide the camshaft out of the engine. We also saw that the cam core was of the pre-'87 design; if it was an '87-up unit, there would be a step on the nose of the cam that indexes with the previously mentioned thrust plate. Because of this reduced-diameter portion of the cam nose, the '87-up cams also use a different cam gear with a smaller bolt pattern.

PARTS AND PRICES

Want to know how much the cam swap described in this story will run you? Here's the cost of everything we needed. Prices are as of press time only and do not include tax or shipping.

Item	PN	Source	Cost
Roller camshaft	50155	Lunati	$256.99
'87-and-up hydraulic roller tappets	72111-2	Lunati	$120.00
7.195-inch pushrods	83132	Lunati	$69.92
Pro Rev valvesprings	73043-1	Lunati	$90.72
7-degree steel retainers	75074-1	Lunati	$48.64
11/32-inch valve locks	77003-1	Lunati	$24.00
Double-roller timing set	93100-9	Lunati	$75.00
Roller cam button	90001	Lunati	$9.40
Retaining plate	90283	Lunati	$2.38
Lifter valley spider	14101116	Chevy dealer	$10.60
Tappet link bar (8)	12550002	Chevy dealer	$21.60
Crane bronze-tipped fuel-pump pushrod	11985-1	Jeg's	$14.99
Standard Abrasives gasket removal kit	260010	Jeg's	$14.99
Standard Abrasives cartridge roll kit	260006	Jeg's	$17.99
Victor Reinz intake gasket	MS-15315	NAPA	$12.42
Victor Reinz timing-cover gasket	JV-1041	NAPA	$10.74
		TOTAL	**$800.38**

Lunati sent stock GM hydraulic roller lifters that dropped into place with no hassles. Remember, roller cams and lifters should be installed using just engine oil as a lube—not moly-type cam lube. Since roller lifters must not rotate in their bores (which would cause the roller to badly gall the cam lobe), each pair of lifters is tied together with stock GM link bars (*arrows*), also called lifter guides. It's only possible to use this design on an '87-and-newer block with bolt holes for the valley spider; to retrofit a roller cam into an older block, you need to use a different lifter design with integral links, unlike the GM type that simply slides over the two lifters and can be removed.

Rocker arms also become an issue. The '87-and-up engines use rocker arms with a small indentation on the nose—you can barely see it on the left as compared to the conventional design on the right. This indentation centers the rocker over the tip of the valve. If you don't use them, then pushrod guideplates are required. And if you use guideplates, then hardened pushrods are required. We just used the stock '87-and-up rockers. With the Lunati cam we picked, the stock slot in the rocker was long enough and the stock range of adjustability was sufficient. Adjustment technique is the same as with flat-tappet cams.

Our last concern before buttoning the engine back up was the compatibility of the cam's distributor-drive gear with the distributor gear. Traditional roller cams require a bronze distributor gear (*left*) because it's a softer material than the cam itself. You'd rather chew a distributor gear than wreck the whole cam. However, Lunati can spec its cams with a ductile-iron drive gear, eliminating the need for a softer distributor gear. Note that a bronze-tipped fuel-pump pushrod must be used with a roller cam. **CC**

Here's the lifter valley spider we mentioned. It bolts to three cast-in bosses in the '87-and-newer blocks and has springy arms that press on each tappet link-bar to keep the bars from coming off as the lifters cycle up and down. This is not needed when using an older block and the corresponding roller lifters with integral links. The '86 blocks have the stands for the spider, but the bolt holes may not be tapped.

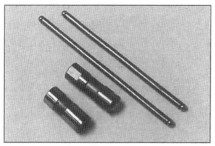

The next concern is the length of the pushrods. Since the roller lifters are longer than the flat-tappet lifters, they require shorter pushrods. In this instance—and with most mild street-roller cams—the stock-length (7.195-inch) '87-and-up Chevy roller-cam pushrods can be used. The standard pushrod length for stock flat-tappet cams is 7.794. Keep in mind that custom-length pushrods may be required depending on your cam grind or milling of the block or heads.

Tools Required

- Air grinder
- Air line setup to fill each cylinder while removing the valvesprings
- Basic sockets and handtools
- Blade-type feeler gauges
- Cartridge roll kit
- Air compressor
- Crankshaft socket
- Gear puller
- Harmonic balancer puller/installer
- In-car valvespring compressor
- Soft-blow mallet
- Standard Abrasives gasket cleanup kit (or gasket scraper)
- Torx bits (for '87-and-up Chevy center-bolt valve covers)

Sources

GM Performance Parts
See your local GM Performance Parts dealer, call 800/577-6888 to find a dealer near you, or visit www.gmgoodwrench.com

Lunati Cams & Equipment
Dept. CC
P.O. Box 18021
Memphis, TN 38181-0021
901/365-0950
901/795-9411 (fax)

Standard Abrasives
Dept. CC
4201 Guardian St.
Simi Valley, CA 93063
800/383-6001
800/546-6867 (fax)

BRUTAL POWER THROUGH CAM DEGREEING

Is Advancing or Retarding a Camshaft Worth Power? This Test May Surprise You

By Marlan Davis

"Throw that cam in 4 degrees advanced—she'll run a lot better!" How often have you heard that hoary bench-racer cliché? Is it just a fable passed down from one car-crafter generation to the next, or is there some validity to the statement?

Understanding Degreeing

Most experienced car crafters know they are able to change the position of the cam's intake and exhaust lobe centerlines (CLs) in relation to the crankshaft during cam installation; the cam can be installed per the manufacturer's specifications ("straight up"), advanced, or retarded. For example, imagine a cam installed straight up at 108 degrees and ground such that the intake valve opens 3 degrees BTDC. Advancing the cam means that the intake and exhaust events occur sooner than the manufacturer's "design" position; therefore, if the cam was advanced 4 degrees to a 104-degree centerline, the intake would open 7 degrees BTDC. Retarding the cam 4 degrees from 108 to 112 would

cause the intake to open 4 degrees later, or 1 degree ATDC.

Advancing or retarding the cam changes neither the lobe displacement angle (LDA—the angular distance, expressed in camshaft degrees, between the camshaft's intake and exhaust lobe CLs), nor lift, duration, or overlap—all these are ground into the camshaft at the time of its manufacture and cannot be altered.

The Theory

Theory says that advancing a cam should produce an improvement in bottom-end torque because peak cylinder pressure is developed earlier in the engine's speed range. In effect, the engine behaves as if the cam has shorter duration. Retarding the cam should have the opposite affect, boosting high-speed power at the cost of some low-end performance; the engine should behave as if the cam has longer duration.

The Test

We decided to find how closely reality matches theory by putting a selected camshaft through a phase. Flowmaster, one of the aftermarket's leading performance muffler makers, maintains an elaborately instrumented Superflow dyno cell, and recently the mufflermen just happened to be testing a stout Chevy small-block 350 engine equipped with extensively ported and polished Corvette alu-

Advancing and retarding a camshaft can alter an engine's power and torque curves, thereby providing yet another tool in the knowledgeable tuner's bag of tricks. For this test, Flowmaster used a prototype Crane hydraulic flat-tappet grind.

minum heads fitted with 2.02-/1.60-inch valves. A Holley 0-4779, 750-cfm double-pumper carb optimized with MaxJets fed fuel to the hungry heads via an Edelbrock Performer RPM intake. GM's HEI ignition system lit the spark before the spent mixture was exhausted through headers, dual pipes, and Flowmaster mufflers. Except for a Milodon oil pan, the lubrication system remained reliably GM-stock.

The engine was equipped with a prototype Crane Compucam flat-tappet hydraulic street cam (see specs table) and Crane 1.6:1-ratio billet aluminum rocker arms. Similar to most street-

			Cam Timing @ 0.050" Tappet Lift				
Position	Valve Lift w/1.6:1 Rockers (Int./Exh.)	Adv. Dur. @ 0.004" Tappet Lift (Int./Exh.)	0.050" Dur. (Int./Exh.)	Intake (Opens/Closes)	Exhaust (Opens/Closes)	Lobe CL (Int./Exh.)	LDA
4° adv.				7° BTDC/35° ABDC	51° BBDC/1° BTDC	104°/116°	
0°	0.480"/0.496"	284°/292°	222°/230°	3° BTDC/39° ABDC	47° BBDC/3° ATDC	108°/112°	110°
4° retard				1° ATDC/43° ABDC	43° BBDC/7° ATDC	112°/108°	

Crane Test Cam Specs

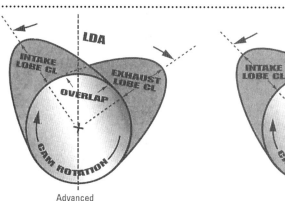

Advanced

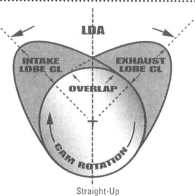

Straight-Up

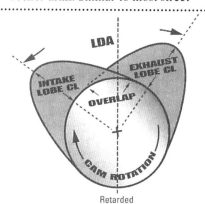

Retarded

PHOTOS BY MARLAN DAVIS

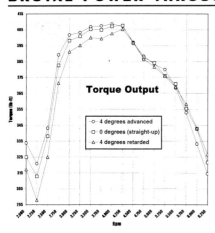

An infinitely adjustable Jesel beltdrive made advancing and retarding the cam a snap on the dyno.

Torque (lb-ft)			
Rpm	4° Adv.	0°	4° Ret.
2,000	333.8	325.0	317.2
2,250	320.9	312.8	297.8
2,500	343.1	338.1	325.0
2,750	389.2	382.6	371.4
3,000	401.6	398.1	391.1
3,250	403.2	400.8	395.1
3,500	406.9	405.3	399.9
3,750	407.4	404.9	399.3
4,000	**408.5**	407.1	402.5
4,250	407.3	**407.6**	**405.3**
4,500	397.0	396.6	396.9
4,750	388.3	387.5	386.6
5,000	383.4	384.1	381.6
5,250	379.9	375.9	375.7
5,500	368.3	370.8	368.8
5,750	352.9	355.4	358.2
6,000	333.2	342.8	343.1
6,250	314.5	321.7	326.7
Avg. thru 4,000	379.4	373.2	369.0
Avg. 4,200-plus	369.4	371.4	371.4
Avg. overall	374.4	373.2	369.0

Duplicating a real-world street-performance engine, the exhaust gases are expunged from the engine by headers (1¾-inch primaries x 3½-inch collectors), 2½-inch dual exhaust pipes, and PN 42553 Flowmaster mufflers.

oriented grinds, the cam's as-ground intake and exhaust CLs were not symmetrical. In other words, installing the cam straight up per the manufacturer's specs actually results in an intake CL that's 2 degrees advanced.

Come again? Crane designed the cam with a 110-degree LDA, but ground it with the intake lobe CL already advanced—so putting the cam in straight up as delivered results in a 108-degree intake lobe CL and a 112-degree exhaust lobe CL ([108 + 112]/2 = 110). For this test series, Flowmaster installed and tested the cam per the manufacturer's specs (108-degree intake CL), 4 degrees advanced from the manufacturer's specs (104-degree intake CL), and 4 degrees retarded (112-degree intake CL). It's important to remember that the 4-degree advance/

retard figures used in the tests are based on the manufacturer's as-intended installation position, not on theoretical split-overlap. Finally, Flowmaster optimized both carburetor jetting and the timing curve for each test.

The Results

As can be seen in the graphs and tables, running the engine 4 degrees advanced yielded the most torque—408.5 lb-ft compared to 407.6 and 405.3 lb-ft for straight up and 4 degrees retarded, respectively. Running the engine 4 degrees retarded yielded the most top-end power—392 hp compared to 386.4 and 391.6 hp for 4 degrees advanced and

straight up, respectively. Exactly as the theory predicts—but which cam position yields the most area under the curve?

To find out, we need to examine *average* torque and power production. Let's first look at average output between 2,000 rpm (the lowest point tested) and 4,000 rpm; this will give a good indication of lower-end performance. In this range, running the cam 4 degrees advanced again yields the most average torque (379.4 lb ft) as well as the most average power (220.4 hp). On the opposite end of the rpm spectrum between 4,250 and 6,250 rpm (the highest point tested), running the cam straight up and 4 degrees retarded yielded an identical 371.4 average torque output. As expected, the 4-degrees-retarded configuration's 368.4 hp proved to be the best high-end power average.

Looking at overall averages throughout the tested rpm range, running the cam 4 degrees advanced yields the best average torque number

(374.4 lb-ft). Both the 4-degrees-advanced and straight-up configurations produced an identical best overall-average power reading of 293.2 hp.

Conclusion

To sum up, running the cam 4 degrees advanced produced leading torque and power average numbers in four out of the six tabulated average categories (outright "wins" in two categories and ties for First in the other two). Straight up and 4 degrees retarded could each manage top finishes in only two out of the six average categories. By this measure, running the cam 4 degrees advanced yields the best overall performance.

Examining the graphs further substantiates this data: The 4-degrees-advanced position maintains higher or substantially equal torque and power output numbers through the bottom-end and midrange, only falling behind over 5,000 rpm. The slight upper-end power gains from retarding the cam are more than offset by the low-end torque losses.

Finally, the data shows that changing cam phasing has little effect on the actual power and torque peak-rpm points—they didn't vary up or down more than 250 rpm. That's because intake manifold plenum volume and runner length, exhaust-system length and diameter, and overall cam profile are the primary determinants of an engine's torque and power peak-rpm points. Instead, advancing and retarding the cam acts similar to a seesaw, skewing the power and torque curves toward the low- or top-end, respectively.

And one last note: Just because this cam behaved as it did, does not mean that different cams will yield similar results. In fact, the

same cam installed in a different engine combo may produce different results. The only way to know for sure is to vary your cam's phasing and see what happens. If you don't have a dyno, try the acid crucible of a real dragstrip! **CC**

With a 1.6:1 ratio, the Crane billet aluminum roller rockers provided additional lift without degrading idle quality. Crane also supplied the other valvetrain parts, including the hardened pushrods, dual valvesprings, keepers, and retainers.

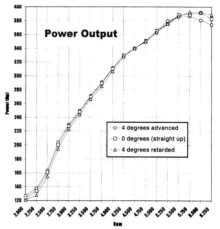

Power Output

Rpm	4° Adv.	0°	4° Ret.
Power (hp)			
2,000	127.1	123.8	120.8
2,250	137.5	134.0	127.6
2,500	163.3	160.9	154.7
2,750	203.8	200.3	194.5
3,000	229.4	227.4	223.4
3,250	249.5	248.0	244.5
3,500	271.2	270.1	266.5
3,750	290.9	289.1	285.1
4,000	311.1	310.1	306.5
4,250	329.6	329.8	328.0
4,500	340.2	339.8	340.1
4,750	351.2	350.5	349.6
5,000	365.0	365.7	363.3
5,250	379.8	375.8	375.6
5,500	385.7	388.3	386.2
5,750	386.4	389.1	392.2
6,000	380.7	391.6	392.0
6,250	374.3	382.8	388.8
Avg. thru 4,000	220.4	218.2	213.7
Avg. 4,200-plus	365.9	368.2	368.4
Avg. overall	293.2	293.2	291.1

Engine Cycle Analysis

So what's a muffler company like Flowmaster doing with a fully equipped Superflow dyno cell? Improving its product, that's what. With available optional instrumentation, the Superflow dyno can run a complete Engine Cycle Analysis (ECA). Sophisticated pressure sensors can actually be inserted into the combustion chamber, cylinder, intake runners, and exhaust headers, where they monitor conditions and deliver real-time data during engine operation. Synched to a crankshaft position sensor that monitors crank position every 0.2 degree of crankshaft rotation, they provide a window into the engine's efficiency throughout the four-stroke combustion cycle. ECA data can record the burn rate, the energy extracted from the

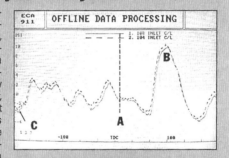

This ECA graphical representation shows the No. 2 cylinder's complete combustion cycle, as monitored by the exhaust sensor. TDC/firing is at the graph's center (A). The exhaust valve opens 180 degrees later, producing an initial positive-pressure spike (B). Negative pressure (C) occurs near TDC/overlap.

A highly accurate crank position sensor (A) works with pressure transducers to precisely monitor the entire combustion cycle. Flowmaster inserted a high-pressure sensor through the back wall of the No. 2 combustion chamber behind the exhaust valve (B), in addition to a low-pressure sensor in the No. 2 primary header tube (C).

quantity of fuel burned, the pumping losses, and the locations of key pressures within the cylinder, exhaust, and intake.

As exhaust specialists, the folks at Flowmaster are particularly interested in analyzing the effects of headers, exhaust pipes, and mufflers on combustion-chamber and exhaust pressures. Higher negative cylinder pressures during intake- and exhaust-valve overlap help the intake tract start to flow, and in some cases can actually boost normally aspirated engine volumetric efficiency beyond 100 percent. All tuned exhaust systems generate a negative pressure wave back up the pipe. By altering the timing of the wave via revisions in header primary tube, header collector, and muffler configuration, you can enhance the suction effect on the intake during overlap. As the only exhaust company to do ECA, Flowmaster is using the generated data to better optimize its exhaust products to aid negative pressure during the overlap period.

Sources

Crane Cams
Dept. CC
530 Fentress Blvd.
Daytona Beach, FL 32114
904/252-1151

Flowmaster Inc.
Dept. CC
2975 Dutton Ave.
Santa Rosa, CA 95407
800/544-4761

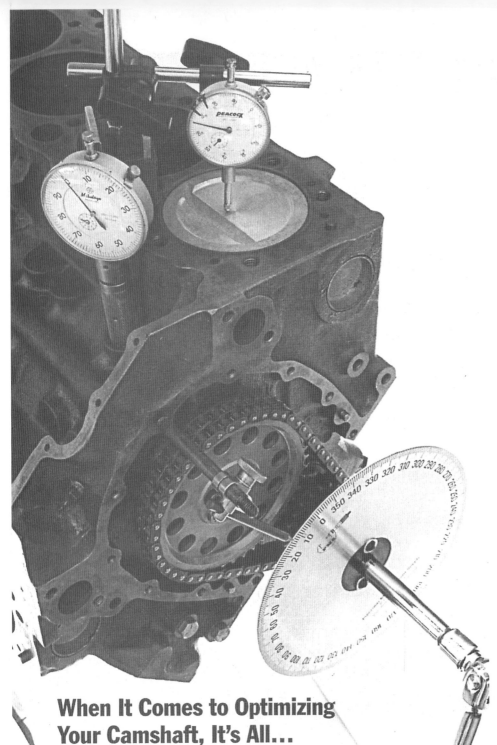

By Marlan Davis

THERE'S A LOT MORE to installing a high-performance cam than merely lining up the timing dots. You've chosen that custom grind in order to maximize your engine's performance potential by ensuring its valves open and close in exactly the right relationship to piston movement. But due to tolerance stackup and manufacturing variations, the only way to know for sure that the cam's timing events occur as intended by the cam designer is to "degree" it in. The two most common degreeing procedures are the intake-centerline method and the intake-opening-and-closing-point method (the latter is also known as the timing card method). Different cam manufacturers prefer different degreeing methods, and it's generally advisable to follow the procedure recommended by your camshaft's manufacturer.

Competition Cams, the manufacturer of the '87-and-earlier small-block Chevy retrofit hydraulic roller cam that serves as the installation example for most of this article's photos, recommends the intake-centerline method for several reasons: it's generally faster than the timing card method; advancing/retarding the intake typically has the most effect on the engine's overall performance characteristics; and, because it is based on merely finding the point of max intake lobe lift in relation to crank degrees After Top Dead Center, this method can be successfully used to degree in the cam, even if you don't have the timing card.

Of course, correctly degreeing the cam is only the first of many checks required when installing a performance cam. You'll also need to take a look at piston-to-valve clearance, potential valvetrain component interference, valvetrain geometry, and (in the case of a roller cam) check for correct endplay. Just think of it as a team with everyone pulling their own weight, working together for the engine's common good. In other words, real camrades in arms.

When It Comes to Optimizing Your Camshaft, It's All...

A Matter Of Degrees

Sources

Competition Cams Inc.
Dept. CC
3406 Democrat Road
Memphis, TN 38118
901/795-2400
800/999-0853

Controlled Induction
Dept. CC
39840 Los Alamos Road,
#3-153
Murrieta, CA 92562
714/677-2332
FAX: 714/677-5472

Kaufmann Products, Inc.
Dept. CC
12400 Benedict Ave.
Downey, CA 90242
310/803-5531 (orders)
310/803-3677 (tech line)

Precision Measurement Supply (PMS)
Dept. CC
P.O. Box 28097
San Antonio, TX 78228
512/681-2405

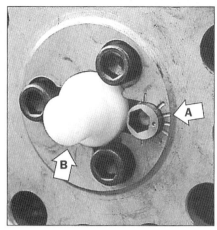

1 Besides the usual multi-indexed crank keyway, Comp Cams' newest "True Roller" timing chain, available for both big- and small-block Chevys, has an infinitely adjustable eccentric dowel pin bushing (arrow A). **Each line represents a 2-degree change in cam timing. Loosening the sprocket mounting screws, then turning the eccentric counterclockwise advances the timing, and vice versa. Roller cams also require a separate anti-walk button** (arrow B). **The billet upper sprocket comes machined for a Torrington thrust bearing.**

2 Begin by installing the crank sprocket, cam sprocket, and timing chain in the engine. The two dots must align. At this point, the line on the eccentric screw of this special timing set should be aligned with the center index mark (see arrow A, above). The #1 piston should also be in place.

MATTER OF DEGREES

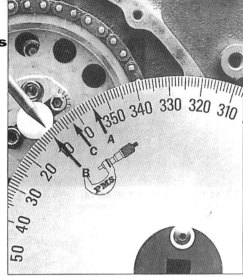

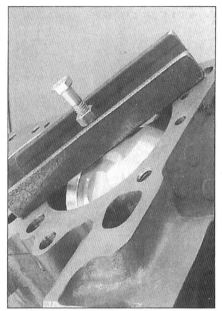

3 Next, accurately locate TDC using a degree wheel, a timing pointer, and a dial indicator mounted on a magnetic stand or bridge. Make a pointer from an old coat hanger or buy an aftermarket adjustable unit. Precision Measurement Supply (PMS) has a degree wheel that's retained on their special crank rotation socket (top right photo) with small set screws, allowing the degree wheel to rotate without disturbing the crank. Kaufmann Products' magnetic indicator stand (bottom right photo) has unique individually adjustable magnetic segments, making it particularly useful on irregular surfaces. Rigidly mount the indicator on the block deck and rotate the piston through its maximum upward travel—this is TDC. Adjust the pointer as close to "0" (TDC) on the degree wheel as you can by eyeballing the indicator. Rotate the engine clockwise all the way around until the indicator reads 0.030-inch before TDC. Record the pointer reading (arrow A: 355 degrees). Continue rotating the engine as the piston passes TDC, until the indicator again reads 0.030. Record the reading (arrow B: 10 degrees). If the numbers before and after TDC don't match, count the number of degrees between the two marks, divide by two (15÷2=7.5), and mark the wheel halfway between the first two marks (arrow C). Rotate the engine clockwise until the pointer aligns with the third mark; then, *without disturbing the crank*, adjust the pointer and/or rotate the wheel so the pointer lines up with "0" on the wheel. Rotate the engine once more through a complete cycle; now the wheel numbers should be equal at the dial-indicator checkpoint on either side of TDC.

4 A rigid piston stop can be used in lieu of a dial-indicator to find TDC. It must be strong enough not to flex. Rotate the engine until the #1 piston is about halfway down the bore, then install the stop to prevent the piston from rising all the way to TDC. Rotate the engine clockwise until the piston gently but firmly contacts the stop, then mark the degree wheel. Turn the engine in the opposite direction until the piston again contacts the stop and mark the wheel. Count the number of degrees between the two marks and divide by two—this is TDC. Remove the stop and adjust the degree wheel as previously.

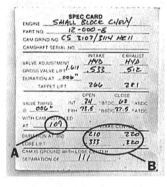

5 The timing card contains all the necessary checking specs. The listed "intake centerline" (109 degrees, A) is the basis for checking the cam by the intake centerline method. The opening/closing point method uses the 0.050 tappet lift numbers (B). This is a Comp Cams custom hydraulic roller grind, generated as the result of Controlled Induction's camshaft profile design program. Comp Cams prides itself on the ability to generate custom non-catalog grinds within 24 hours.

7 Competition Cams offers a cam degreeing kit complete with handy carrying case. Optimized for checking the cam on an engine with heads already installed, its dial indicator mounting fixture screws into a rocker cover mounting bolt hole. It also has a piston stop that screws into the spark plug hole. Many pros running big cams and springs prefer to mock up the entire valvetrain and take the reading off the valvespring retainer in order to compensate for "real world" valvetrain flex.

6 To check the cam phasing, a solid tappet is required. Use a solid flat tappet with a hydraulic or solid flat-tappet cam; use a roller tappet with a hydraulic roller or solid cam. *Do not use hydraulic lifters or your readings will be inaccurate.* Place the lifter in the #1 intake tappet bore. (Careful—the first lobe isn't always the intake!) Position the dial indicator and magnetic base so that the indicator's stem matches the particular engine's pushrod angle. With the lifter on the base circle, place the dial indicator at "0." Rotate the engine through the complete cam lobe opening-and-closing cycle until the lifter returns to the base circle. The indicator should again read "0." If it doesn't, the fixture setup is not rigid enough and needs to be readjusted, or the lifter is hanging up in the bore.

8 Achieving adequate dial indicator rigidity with the typical magnetic base, long stem, and lifter cup is often difficult. The best solution we've seen is this fixture offered by PMS and Comp Cams. It fits inside the lifter bore, held snug by captured O-rings. Different-diameter interchangeable feet are offered that simulate flat or roller lifters for GM, Ford, or Chrysler engines. A standard dial indicator attaches to the top. The result is an extremely accurate and rigid cam-check tool.

9 To degree the cam using the intake centerline method: Rotate the engine clockwise until the dial-indicator pointer reads about 0.025-inch before max lobe lift. Record this location on the degree wheel (83 degrees in example, A). Continue rotating the engine in the same direction past maximum lift until the pointer falls back to your previous checkpoint. Mark the degree wheel (140.5 degrees, B). Add the two readings and divide by two—the result is the intake centerline (111.75 degrees, C). According to the timing card (see 5, on previous page) the correct centerline for this cam is 109 degrees (D), so you must advance the cam 3 degrees. If checking the cam using the 0.050-inch opening and closing points, rotate the engine clockwise until reaching the 0.050-inch check points, compare the numbers observed on the degree wheel at the appropriate check points to the numbers listed on the timing card, write down the difference in terms of degrees advanced (early) or retarded (late), and average all the results to determine if the cam needs to be advanced or retarded.

10 While our new-design chain has an adjustable dowel bushing, more traditional methods of correcting cam timing errors include: crank sprockets with multiple keyways, offset cam-sprocket dowel-pin hole bushings, or offset crank-sprocket keys. After correcting the cam timing, the intake centerline should check to the published card spec. The exhaust centerline should likewise equate to double the cam lobe separation spec minus the intake centerline spec (on the timing card shown in 5, that would be: [111x2] – 109 = 113]. If it doesn't, the cam is incorrectly ground and should be returned to the manufacturer.

11 Check piston-to-valve clearance only after your cam is degreed in, since advancing or retarding the cam will change this clearance spec. While clay or checking springs can be used for this procedure, on unassembled engines we prefer to use the "valve drop" method as this positively avoids any chance of mechanical bind. With the heads off and the dial indicator attached to the appropriate cam lobe, record the intake lobe lift numbers in 5-degree increments from 25 degrees before TDC to 25 degrees after TDC during the transition from the exhaust stroke to the intake stroke. Repeat this procedure for an exhaust lobe. Install the head gasket and cylinder head, using wooden clothes pins to retain the valves in the head. Holding the intake valve fully closed, install and zero the dial indicator on the valve stem top. Using the same 5-degree-incremental checkpoints as you did with the cam lobes, carefully let the valve drop fully until it contacts the piston top and record the observed indicator readings. Do this for at least one intake and one exhaust valve, although it's a good idea (because of rod length, piston deck height, and valve seat location variations) to check all the valves. Once these figures are known, determine piston-to-valve clearance at the various check points: Valve drop – ([Cam lift x rocker arm ratio] – valve lash) = Clearance. At least 0.100-inch is required. If you have less, machine deeper valve notches in the piston top.

12 On engines with rear-mounted distributors, roller cams tend to walk forward in the block because no taper is ground onto the lobe. Acceptable roller cam endplay is between 0.005-0.010-inch. To check: Install a dial indicator on the rear of the cam, then use a screwdriver to carefully pry the cam back and forth with the front cover and gasket installed. Stock sheetmetal covers tend to flex, so you'll need to use a racing short water pump with a countervailing stop screw, or aftermarket billet or cast cover. Reduce clearance by shimming the front anti-walk bushing; increase clearance by milling the bushing, machining the inside of the cover, or tightening the short water pump's stop screw.

13 The valvesprings must not go into coil-bind (stack solid) at max cam lift. You can check this by using a vice to compress the spring to the length it would be at max valve lift (Spring installed height – [Cam lift x rocker arm ratio] = Spring height at max lift). Then use feeler gauges to verify there's at least 0.080-inch clearance between the center coils. If there isn't, you'll need to get a different valvespring.

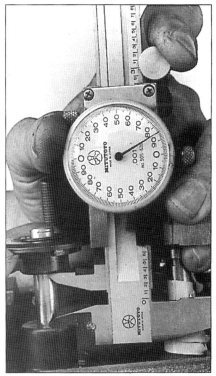

14 At max valve lift there should be at least 0.080-inch clearance between the bottom of the retainer and top of the valve guide/seal (Measured retainer-to-seal clearance – [Cam lift x rocker arm ratio] = Clearance at max lift). If there isn't, you'll need to get a different seal and/or machine down the valveguide boss. Also check that the rocker arm body does not contact the retainer and (with higher-than-stock rocker arm ratios) that the pushrod doesn't rub against the head. Finally, verify overall valvetrain geometry as shown in "Valve Training," CC October '92.

Easily one of the most baffling aspects of building a performance engine is selecting a camshaft. With well over a dozen reputable camshaft companies offering many cams for each engine, choosing the best camshaft for your application can be a mind-numbing proposition. Competition Cams alone offers over 130 different camshafts for the small-block Chevy. So where do you start?

Since each engine application has different requirements, three cam companies have developed computer software to help make the best camshaft choice. Programs designed by Crane Cams, Competition Cams and Wolverine/Blue Racer are self-prompting, menu-driven programs that are easy to use and offer professional suggestions based on a number of inputs. The programs are primarily intended for the entry-level street enthusiast.

Beyond the basic cam-selection programs are a couple of programs from AutoWare, Racing Systems Analysis and Controlled Induction that are simplified engine-power simulations. These programs sacrifice accuracy for ease of use but can still be considered educational.

All of these programs are designed for IBM-compatible computers, usually PC-XT or AT versions. They might be the best learning tool you buy short of a subscription to HOT ROD magazine!

NEW TECH

COMPUTERIZED CAM SELECTION

COMPUTER PROGRAMS TAKE THE MYSTERY OUT OF CHOOSING A CAM

By Jeff Smith

Crane's CamChoice offers cam selection based on a number of vehicle inputs. Here, the combination determined that an HMV-272 hydraulic would work best.

CamChoice also offers electronic timing-card access so you can more closely evaluate the camshaft based on both advertised and .050-inch tappet-duration numbers, lobe-lift figures and valvespring recommendations.

CRANE CAMCHOICE

As with most of the cam-selection programs, CamChoice starts with the basic questions of cruise rpm at 60 mph (to establish gear ratio), compression, transmission type, vehicle weight and engine modifications. Those and a few other inputs establish the parameters that the program uses to determine the camshaft that's best for your application. For example, a 9.0:1 350 Chevy engine in a 3500-pound Chevelle with 3.08 gears and a stock Turbo 350 transmission produces a suggestion for an HMV-260-2-NC with 204/216 degrees of duration at a .050-inch tappet lift with lift figures of .427/.454 for intake and exhaust respectively and a lobe-separation angle of 112 degrees. This is a conservative cam selection and is typical of Crane's approach to prevent overcamming an engine. The program is easy to run and allows you to quickly make changes to evaluate how the different variables affect the selection of a cam.

COMPETITION CAMS CAMQUEST

While it's not quite as much fun as some video games, CamQuest is far more practical. The cam suggestions are only slightly more aggressive than Crane's but less so than the Wolverine program. CamQuest also takes into account specific engine pieces, such as intake-manifold configuration, identifying specific intake-mani-

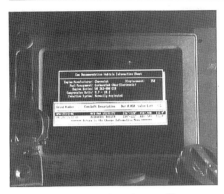

Competition Cams' CamQuest offers cam-timing recommendations as well as integrating specific brand-name components, such as intake manifolds, to more closely predict the best cam to use. For example, there is a distinct power difference between an Edelbrock Performer and a Performer RPM, even though they are both dual-plane intakes.

fold designs to help profile the cam more closely. Since cams and converters are often matched for strong performance, CamQuest also offers input and suggestions for coordinating those components. In addition to the cam-selection program, CamQuest also offers quarter-mile e.t. and speed estimates, optimal carburetor cfm suggestions, handy displacement and compression-ratio programs and a number of other useful performance calculations. They make CamQuest a useful tool for any hot rodder.

Competition Cams also offers cam-selection help over the telephone with Cam Help—a toll-free cam-selection and technical-assistance hot line. The Cam Help line is available from 8 a.m. to 5 p.m. (CST) Monday through Friday and is staffed with experienced technical personnel to help you either choose a cam or solve a camshaft-related technical problem.

WOLVERINE CAM SELECT

The Wolverine program is similar to the Crane and Competition Cams programs, although the selections may be more aggressive than the other two. Using the same 350 Chevy example as in the Crane approach, the Wolverine program suggested 214/224 duration at .050 cam with .443/.465 lift and a 112-degree lobe-separation angle. Like the other programs, the Wolverine/Blue Racer software offers a multitude of utility programs such as compression ratio, gear-ratio calculations, displacement and dozens of others. The Cam Select program also offers submenus for competition, circle-track and sports-car applications.

CONTROLLED INDUCTION JR. AND THE DYNO 2

Rick Jones' Dyno 2 program is tons of fun to use, and you can learn much from its output. Input is shown on three screens for short-block data, cylinder-head flow and valvetrain information. The fun part comes with the Dyno Test. You tell the program at what rpm you want the test to start, and the computer spits out a complete dyno-run sheet simulation for Corrected Torque, Corrected Horsepower, Brake Mean Effective Pressure (BMEP), CFM, Volumetric Efficiency and more, just like an actual dyno sheet. Plus, the program simulates the actual pull on the dyno, including the sound of the engine running through the 250-rpm steps to maximum power! We simulated a 350 Chevy and found the numbers often within 5 percent of power we've made on a real engine. The Dyno 2 will also calculate the rpm where valve float should occur and will indicate it with a horrible crashing sound when your valve smacks a piston! For its under-$70 price tag, the Dyno 2 is certainly worth the investment.

RACING SYSTEMS ANALYSIS ENGINE JR.

More-computer-literate hot rodders are probably aware of Patrick Hale's slick Quarter and Quarter Jr. programs, which simulate vehicle performance on a dragstrip. Hale has now entered into engine simulation with a simple program called Engine Jr. The single-screen input requires similar inputs compared to Controlled Induction Jr., and we found it simple to use and very straightforward. All of the classic inputs

```
Controlled Induction Software                          Phone (909) 677-2332
                        THE DYNO 2

                        DISPLACEMENT: 355.12
BORE: 4.030  STROKE: 3.480          ROD LENGTH: 5.700        MCR: 9.70

    INTAKE VALVE DIAMETER: 2.020 CARBURETOR CFM: (1.5 in./hg): 750
              INTAKE                                   EXHAUST
PORT FLOW: 254 CFM (28 IN/H2O @ .500 LIFT)            PORT FLOW: 188 CFM
    .502                    NET VALVE LIFT                 .512
    1.60                    ROCKER RATIO                   1.60
    .005                    VALVE LASH                     .005
    107                     LOBE CENTER                    111
    219                  DURATION @ .050                   221
```

RPM	CTORQUE	CHP	BMEP	CFM	BSAC	VE	MANI HG
3000	370.0	211.4	143.0	296.7	6.431	96.3	0.246
3250	381.4	236.0	1144.5	326.4	6.335	97.7	0.293
3500	392.0	261.2	145.7	356.3	6.248	99.1	0.0345
3750	401.8	286.9	146.8	386.3	6.167	100.2	0.400
4000	410.9	313.0	147.8	416.3	6.093	101.3	0.460
4250	401.0	324.5	147.2	442.4	6.244	101.3	0.520
4500	391.0	335.0	145.6	464.9	6.357	100.5	0.578
4750	381.4	344.9	144.0	486.9	6.465	99.8	0.639
5000	372.3	354.4	142.3	508.3	6.570	98.9	0.702
5250	363.5	363.3	140.7	529.1	6.671	98.1	0.768
5500	355.0	371.8	139.0	549.3	6.768	97.2	0.835
5750	346.8	379.7	137.3	568.9	6.863	96.3	0.904

Controlled Induction's Dyno 2 appears to be more accurate than the CI Jr. program, mainly because of its more in-depth, three-screen inputs. The fun part of this program is the Test mode. The computer simulates a 250-rpm-step dyno pull complete with sound effects!

are there, including intake-port-flow data and cam duration at .050. None of the simplified programs take into account intake-manifold port length or port size, which dramatically affect the torque curve, but even without those inputs, the data is close. The numbers are conservative, which means that the program makes you feel like a hero when your engine makes more power than the program predicts. Output includes horsepower and torque at their rpm points and redline. **HR**

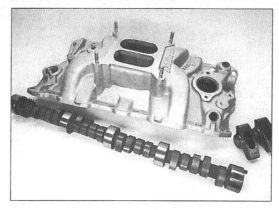

As you improve the integration of intake manifold, cylinder head and exhaust flow with cam timing, power will increase. For an entry-level enthusiast, computer programs offer an easy way to learn how these relationships work.

Computers aren't carnivorous. They don't bite (byte?), so don't be afraid to sit down in front of one. All of the programs in this story are easy to operate and fun to use. Have a friend help you get started and then you can learn at your own pace.

SOURCES

Included in this Source guide are companies that have created more-extensive computer programs than space allowed us to mention. These programs are more complex engine simulations requiring extensive engine-building knowledge and experience.

SOURCES

Allan Lockheed & Associates (Engine Expert)
Dept. HR02
P.O. Box 10828
Golden, CO 80401-0620
303/238-2414

AutoWare
Dept. HR02
7624 Verona N.W.
Albuquerque, NM 87120
800/647-2392 (orders)
505/899-1520

Competition Cams, Inc.
Dept. HR02
3406 Democrat Rd.
Memphis, TN 38118
901/795-2400
800/999-0853 (Cam Help)

Controlled Induction
Dept. HR02
24650 Leafwood
Murieta, CA 92562
909/677-2332

Crane Cams
Dept. HR02
530 Fentress Blvd.
Daytona Beach, FL 32114
904/252-1151
904/258-8846 (24-hour Dial-A-Cam)

Performance Trends, Inc. (Engine Analyzer)
Dept. HR02
Box 573
Dearborn Heights, MI 48127
313/473-9230

Racing Systems Analysis
Dept. HR02
P.O. Box 7676
Phoenix, AZ 85011
602/241-1301

Wolverine/Blue Racer
Dept. HR02
4790 Hudson Rd.
Osseo, MI 49266
800/248-0134
517/523-3611

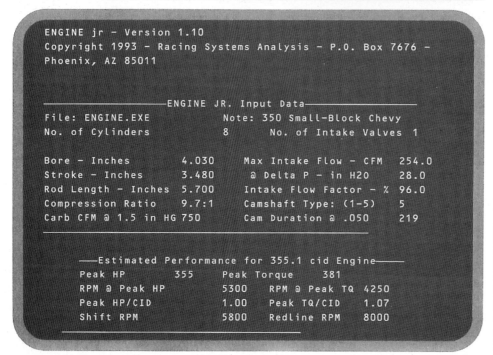

```
ENGINE jr - Version 1.10
Copyright 1993 - Racing Systems Analysis - P.O. Box 7676 -
Phoenix, AZ 85011


───────────────────ENGINE JR. Input Data───────────────────
File: ENGINE.EXE              Note: 350 Small-Block Chevy
No. of Cylinders         8       No. of Intake Valves  1

Bore - Inches          4.030   Max Intake Flow - CFM    254.0
Stroke - Inches        3.480   @ Delta P - in H20        28.0
Rod Length - Inches    5.700   Intake Flow Factor - %    96.0
Compression Ratio      9.7:1   Camshaft Type: (1-5)       5
Carb CFM @ 1.5 in HG   750     Cam Duration @ .050       219


─────Estimated Performance for 355.1 cid Engine─────
Peak HP          355     Peak Torque        381
RPM @ Peak HP    5300    RPM @ Peak TQ    4250
Peak HP/CID      1.00    Peak TQ/CID      1.07
Shift RPM        5800    Redline RPM      8000
```

Engine Jr. is similar to the Dyno 2 program except without the dyno curve. This program from Patrick Hale is another easy-to-run program that allows you to configure items such as bore, stroke, compression, cylinder-head flow and cam timing to evaluate the effect these items have on engine power.

SECRETS
OF CAMSHAFT
POWER

BY MARLAN DAVIS

Photos by Marlan Davis

Illustrations by Comp Cams and Steve Amos

Special thanks to Billy Godbold at Competition Cams and Mike Golding at Crane Cams for their assistance in the preparation of this article.

Car magazines have published rain-forest-loads of issues dealing with camshafts. Why? Because the cam is one of hot rodding's most common, most visceral, and most baffling upgrades.

Camshaft issues always sell magazines, and readers always ask for more. Just when we thought you were sick of it, our most recent readers' poll demanded even more info on how cams work. That's why this story will offer more on the hows and whys of camshaft specifications than any other in recent memory. This time we'll count on you to know the basic definitions of terms such as intake opening, duration, and lift as we go into the theory of how each aspect of cam design tends to affect engine power.

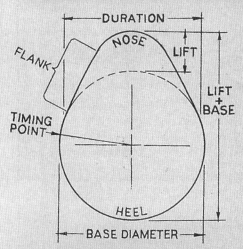

This illustration shows the basic parts of a cam lobe. The nose height compared to the base circle determines the lift generated by the lobe. The overall lobe width establishes how long the valve stays open—aka duration.

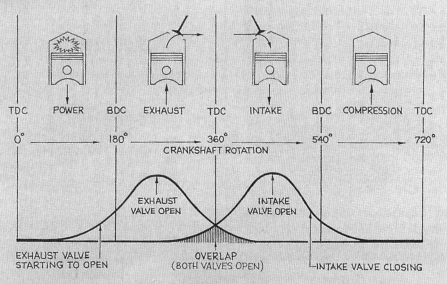

The valves' opening and closing points are tied to the four-stroke engine's combustion cycle. All modern cams have an overlap period during the crossover between the exhaust and intake stroke where both exhaust and intake valves in the same cylinder are open.

Intake Opening

Looking at the intake valve first, its opening point is critical to vacuum, throttle response, emissions, and gas mileage. At low speeds and high vacuum conditions, premature intake opening during the exhaust stroke can allow exhaust gas reversion back into the intake manifold, hurting the intake pulse velocity, and contaminating the fresh intake charge. A late-opening intake gives smooth engine operation at idle and low rpm, plus it ensures adequate manifold vacuum for proper accessory operation (assuming the other three valve opening and closing points remain reasonable).

As rpm increase, air demand is greater. To supply the additional air and fuel, designers open the intake valve sooner, which allows more time for the intake charge to fill the cylinder. With an early-opening intake valve, at high rpm the exiting exhaust gas also helps draw the intake charge through the combustion chamber and out the exhaust—that's good for purging the cylinder of residual gas, but it also increases fuel consumption by allowing part of the intake charge to escape before combustion and can make for a rough idle.

Intake Closing

The intake closing point has more effect on engine-operating characteristics than any of the other three opening and closing points. The earlier it occurs the greater the cranking pressure. Early intake closing is critical for low-end torque and responsiveness and provides a broad power curve. It also reduces exhaust emissions while enhancing fuel economy.

As rpm increase, intake charge momentum increases. This results in the intake charge continuing to flow into the combustion chamber against the rising piston far past BDC. The higher the engine's operating rpm, the later the intake closing should be to ensure all the charge possible makes it into the combustion chamber. Of course, closing the valve too late will create significant reversion. It's a fine balancing act.

In a perfect world, the optimum intake closing point would occur just as the air stops flowing into the chamber; would get the valve seated quickly and not waste time in the low lift regions where airflow is minimal and there is no compression building in the cylinder; wouldn't be so fast that the valve bounces as it closes, allowing the charge to escape back into the intake port and disturb the

next charge; and, in hydraulic street cam applications, would ensure the closing ramps are not so fast that they result in noisy operation.

Exhaust Opening

Overall, the exhaust valve opening point has the least effect on engine performance of any of the four opening and closing points. Opening the exhaust valve too early decreases torque by bleeding off cylinder pressure from combustion that pushes the piston down. Yet the exhaust has to open early enough to provide enough time to properly scavenge the cylinder. An early-opening exhaust valve may benefit scavenging on high-rpm engines because most useful cylinder pressure is used up anyway by the time the piston hits 90-degrees before BDC on the power stroke. Later exhaust valve opening helps low rpm performance by keeping pressure on the piston longer, plus it reduces emissions.

Exhaust Closing

Excessively late exhaust valve closing is similar to opening the intake too soon—it leads to increased overlap, allowing either reversion back up the intake, or the intake mixture to keep right on going out the exhaust. On the other hand, late closing events can help purge spent gasses from the combustion chamber and provide more vacuum signal to the intake at high rpm. Early exhaust closing yields a smoother operating engine. It does not necessarily hurt the top-end, particularly if it's combined with a later intake valve opening.

As engine operating range increases, designers must move all the opening and closing points out to achieve earlier openings and later closings, or design a more aggressive profile to provide increased area under the curve without seat timing increases.

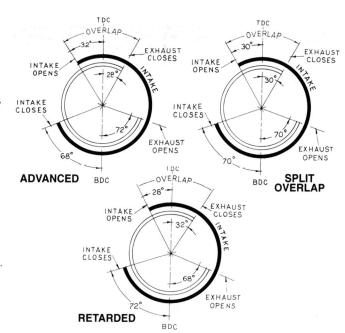

Shown are timing figures for a theoretical cam installed advanced, at split overlap ("straight-up"), and retarded. Most street cams already have some advance ground in at the factory.

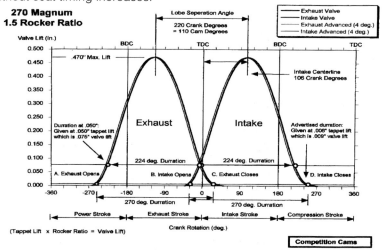

This cam is ground with a 110-degree lobe displacement angle, but 4 degrees advanced (106-degree intake/114-degree exhaust lobe centerlines, *heavy lines*). If the installer advanced it another 4 degrees (8 degrees total, *light lines*), the intake and exhaust centerlines move to 102 and 118 degrees, respectively, but the LDA is still 110 degrees.

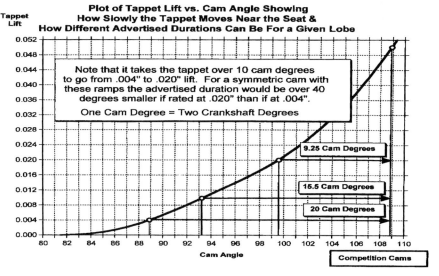

Plot of Tappet Lift vs. Cam Angle Showing How Slowly the Tappet Moves Near the Seat & How Different Advertised Durations Can Be For a Given Lobe

Note that it takes the tappet over 10 cam degrees to go from .004" to .020" lift. For a symmetric cam with these ramps the advertised duration would be over 40 degrees smaller if rated at .020" than if at .004".

One Cam Degree = Two Crankshaft Degrees

Competition Cams

Off the valve seat, relatively small changes in the advertised duration lift rating point can cause a big change in the cam's published advertised duration numbers.

Lobe Centerline

Tailoring the valve opening and closing points on an actual camshaft is accomplished by varying the lobe centerline location, changing the LDA, and refining the profile shape itself. We'll consider changing the centerline location first. Advancing the cam moves both the intake and exhaust centerlines an equal amount, resulting in earlier valve timing events. Engines typically respond better with a few degrees of advance, probably due to the importance of the intake closing point on performance. For racing, advanced cams benefit torque converter stall, improve off-the-line drag-race launches, and help circle track cars come off the corner.

Cam companies often grind their street cams advanced (4 degrees is typical), which allows the end-user to receive the benefits of increased cylinder pressure, yet still install the cam using the standard timing marks. One exception is Crane's CompuCam series, which varies because of the vacuum signal requirements of the ECMs it's designed to operate with.

Lobe Displacement Angle

Although the installer can advance and retard the lobe centerlines, the displacement angle between the centerlines is ground into the cam at the time of manufacture and cannot be changed by the end-user. Narrow LDAs tend to increase midrange torque and result in faster revving engines, while wide LDAs result in wider power bands and more peak power at the price of somewhat lazier initial response.

A street engine with a wide LDA has higher vacuum and a smoother idle. On the street, LDA should be tailored to the induction system in use. According to Comp Cams, typical carbureted, dual-plane manifold applications like 110-112 LDAs, while fuel-injected combos want slightly wider 112- to 114-degree LDAs. Fuel-injection doesn't require the signal during overlap that carburetors need to provide correct fuel atomization, and most computer controllers require the additional idle vacuum that results from decreased overlap.

Bracket racers with higher stall-speed converters, high compression, single-plane intakes, and large carbs usually want 106-110-degree LDAs. Engines equipped with blowers or turbos, or used primarily with nitrous oxide, typically work best with wider 110- to 116-degree separations. Race engine speeds have increased over the years causing a corresponding upward creep in LDA and duration.

Duration

Duration has a marked effect on a cam's power band and driveability. Higher durations increase the top-end at the expense of the low-end. A cam's "advertised duration" has been a popular sales tool, but to compare two different cams using these numbers is dicey because there's no set tappet rise for measuring advertised duration. Measuring duration at 0.050-inch tappet lift has become standard with most high-performance cams. Most engine builders feel that

0.050 duration is closely related to the rpm range where the engine makes its best power. Typical daily driven, under-10.25:1-compression ratio street machines with standard-size carbs, aftermarket intakes, headers, and recurved ignitions, like cams with 0.050-inch durations in the 215- to 230-degree range if using a hydraulic grind, or 230- to 240 degrees with a solid.

When comparing two different cams, if both profiles rate the advertised duration at the same lift, the cam with the shorter advertised duration in comparison to the 0.050 duration has more aggressive rmp. Providing it maintains stable valve motion, the aggressive profile yields better vacuum, increased responsiveness, a broader torque range, and other driveability improvements because it effectively has the opening and closing points of a smaller cam combined with the area under the lift curve of a larger cam.

Engines with significant airflow or compression restrictions like aggressive profiles. This is due to the increased signal that gets more of the charge through the restriction and/or the decreased seat timing that results in earlier intake closing and more cylinder pressure.

Big cams with more duration and overlap allow octane-limited engines to run higher compression without detonating in the low- to mid-range. Conversely, running too big a cam with too low a compression ratio leads to sluggish response below 3,000 rpm. Follow the cam grinder's recommendations on proper cam profile-to-compression ratio match-up.

Lift

Another method of improving cam performance is to increase the amount of lobe lift. Designing a cam profile with more lift results in increased duration in the high-lift regions where cylinder heads flow the most air. Short duration cams with relatively high valve lift can provide excellent responsiveness, great torque, and good power. But high lift cams are less dependable. You need the right valvesprings to handle the increased lift, and the heads must be set up to accommodate the extra lift. There are a few examples where increased lift won't improve performance due to decreased velocity through the port; these typically occur in the race engine world (0.650-1.00-inch valve lift). Some late model engines with restrictive throttle-body, intake, cylinder head runner, and exhaust

Aggressive lobe ramps allow the valve to reach maximum velocity more quickly, generating more area for a given duration.

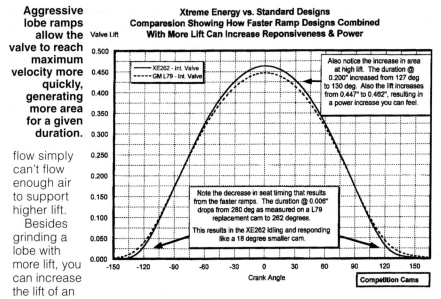

Xtreme Energy vs. Standard Designs
Comparesion Showing How Faster Ramp Designs Combined With More Lift Can Increase Reponsiveness & Power

Valve Lift

- XE262 - Int. Valve
- GM L79 - Int. Valve

Also notice the increase in area at high lift. The duration @ 0.200" increased from 127 deg to 130 deg. Also the lift increases from 0.447" to 0.462", resulting in a power increase you can feel.

Note the decrease in seat timing that results from the faster ramps. The duration @ 0.006" drops from 280 deg as measured on a L79 replacement cam to 262 degrees.

This results in the XE262 idling and responding like a 18 degree smaller cam.

Crank Angle

Competition Cams

flow simply can't flow enough air to support higher lift.

Besides grinding a lobe with more lift, you can increase the lift of an existing cam profile by going to a higher rocker arm ratio. For example, small-block Chevys where the cylinder head runners are not maxed out may benefit from moving up from the stock 1.5:1 ratio to 1.6:1 rockers. But going up more than one tenth in rocker ratio can lead to trouble; there's a limit to how fast you can move and accelerate the valve before the valvespring can no longer control the system. If a profile was a good design with 1.6:1 rockers, it'll probably be unstable with 1.8:1 rockers. The correct solution is to design the profile from the ground up for use with high-ratio rocker arms.

Overlap

Duration, lift, and LDA combine to produce an "overlap triangle." The greater the duration and lift the more overlap area, LDAs remaining equal. Given the same duration, LDA and overlap are inversely proportional: Increased LDA decreases overlap (and vice versa). More overlap decreases low-rpm vacuum and response, but in the midrange overlap improves the signal provided by the fast-moving exhaust to the incoming intake charge. This increased signal typically provides a noticeable engine acceleration improvement.

Less overlap increases efficiency by reducing the amount of raw fuel that escapes through the exhaust, while improving low-end response due to less reversion of the exhaust gases back up the intake port; the result is better idle, a stronger vacuum signal, and improved fuel economy.

Due to the differences in cylinder head, intake, and exhaust configuration, different engine combos are extremely sensitive to the camshaft's overlap region. Not only is the duration and area of the overlap triangle important but also its overall shape. Much recent progress in cam design has been due to careful tailoring of the shape of the overlap triangle. According to Comp, the

most critical engine factors for optimizing overlap include intake system efficiency, exhaust system efficiency, and how well the heads flow from the intake toward the exhaust with both valves slightly open.

Asymmetric Lobes

In the past, both the opening and closing sides of a cam lobe were identical. More recently, designers developed asymmetric lobes, wherein the shape of the opening and closing sides differ. Asymmetry helps optimize the dynamics of a valvetrain system by producing a lobe with the shortest seat timing and the most area. The designer wants to open the valve as fast as possible without overcoming the spring's ability to absorb the valvetrain's kinetic energy, then close the valve as fast as possible without resulting in valve bounce. There are many different theories about how to design the most aggressive, stable profile.

Asymmetric lobes can better tailor the cam to specific cylinder head idiosyncrasies. To optimize airflow, some heads may need a slow opening intake, or a slower-closing exhaust.

Hydraulic lifters can provide quiet valvetrain operation only if the closing velocity is kept below a certain threshold. However, the opening velocity can be higher and still provide quiet operation. Almost all modern hydraulic profiles have some asymmetry.

Dual-Pattern Cams

If an engine has equal airflow potential on the intake and exhaust sides, a single-pattern cam is sufficient. When the airflow differs markedly between the intake and exhaust, a dual-pattern cam should be used to balance flow through the engine. In street applications, they help compensate for a full exhaust system. The amount of difference between the intake and exhaust lobes is based on the cylinder head's characteristics, the intake and exhaust system design, and whether the engine is normally-aspirated, blown, or nitrous-injected.

A recent trend in dual-pattern street cams is to use unique-profile intake and exhaust lobes. Not only does the duration and/or lift of each lobe differ, but the overall lobe shape is specifically optimized for use on the intake or exhaust side. Comp's Xtreme Energy series is an example of this approach. The intake profiles minimize seat timing and maximize area, and the exhaust profiles promote excellent scavenging, increased signal, and maximum airflow. **CC**

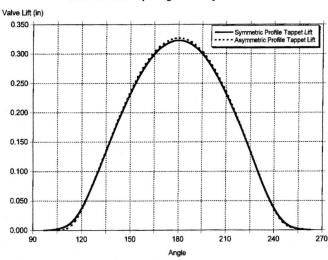

Comparison of Symmetric and Asymmetric Hydraulic Profiles
Note the Latter Opening of the Asymmetric Profile

Valve Lift (in)

- Symmetric Profile Tappet Lift
- Asymmetric Profile Tappet Lift

Angle

In an effort to increase the engine's power potential, designers often skew the cam's timing points. This requires an asymmetric design. The later opening asymmetric lobe improves low-end performance without sacrificing total area under the curve.

SOURCES

COMPETITION CAMS INC.
Dept. CC
3406 Democrat Rd.
Memphis, TN 38118-1577
800/365-9145
www.compcams.com

CRANE CAMS
Dept. CC
530 Fentress Blvd.
Daytona Beach, FL 32114-1200
904/252-1151
www.cranecams.com

LUNATI CAMS
Dept. CC
4770 Lamar Ave.
Memphis, TN 38118
901/365-0950

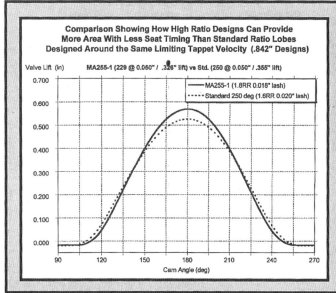

A cam lobe specifically optimized for high-ratio rocker arms can provide more area with less seat timing than standard ratio lobes designed around the same limiting tappet velocity. Both these lobes were designed for GM's typical 0.842-inch tappet foot diameter.

Tappet Dancing

Flat Tappets

Hydraulic flat-tappet camshaft and lifter systems are the most popular configuration for street applications. They provide quiet operation, low maintenance, easy installation, great response, and good power. But hydraulics can "pump up" at high rpm, leading to rapid power loss caused by valve float.

Solid flat-tappet lifters offer a stiff system that can more easily maintain control at high rpm. They require periodic valve lash adjustments, but these can be minimized with good rocker adjustment locking devices. For street use, the crossover point between hydraulic and solid lifters is somewhere between 6,000 and 7,000 rpm, depending on the engine's specific valvetrain configuration and weight.

Mechanical cams usually need about 8-10 degrees more duration to have a comparable power band to a hydraulic lifter cam in the same engine. Also, a mechanical cam's gross valve-lift figures don't include lash, so the recommended lash must be subtracted to come up with the theoretical valve lift.

With flat-tappet cams, the maximum velocity allowed by the tappet before the contact point between the tappet and lobe skates off the edge and causes failure is directly proportional to the tappet diameter. A larger diameter tappet allows the use of a profile with higher maximum velocity. Profiles designed with higher maximum velocity can have more area and more lift for a given duration than similar profiles with less maximum velocity. Most GM applications use a 0.842-inch lifter foot diameter, but Fords and Chryslers use 0.875-inch and 0.904-inch, respectively. This gives these engines a theoretical advantage (albeit at the cost of a slightly heavier lifter) when restricted to a flat-tappet profile if the profile is ground to take advantage of it.

Roller Tappets

Tappet diameter becomes irrelevant with roller lifters. Solid roller lifters allow much higher velocities than flat-tappets and can tolerate the increased spring forces necessary to maintain valvetrain control with these extremely aggressive designs. The typical powerband of flat tappets is 3,000- to 3,500-rpm wide, yet roller lifters usually have a 4,000-4,500-rpm wide band. This is because rollers can hold the valve on the seat longer, then open it quicker. However, the initial departure from the valve seat is slightly slower than a flat tappet because of geometrical limitations. At some point, as rollers are designed for quicker and quicker acceleration off the seat, the designer

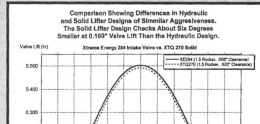

Due in part to its lifter's hydraulic action, don't compare a hydraulic grind directly against a solid grind. This illustration shows the differences between hydraulic and solid lifter profiles of similar aggressiveness. The solid lifter design checks about 6 degrees smaller at 0.100-inch valve lift than the hydraulic.

must go to an inverted ramp profile. There is a limit to how much inversion is possible before the flanks become too difficult to grind. Overall, the increased area permitted by the roller's higher average velocities more than compensates for its slower initial acceleration. Lifter wear was the main drawback to rollers, but new lifters are being introduced that provide greatly increased durability. Currently, the main drawback is cost.

Hydraulic roller lifters provide many of the same advantages as solid roller lifters. However, they are more rpm-limited than hydraulic flat tappets. This is due to the hydraulic roller's higher overall weight, which makes it hard to utilize the more aggressive potential of rollers and maintain stability over 6,500 rpm without relying on very high spring forces that tend to collapse the hydraulic plunger. Further development may lead to improvements in this area, but cost still remains a problem.

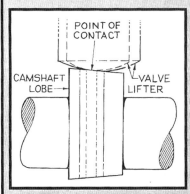

A larger diameter flat-tappet has a greater contact area on the cam lobe than one of smaller diameter. The greater contact area permits the design of a more aggressive profile without decreasing its reliability.

SHOP SERIES

UNDERS

by Jim McFarland

Do You Know?

Answer True or False

☐ 1. Net valve lift is the amount of lift (imparted to a valve) as measured at the camshaft lobe.

☐ 2. Valve duration is the period of time during which a given valve is off its respective seat and relates directly to the points on a lobe where the lift flank (ramp) begins and ends.

☐ 3. Valve overlap is a time during which the exhaust valve is beginning to open and the intake is beginning to close, resulting in both valves being off their seats.

☐ 4. Cams with long overlap periods tend to improve volumetric efficiency (torque output) at low engine rpm.

☐ 5. For street-driven engines, high compression ratio is more compatible with long overlap periods than comparable cam designs utilizing short overlap periods.

☐ 6. The larger the lifter base diameter, the more the lifter tends to act like a roller lifter.

☐ 7. Lobe centerline displacement angle is not related to the amount of overlap a particular camshaft design may incorporate.

☐ 8. A camshaft's base circle is that portion of the lobe on which a lifter rides during the time the valve is on its seat.

☐ 9. Dual-pattern camshafts have lobes that open valves more quickly than they are closed.

☐ 10. Under certain conditions, it's possible to pass raw air and fuel mixture through the induction system, past the cylinder, and out the exhaust system if the overlap period vs. piston motion supports this condition.

☐ 11. By advancing a given camshaft, power (torque) can be moved to a higher-than-previous engine rpm.

☐ 12. Switching from one camshaft to another has little or no effect on carburetor calibration (jetting in particular).

Answers at end of article.

Ah, the mythical camshaft. Considered by many in the same light as a television set: When it works, it works, and when it doesn't, some sort of magic is required to bring it back into focus. This month we'll lay bare some of the essentials in understanding how cams work, and why they sometimes don't.

In an earlier Shop Series it was noted that air flow into an engine is closely related to the rate and amount of pressure differential (drop) developed across the induction system. And, further, the amount of combustion residue that passed out of the engine during the exhaust cycle was also related to some amount of pressure drop (this time positive in nature) across the exhaust path. Simple in theory, it becomes a little more involved when you consider how intake and exhaust valve timing figure into these pressure drop relationships. But before we get down to specifics, let's examine some of the basic terminology associated with an engine's camshaft so that we can understand the relationships once they are discussed.

In no particular order, "net valve lift" comes first. This is the amount of lift as seen by the *valve*. Depending upon the type of valve lifting mechanism (lifter/pushrod, cam lobe rocker arm, etc.), there will be some amount of flex or clearance or deflection of valvetrain components. The amount of such lift loss depends in no small part upon valve spring pressure and engine rpm; but it exists. Consequently, a cam designed with 0.500-inch lobe lift would impart 0.750-inch valve head movement if used with a rocker arm ratio of 1.5:1. But such is not the case.

Rocker arm geometry integrity, pushrod flex, valve spring deflection and/or surge, and a variety of other lift-reducing variables can enter the picture, resulting in valve head movement (net lift) less than that intended

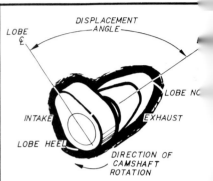

FIGURE 1—Displacement angle is the measurement between the lobe centerlin of the intake and exhaust lobes for each an engine's cylinders. Note also the "lob heel" point, which is at BDC of the lobe (regardless of piston position).

by the cam manufacturer. So what y read isn't necessarily what you get.

Everybody knows what *duration* right? Well, it can vary from "ca specification," too. As an exampl let's define duration as, "the tot amount of time a valve is off its valv seat." Owing to the same conditions "slack" in a valvetrain assembly, valv movement may not track exactly wi lobe design, resulting in somethin less than design duration when mea sured at the valve head. The highe the rpm and/or valve spring pressure the more duration can vary from de sign limits. Typically, timing is mad shorter.

By definition, *overlap* is the perio of time (degrees of crankshaft or can shaft rotation) during which both in take and exhaust valves are unseated More precisely, it is the time when th exhaust valve is closing (ending th exhaust cycle) and the intake is begin ning to open (start of the inlet cycle) During this period, there is a pressure flow relationship between the intake and exhaust systems with results we'l touch on shortly.

As the overlap period is increased effective cylinder pressure is usually reduced at the lower engine speeds Stated another way, high-degree-of overlap cams require elevated engine rpm to produce good cylinder pres sure (or power). As overlap is de creased, low rpm cylinder pressure builds, resulting in the so-called RV or torque/mileage cams of recent times.

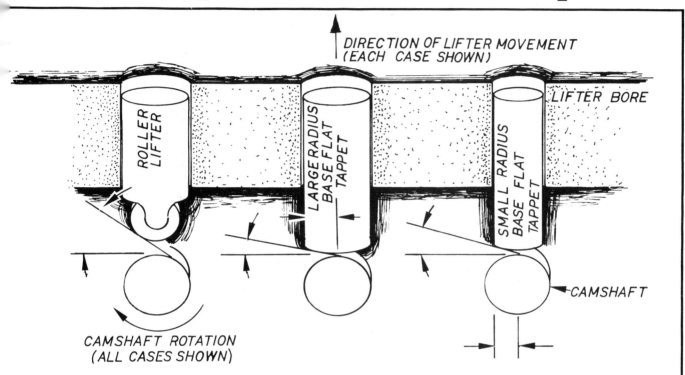

DIRECTION OF LIFTER MOVEMENT
(EACH CASE SHOWN)

ROLLER LIFTER

LARGE RADIUS BASE FLAT TAPPET

SMALL RADIUS BASE FLAT TAPPET

LIFTER BORE

CAMSHAFT

CAMSHAFT ROTATION
(ALL CASES SHOWN)

FIGURE 2—This is a little tricky and can lead to some misunderstanding. The point to be emphasized is that there is a difference among roller, large-base, and small-base lifters relative to the amount of lifter movement generated vs. camshaft rotation angle. Notice that we are dealing with the opening flank of the camshaft lobe in each instance. The large-base flat tappet picks up the opening flank of the cam sooner than the small-base tappet. Thus, opening rate can be increased. In the case of the roller lifter, initial opening point may not be as early, but the rate of valve opening can be made much quicker than for either of the flat tappets. To avoid confusion, just study the relationships among the three methods.

A short overlap cam tends to make an engine "think" it has a higher mechanical compression ratio than it actually does. Conversely, you can run high compression ratios with cams of long overlap periods, allowing the use of lower-than-race grades of gasoline. It's pretty much a matter of effective cylinder pressure within the range of intended engine rpm. And one sensible approach to camshaft selection is consideration of where the engine will be run (for rpm) the majority of the time. Boosts in torque are associated with attending increases in cylinder pressure, and the choice of camshaft overlap characteristic relates directly to this pressure condition.

Now let's talk about *displacement angle*. There's often confusion regarding this term. If you'll consult the appropriate illustrations, you'll note there is a specific angular relationship between the lobe centerline of the intake and the lobe centerline of the exhaust lobes. This "spread" of centerlines relates to the amount of overlap and is expressed in degrees. The point of confusion seems to arise when considering how displacement angle affects an engine's ability to make power relative to where (in rpm) it makes this power.

For example, let's say we have a camshaft ground on a displacement angle of 104 degrees. This establishes an overlap period that includes the profiles (shapes) of both intake and exhaust lobes. If we increase the displacement angle to 108 degrees, there will be a resulting decrease in overlap period and a lowering (in rpm) of the point at which high torque (or power) efficiency is achieved. (There is an argument that an increase in displacement angle will *raise* this range of power efficiency. It's pretty much a matter of how you view the lobe relationship and whether you are referencing crankshaft degrees of rotation or cam degrees. If you'll simply tie it all back into the changes caused in the overlap period and accept that short periods are associated with lower power output, in terms of rpm, than periods of long overlap, it should make sense.)

Next up is the *rate of valve movement*. Here, lobe profile and type of valve lifter (tappet) both affect the velocity and acceleration of a particular valve. Basically, there are two types of lifters, roller-tipped and non-roller. As you'll note in the illustration, side-thrust loading is increased as a function of lifter base size. The wider the base (greater the base diameter), the more rapid the lifter movement, up or down (or positively and negatively in terms of velocity and acceleration). Roller lifters will accept very high rates of movement since sliding friction is replaced by rolling friction and lateral (or side) loading can be greatly increased without attendant lifter/lobe wear.

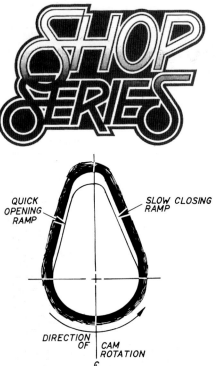

FIGURE 3—This is the asymmetrical lobe design with its rapid opening rate and much more gradual (slower) closing ramp rate. There seems to be some advantage to this design in utilizing kinetic energy forces (cylinder filling) during the last stages of the induction and exhaust cycles.

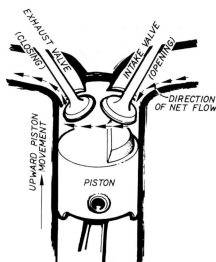

FIGURE 4—Here's the "over-scavenge" condition mentioned. The reason for inclusion of this set of flow relationships is to show that camshafts with too much overlap (for the rpm range of operation) can reduce net engine power by the passage of unspent fuel/air mixture right out of the exhaust system. Increased overlap periods may be good for high rpm power output, but they're death to low rpm operation and should be considered when selecting a cam for your particular engine.

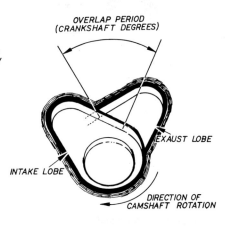

FIGURE 5—Overlap is that period when both intake and exhaust valves are off their respective seats. Failure to examine this aspect of a camshaft can lead to lost (or misapplied) torque and diminished engine performance (including fuel economy). The lower the rpm, the less the overlap there should be.

Generally, roller cams require fairly high valve spring pressures just to keep the lobes and lifters "stuck" together at the higher engine rpm. Remember, high rates of valve acceleration develop high levels of kinetic energy in the valvetrain, especially the valve itself. So there's a possibility of lobe/lifter and rocker/valve separation when the cam lobe is passing over its "nose" position at or near maximum valve lift. However, excessive valve spring pressure can accelerate lobe wear and flush metal throughout an engine's oiling system. And unless you're on an unlimited budget and enjoy rebuilds, this might be a condition you'll want to avoid.

What's a "nose" and a "base circle" and a "flank"? The *base circle* is the point at which the flank begins and the surface on which the valve lifter (or rocker arm) rides during times when the valve is seated. The *flank* is that surface over which the lifter (rocker) passes as the valve is opened and closed. And the point during which the valve acceleration and velocity becomes zero is maximum lift and the *nose* of the lobe in question. Could it be simpler?

Single-pattern cams are those for which the intake and exhaust lobes are the same (lift, duration, rates of lift, etc.). Dual-pattern camshafts utilize intake and exhaust lobes of differing designs, and this is of particular value when considering cylinder head flow capability that is not the same from intake to exhaust—especially if no cylinder head modifications are allowed. Example? Let's say you're limited to a stock cylinder head and are trying to optimize net port flow (intake and exhaust). If the head being used is more restrictive on the exhaust side than the intake, it might be advantageous to have more exhaust timing duration than intake. Thus, a dual-pattern camshaft.

Furthermore, let's assume we'd like to utilize some of the kinetic energy developed during the induction cycle while the intake valve is closing. A common approach here is to delay the rate of intake closing so that the flow energy level achieved before maximum lift is allowed to "work" a little longer before the inlet valve is seated. Such lobe profiles are often called "asymmetrical" inasmuch as opening lift rates are quicker than those on the closing side. Similar lift rate treatment can be applied to the exhaust lobe wherein quick opening rates and slow closing rates help (1) purge the cylinder during early, high-pressure exhaust gas flow and (2) aid gas flow velocity by getting the valve near its seat during the time when upward piston motion is "pumping" combustion residue out of the cylinder.

It was mentioned that the overlap period is a time when the intake and exhaust systems are exposed to each other. More specifically, when the intake valve first begins to open, pressure in the cylinder (combustion space) is higher than in the induction system (assuming the engine is normally aspirated). Depending upon the exhaust gas flow rate, there will be a time when fresh incoming air and fuel may be passed right out through the exhaust port (a consequence of gas flow dynamics in the exhaust system). Such an "over-scavenging" condition can reduce the amount of fresh air/fuel mixture that will remain in the cylinder after closing of the exhaust valve, resulting in lost power and efficiency.

Of the various valve timing conditions that can produce lost cylinder pressure during combustion, the overlap period is of particular significance. For the longer the overlap period, the higher the engine rpm at which acceptable levels of cylinder pressure are once again achieved. Fuel and air that pass right through an engine don't contribute to usable power.

The potpourri for this month? Well, here they come . . . . Don't mix used camshaft and lifter parts. Fresh pieces and a break-in period of no less than 15 minutes at 2000-plus rpm help ensure long component life. For radical camshafts, break-in should be accomplished using valve springs of much lower than required pressure. A set of outers (asuming double or triple will later be used) works well. When you anticipate re-using a camshaft and lifters, be certain all lifters are returned to their previous lifter boss and check lifter bases for proper lifter rotation. If there's a concentrated wear spot on the face of the lifter base, throw immediately into the trash can and replace with a new part.

114

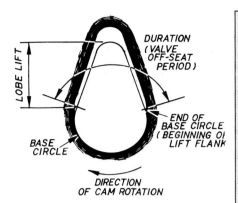

FIGURE 6—Here you can see the dimensions that establish camshaft lobe lift and overall valve duration (as determined by the camshaft). Note that any increase in base circle dimension is the initiation point for flank surface (or termination of it if on the closing side).

Advancing a camshaft increases low rpm cylinder pressure (torque) while retarding the cam increases the rpm point at which the same levels of cylinder pressure are achieved. Increasing valve lash effectively shortens valve timing while decreasing lash increases duration. This is a quick and effective method for evaluating a given camshaft, and determining whether a camshaft with different timing should be installed. Such lash exercises also affect net lift, but the duration changes appear more significant.

And, don't overlook the fact that a camshaft change can have a material effect on carburetor calibration. Extended valve timing reduces the fuel metering signal while shortened timing tends to increase the amount of fuel flow. If you really want to polish all this off with a couple of thought-provokers, consider the effects of 180-degree headers vs. four-into-one systems. Engines fitted with the 180-degree exhaust systems tend to broaden the power curve, allowing use of larger camshafts (with 106 to 108-degree displacement angles) than the more conventional four-into-one systems that depend more on lobe designs and arrangements for torque in a specific range of rpm.

Finally, there's the engine builder who decides his V8 needs to produce power over a very wide range of rpm. So to accomplish this, he treats the engine like two V4s. The camshaft is "split" (in terms of timing patterns), the exhaust system gets similarly split as does the induction system. And all of a sudden we're right back to that mythical camshaft. Entirely *unlike* the analogy with the television set, but certainly an engine part for which you get the picture. **HR**

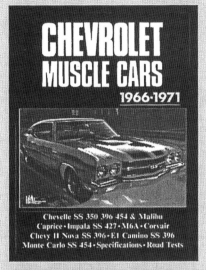

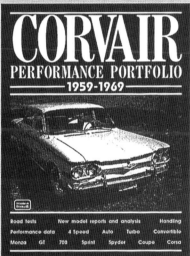
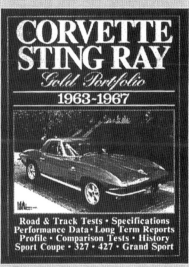
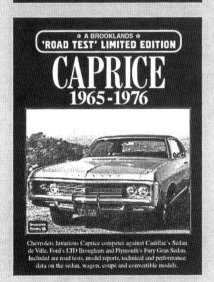
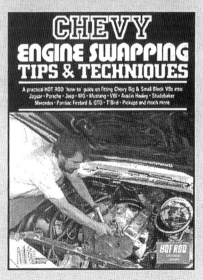
115

To many of us, knowledge of an engine's camshaft stops at lift and duration. Or perhaps it doesn't even really go that far. So often, it seems, we tend to understand and select a particular cam on its merits as told to us by someone else, perhaps one whose engine combination is especially applicable to the cam he's using, but not necessarily best suited to our specific engine.

The subject of cam function and design is a rather large one, so it is the intent of this month's Series to deal with the ground-level basics of cams: What they do. How they do it. What terms are used to describe their parts. And what these terms mean. So that by the time you get around to picking your next cam, there'll be a little more substance to your selection than, "Gimme that one 'cause I like its looks." We know because we've been there. First of all, suppose we discuss what a camshaft is supposed to do in an internal combustion engine.

Air and fuel pass into an engine and spent exhaust gas leaves it. And since the combustion process deals with very high cylinder pressures, intake and exhaust valves must seal and hold this pressure to provide usable power. Other than during these times, intake and exhaust valves must be opened and closed to allow the passage of air/fuel mixtures and exhaust gas into and out of the engine's cylinders. Couldn't get much simpler, right? But it is the *timing* of these openings and closings and the *duration* of these events that govern how a given camshaft affects power output.

On a common shaft there are typically located several noncircular lobes. As the shaft turns (make a good soap opera title, wouldn't it?), each of these lobes can impart motion to a follower (lifter) that causes a rocker arm to open and close a particular valve. In pushrod engine design, there's no direct contact between follower and rocker arm (a pushrod connects them). In overhead cam engine design, camshaft lobes impart direct motion to rocker arms.

But regardless of the specific method of valve operation, camshafts with lobes cause valves to (1) open, (2) close, (3) remain open, (4) be lifted a specific amount from the valve seat. Obviously, it is the design (shape) of each lobe and its position relative to other lobes on the shaft that affect valve motion and the effects of valve timing on engine performance.

Perhaps the most important aspect of camshaft design, selection and understanding is where in an engine's rpm range are optimum volumetric efficiencies going to be required. Cams designed for low-rpm engine operation are not the same as those intended for higher rpm use. Discussion of differences among these types will follow. But to get us into that, let's now spend a few minutes talking about some of the terminology relative to cam design.

Base circle is not the ring drawn on the ground to locate home plate. It's the lobe circle (as shown in the illustrations) from which additional radiuses are referenced to cause

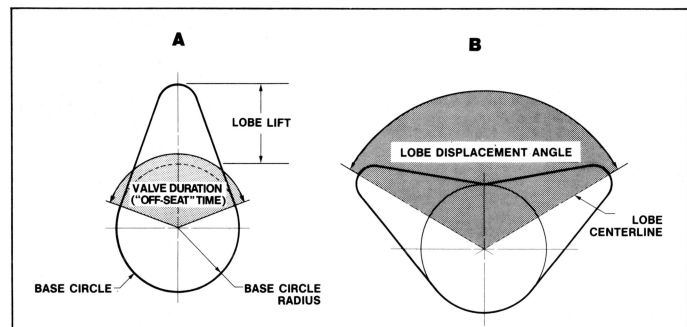

A. Here you can see the relationships of base circle, lobe lift and valve duration. During times when a valve is in its closed position, follower (or lifter) travel is along the base circle surface of the lobe. From the time when a valve leaves its seat to when it is seated again, "off-seat" time (or valve duration) allows mixture/gas flow. Note that net lobe lift is measured from base circle radius to optimum lift, not from the point at which lift motion begins. **B.** The angular measurement (in crankshaft degrees) from the centerline of an intake valve lobe to the centerline of a corresponding exhaust valve lobe is called "lobe displacement angle." Variations of this relationship govern the amount of "overlap" between intake and exhaust valves.

ILLUSTRATIONS: LARRY D. RODGERS

A CAMSHAFT PRIMER: THE MYSTIQUE OF VALVE MOTION . . . AS REGULATED BY THE SHAFT WITH THE CAMS ON IT

By Jim McFarland

valve motion. It's also the portion of a cam on which the follower rides during times when the valve is seated. At the first increase of this base circle dimension, a given cam follower begins motion up the lobe "flank." This ascension continues until the follower reaches the maximum amount of displacement up the flank (maximum lift), after which it continues down the "closing side" of the cam flank. When the follower once again reaches the base circle, the valve is seated and will remain so as long as the follower rides the base circle. It is the shape of the opening and closing flanks that determines rate of valve motion and, therefore, the rate at which the flow passage around a particular valve and seat can develop. Cams that have quick lift rates expose flow paths quickly, while those with slow rates offer more flow restriction at the valve/seat junction.

Duration is the measure of time a valve is off its seat and usually relates to degrees of crankshaft rotation. Since most cams rotate at one-half crankshaft speed (one cam revolution for every two turns of the crankshaft), it's understandable that as much as 300 degrees of valve duration can exist and still have time for the compression and power strokes of the piston. It's simply a matter of reference. The crankshaft controls piston movement, and because cranks normally drive the camshafts, valve timing figures are noted in degrees of crank rotation.

Lobe displacement angle and intake lobe centerline are often confused in discussions of cam basics. Displacement angle is the angular distance between the intake and exhaust lobes for a single cylinder of the engine. For example, if a cam is ground with a displacement angle of 110 degrees, this means there are 110 degrees of crankshaft rotation between the centerlines of a pair of intake and exhaust lobes (see illustration). If you'll take a moment to study Figure C, it's obvious that there is also an angular relationship between the opening point of the intake lobe and the closing point of the exhaust lobe. It is during this time that both intake and exhaust valves are unseated (intake opening, exhaust closing). This is called the overlap period, and it can be determined by numerically adding the value of the intake opening point (before top dead center piston position) to the exhaust closing after TDC piston position. Let's say a cam is ground with an intake event of 36

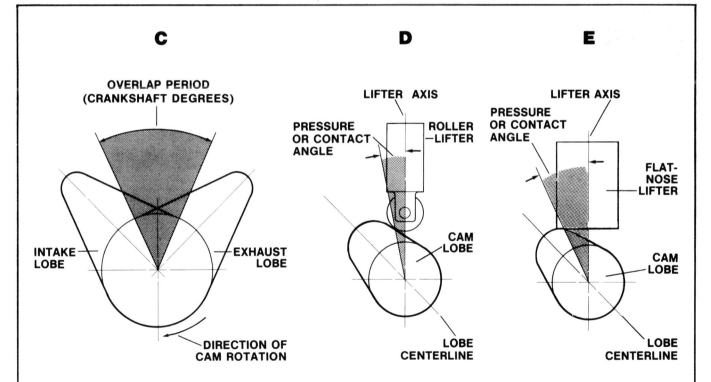

C. This is an illustration of "overlap" between intake and exhaust valves. Note the direction of cam rotation and you'll see that as the exhaust valve is closing (downside on the exhaust lobe), the intake valve begins to open. From this point until the exhaust valve closes, both valves are off their respective seats. You might also note that the earlier an intake valve opens, the greater will be the cylinder pressure exposed to the intake manifold. This is reversion pressure, and it can lead to contamination of subsequent cylinder fillings. **D.** Here's a roller follower (lifter) and its basic relationship to a camshaft lobe. Note that the amount of angular relationship between lifter axis and roller contact on the cam lobe is relatively small. This measurement, called pressure or contact angle, relates to the amount of side-thrust imparted to the lifter during times when the lifter is off the cam's base circle. **E.** Flat-lifters such as conventionally found in solid or hydraulic follower designs usually cause greater pressure or contact angles than roller types. This increases the amount of side-load on the lifter, resulting in more force (or required engine power) to operate a given valvetrain at high rpm. It also means that valve lift rates are limited to cam/lifter materials and engine rpm.

degrees opening before TDC and an exhaust closing event of 40 degrees after TDC. Overlap period would be 76 crankshaft degrees.

As the overlap period increases, there is less valve seated time available, resulting in higher engine rpm required to generate adequate cylinder pressure. For example, race cams usually have more overlap than those intended for stock applications. Think of it in terms of how long overlap periods allow usable cylinder pressure to be lost to atmosphere and the whole soggy mess gets a little clearer.

Intake lobe centerline has to do with the position of the camshaft as installed in an engine. It simply means that the centerline of a cam's intake lobe (usually the No. 1 cylinder) is related to the position of the crankshaft (thus, piston position). Moving the camshaft ahead of this initial position is called "advancing" the cam and tends to help low-rpm power output. Moving the cam behind this initial position is called "retarding" the shaft and generally helps power at higher rpm. Functionally, advancing a cam increases low-rpm cylinder pressure, thus aiding fuel economy and throttle response. Retarding a cam increases the rpm point at which optimum volumetric efficiency is achieved, thereby raising the point of peak power. And whether the cam is of race design or a stocker, the same effects can be expected.

Okay. We've touched on lift, duration, overlap, displacement angle, lobe centerlines, advancing and retarding, and primary functions of a camshaft. Now suppose we work our way through the three basic types of camshaft lobe followers and see how each affects the performance of a particular lobe design.

All three of these types can be classified as radial followers. That is, each involves a follower that is held in some form of bushing (lifter or follower bore in the engine's cylinder block) and actuates a valve based on radius changes in the lobe while the camshaft rotates (see illustration because this may not be a clear description). One, with a flat face, is typical of most "flat-tappet" design followers. The next, with a spherical face, is called a "convex" lifter and tends to provide increased rates of valve motion as compared to flat-faced followers. And the third, which incorporates a roller (or wheel) that follows lobe shape, is used primarily for exceptionally high rates of valve motion where lifter/lobe contact pressures can be minimized, particularly at high engine rpm.

Assume for a minute that we have an engine operating at 4000 rpm. At this speed (or any other), there is a specific amount of time in terms of crankshaft rotation in which to operate the intake and exhaust valves for a particular cylinder. To optimize the amount of intake and exhaust flow, it may be necessary to open, hold open, and delay closing of the valves to achieve maximum cylinder filling (volumetric efficiency). Since there is only a specific amount of time in which to do this, it may be good to have quick valve motion so that the valve/seat relationship offers the least amount of impedance to net flow. Such valve action tends to increase contact pressure (friction load or drag) between follower and lobe, suggesting the use of a roller design follower instead of a flat-faced one.

Such is the case with race-type camshaft lobes. And as a compromise, because the spherical lifter face imparts something of a "roller effect" to valve, the convex follower is frequently used in race cam design. This offers a degree of roller action without the need for a true roller tappet. Grand National NASCAR engines are a predominant user of this type of camshaft.

Also with respect to roller cam followers, the line of action (force) from the cam lobe to the follower cannot be along the follower axis, except when the follower is at or near maximum lift. It is at this point when the valve is being "dwelled" in its open

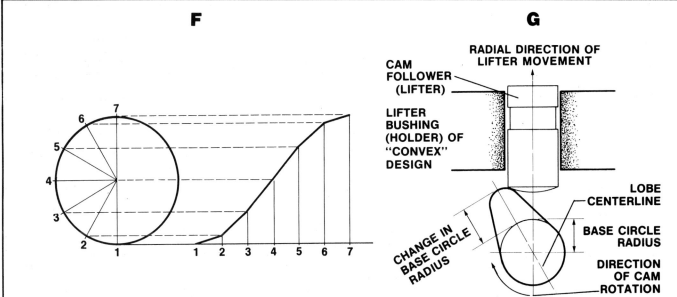

F. This is simple harmonic motion. We included such an illustration to show typical valve motion relative to camshaft rotation. The "slope" of the curve (angle relative to the horizontal axis) indicates how fast valve action is taking place. The more vertical the slope, the faster the valve action. Note that maximum valve movement takes place during the midpoints of the lift curve. The more vertical the slope, the faster the valve action. This is a basic lift curve. As mentioned in the story, variations of simple harmonic motion produce specific valve motion relative to specific engine requirements. **G.** This is the typical "convex" tappet design. Compare this type of lifter with the design shown in Figure E. This lifter design is one method of cheating roller-vs.-flat-tappet capabilities to use more radical profiles. Besides all this, cams designed for use with convex lifters really get the job done.

position—no (or relatively little) upward or downward motion—that the line of action between cam lobe and lifter lies along the follower's axis.

At all other times, there is a "pressure angle" (as shown in the illustrations) that tends to produce a side thrust motion in the lifter. This increases lifter drag or friction in its boss and should be avoided where possible by designing lobe profiles that produce the greatest amount of linear lifter travel for a given amount of lift. And while this may seem momentarily deep, it is meant to point out that the relationships between lobe shape and lifter design (and type) are critical to best valve action and maintaining continuous contact between lobes and lifters, especially when lift rates and engine rpm are high. Valve springs can be depended upon to do just so much, and even these have limits of performance, as many a drag racer's parts budget reflects. Of the various types of basic lobe shape, perhaps the parabolic (with constant acceleration and deceleration of follower motion), parabolic with constant velocity, and simple harmonic motion are the more common in automotive applications.

At least in theory, parabolic lifter motion has the least amount of follower acceleration for a specific lobe lift and engine speed. A standard deviation of this method includes periods of constant lifter velocity, in addition to parabolic motion, where it may be useful to have zero lifter acceleration and constant velocity along an opening or closing ramp. This is the second basic lifter motion method.

Simple harmonic motion of a follower is especially suited to roller lifters, since maximum pressure angles will normally be smaller than with either types of parabolic motion. This also means that there will be less power required to rotate the camshaft, which is of particular benefit when either rpm or valve spring pressures are made high. Cams are frequently designed using combinations of these methods of follower control, and further examination of the theoretical aspects of each is beyond the scope of the Series. Just keep in mind that from the initiation of valve lift, up to a maximum, and down to the end of lift, we are dealing with an "elastic" system of energy in which there is damping, harmonics (especially since we are concerned with valve springs), and a general transfer of forces into and out of an entire valvetrain assembly. Aside from all

this, the prevailing objective of the camshaft is to provide the proper amount of valve timing and lift to optimize cylinder filling *in a specific range of engine rpm.*

Such variables as total piston displacement, span of rpm, geometric relationship of crankshaft stroke and connecting rod lengths, cross-sectional size of intake and exhaust port passages, size of intake and exhaust valves, and compression ratio can each or all affect valve timing requirements. Thus, a particular lobe design and arrangement for one engine can perform totally differently in another. A cam that's "big" in a 350-c.i.d. engine gets even "bigger" in an engine of smaller displacement. And one that's "big" in a small engine becomes effectively "smaller" in a larger engine.

In many respects, we can return to a previous Series where it was suggested that atmospheric pressure "forces" air into an engine; and that the ability of atmospheric pressure to accomplish high levels of cylinder filling depends upon the difference in pressure between cylinder and atmospheric pressures; and that there is no such thing as vacuum, only the absence of atmospheric pressure.

Camshafts control valve motion. If an intake valve is opened too early (relative to some rpm), some amount of cylinder pressure will be lost into the induction system (reversion, if

you will). If it opens too late, some time is lost in which to load the cylinder. Should an exhaust valve open too early, some effective "work pressure" will bleed to the atmosphere and power will suffer. And if it closes too late, there's a good chance of drawing some residual exhaust gas back into the cylinder (since the piston will have already begun the intake stroke).

So aside from the criticalness of designing suitable valve motion dynamics into a particular lobe, precise valve timing is required to optimize engine performance. It was the intent of this month's Series to point out some of the basic terms and how they relate to specific camshaft functions. Should you decide that a more analytical or mathematical exploration of the subject would be to your liking, we suggest locating basic textbooks on the dynamics of mechanisms (found in most libraries).

Meanwhile, you'll now be able to dazzle the guy behind your favorite parts counter with some fresh terms and knowledge. And when you've finished finding out what he knows about pressure angles and parabolic follower motion, you can still point to the cam you've chosen and say, "Gimme that one. I still like the way it looks." **HR**

REVIEW QUESTIONS: True or False

1. A flat-nose lifter can normally bench-press more than 340 pounds.
2. Duration is measured in crankshaft degrees and relates to the amount of time required for either an intake or exhaust valve to reach maximum lift.
3. Lifter (or follower) motion off the lobe base circle is when valve lift usually begins.
4. Opening and closing "flank rates" have little to do with rate of lifter acceleration.
5. Camshafts typically rotate at twice crankshaft speed.
6. Camshaft lobe displacement angle and lobe centerline are terms that mean the same thing.
7. A camshaft ground with a displacement angle of 108 degrees means that there are 108 crank degrees between the intake lobe spacing of any two adjacent cylinders.
8. Valve overlap periods are normally long for street-type cams and short for race-type, high-rpm engines.
9. Advancing a camshaft (relative to piston position) tends to improve high-rpm power with little effect on low-rpm torque.
10. Convex valve lifters provide valve action similar to that of roller lifters.
11. Spherical followers and convex followers are the same thing.
12. When a valve (or follower) reaches the nose of a given lobe, it is said to be in its "dwell" position, where there is little or no upward or downward motion taking place.
13. Theoretically, parabolic follower motion provides the greatest amount of lifter acceleration, making it well-suited to race lobe designs.
14. Simple harmonic lifter motion is well-suited to flat-nose follower designs, especially where hydraulic lifters are used.
15. Connecting rod and crankshaft stroke relationships are about the only two primary engine variables not affected by camshaft design.

Answers to Review Questions: 1. Well, maybe he could. 2. False, 3. True, 4. False, 5. False, 6. False, 7. False, 8. False, 9. False, 10. True, 11. True, 12. True, 13. False, 14. False, 15. False.

A GUIDE TO CAMSHAFT AND VALVETRAIN TRICKERY

Camshafts are probably the number-one bench racing topic in America. While many secrets lie in the actual design of the bumpstick, there are additional tips that apply to the valvetrain. In this builder's guide, we'll give you a few tips on how to get the most from your cam of choice.

ECCENTRIC TIMES

16 LASHES

One of the biggest hassles with a solid (mechanical tappet) cam is the need to regularly readjust valve lash, a task usually associated with an aggravating hot oil bath. The best method of setting lash doesn't rely on sequencing charts, and doesn't require the engine to be running. Simply set intake lash just as the exhaust valve opens, and set exhaust lash just as the intake valve is near closing. You can ignore firing order, and it works with any number of cylinders on any engine. If you want to set lash with the engine hot, which you should, then warm it up before you pop each valve cover. This works equally well when setting hydraulic lifters.

FLOAT RAINS ON YOUR PARADE

If you've heard about valve float, but aren't sure how root beer and ice cream go with car parts, then we'll fill you in. When an engine over revs, the inertia of the valves can exceed the valvesprings' ability to keep them in phase with the cam. In valve float, oftentimes the cam lobe tries to open the valve, while the spring is trying to close it. Just one healthy valve float can substantially damage springs, lowering the rpm at which valve float will occur next time. Check or replace the springs, especially stock ones, if valve float has occurred. Your

springs should have enough tension to prevent float, but they also need to be light enough to keep the lifters from wearing out the cam. The manufacturer of your cam will be able to recommend the appropriate valvespring. Crane's new H-11 tool steel springs may be what you need for a high-tension spring in a stock diameter for small- and big-block Chevys.

FASTER FASTENERS

Ever since you were a kid, you've probably eyeballed those orange drawers in the local parts store. Drawers filled with Dorman brand treasures of all kinds: clamps, fasteners, couplers, fittings, and the like. Now Dorman has entered the performance market with fastener packages to make cam swaps easier. You can now choose packages for valve covers, rocker studs, timing covers, and cam bolts, and most are available in a variety of finishes. Best of all, Dorman's HPX line has individual pieces so you only have to buy what you need, and they're all made in America!

CLEVER LEVER

Give your cam a lift with the mechanical advantage of higher-ratio rocker arms. Adding one tenth of a point of rocker arm ratio will increase lift by about .030 inch. For example, a small-block Chevy has 1.5:1 ratio rockers, and we'll assume a .475-inch lift cam. Installing 1.6 rockers would increase lift to around .505 inch. Duration would remain the same, so the rate of lift at the valve would increase. This faster  valve acceleration can cause valve float, and the added lift would require you to check valve-to-piston clearance. This tuning tip is most helpful on small-block Chevys and Fords that can use a little extra flow on the exhaust ports. Crane's 1.6 small-block Chevy stamped-steel rockers even make this an affordable proposition!

NO FEAR GEAR

If you've ever run a steel billet roller cam, you've either wasted cam gears or learned to live with soft bronze distributor drive gears. Competition Cams has solved this problem with a new hardening process called austempering. This new system allows you to use strong roller cams that don't require trick distributor gears. Just toss in the cam, bolt up the stock distributor, and you're ready to go! These new, user-friendly rollers are currently available for big-block and small-block Chevys.

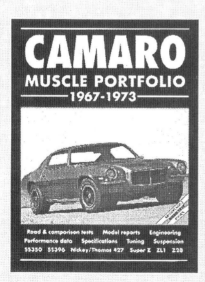

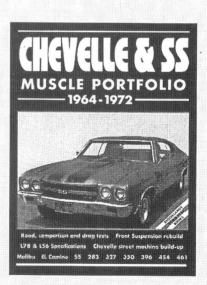

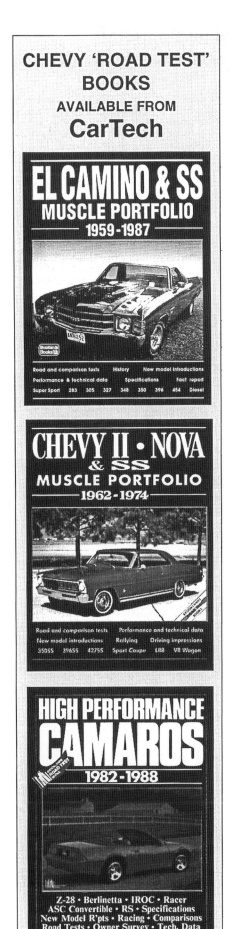
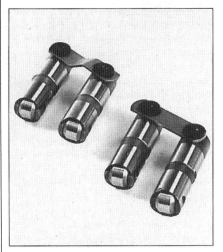

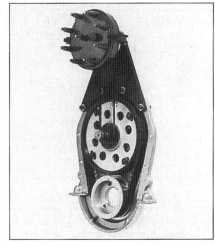

ROLLIN', ROLLIN', ROLLIN'

Keep them lifters rollin'! If you were excited when Chevy introduced factory roller cams, then you were probably disappointed to discover that stock rollers won't retrofit into older blocks due to the taller lifter bores on the new engines. Competition Cams has solved the problem with new hydraulic roller-lifter technology for older small-block and big-block Chevy engines. The hydraulic rollers offer the advantages of being able to use faster ramps on the cam, as well as quieter operation and increased dependability.

GET BELTED

If you're the type who plays with cam timing like changing plugs, then the Jesel beltdrive may be the hot ticket. This external cam drive offers simple timing adjustments in two-degree increments through a 20-degree range. Jesel's billet pulleys and 25mm belt will accurately motivate your cam, without imparting evil crankshaft vibrations to the bumpstick. If the idea of a belt spinning your cam worries you, don't sweat it—lots of NASCAR racers rely on these units for long-duration events. Jesel recommends replacing the belt yearly. If you want to get double-trick, tack on Jesel's new beltdrive distributor kit.

JUICE LIFTER TECH

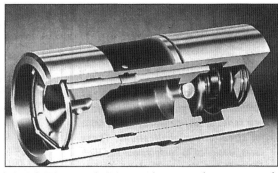

While hydraulic cams are run at zero lash, there are bleed-down lifters available that can be used as a tuning tool to cut down low-rpm lift and duration. Crane's Hi Intensity lifters are a good example. These tappets allow a slight oil bleed down at low rpm to reduce lift and duration—kind of like a shock absorber between the cam and the pushrod. The result is more low speed vacuum and torque. As rpm increases, there is less time for the lifter to release pressure, so you get the full lift and duration ground into the cam. These lifters may be used only on the intake lobes as a tuning device, and you can experiment with different viscosity oils to alter the bleed-down rate.

IT'S MANLEY, MAN

If you'd like more cylinder head flow, but don't want to change your heads, try Manley's Pro Flow or Race Flow valves for "free" flow. These valves have a standard diameter stem with an undercut in the bowl area. This, combined with the valves' swirl polished head and three-angle valve job, can increase low-lift flow dramatically, according to Manley. Best of all, they fit right up without any high-dollar modifications. Consider these valves as a next-step benefit the next time you go through your heads, or get really trick by capping them off with Manley's full line of valvetrain hardware.

BREAK IN VS. BROKEN

Anyone who's read more than a few issues of HOT ROD knows that it's vital to use a break-in coating on a new cam. However, dipping the bumpstick in lube and pouring goo down the oil filler isn't the only answer to properly breaking in a cam. First, you should make sure the engine is going to fire up on the first try. Don't turn the motor over by hand, or you'll wipe the pre-lube off the lobes, which could waste the cam before the engine even runs. Once the cam is coated with a moly disulfide assembly lube, add a can of zinc dithiophosphate antiwear additive and fire up the engine. Immediately bring it up to speed and vary the rpm between 1500 and 2000 rpm for 15 minutes. This ensures that oil will splash all over the cam instead of in a single pattern. Change the oil when you're done, and the cam should last a lifetime.

TIPTOE THROUGH THE TULIPS

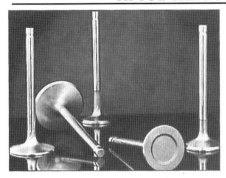

In a race engine, or even a severely loaded street engine, the exhaust valve can be the hottest part of the engine. Two-piece welded valves that are commonly used in stock applications can warp due to lack of cooling, and a warped valve has even less heat-transferring contact area on the seat. Wolverine has attacked the performance cam and valvetrain market with the Blue Racer line. One of its products is a one-piece forged austenitic stainless-steel valve that offers better heat transfer through the stem. With performance claimed to be second only to titanium, the Blue Racer valves could be the solution to your problems.

LASHING OUT

Did you ever wish you could change cam duration without swapping cams? With a solid-lifter cam, you can! If your recommended lash is .022 inch, then you can kill duration and retard valve opening a few degrees by increasing lash to .026 inch. This will help smooth out a rough idle, although valve noise will increase. Conversely, reducing lash to .018 inch will slightly increase duration and advance the valve opening point. Intake and exhaust clearances don't have to be the same, so you can stagger lash to reduce intake duration, while increasing exhaust duration as a no-cost tuning aid. This is a very subtle technique best used to tune in a good cam—it's not a fix to a grossly overcammed engine.

NIFTY LIFTER

Accurately degreeing a cam by using a hydraulic lifter as a checking tappet is impossible because of clearances inside the lifter. To remedy the situation, take one of your old lifters and remove the snap ring so you can dump the piston and spring out of it. Clean out the empty lifter and then flip over the pushrod cup (concave side down) and glue it to the seat in the top of the lifter. Now the lifter is a solid piece for repeatable measurement, and the oil hole that was on the

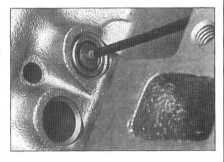

underside of the pushrod cup makes a perfect perch for the dial-indicator tip. Make sure you glue the lifter together, or the cup may fall inside the engine, negating the benefits of a perfectly cool idea.

PREVIEW OF CAMMING ATTRACTIONS

If these tidbits of cam tuning trivia have whet your appetite for more, then stay tuned for next month's story on cam selection! We'll sort through the sometimes scary, always vital details of choosing the right cam for your needs. You, too, will learn such camspeak as "duration at .050," "lobe separation angle," and "base circle." It will be a veritable bonanza of valve actuation information! **HR**

New Camshaft Selection Software From Competition Cams

By Chuck Schifsky

HOW OFTEN HAVE YOU PAGED through a stack of catalogs trying to find the best camshaft for your street machine, only to be confused about how your gear ratio or bolt-on carburetor could affect your choice? Well, Competition Cams is attempting to help performance enthusiasts who have access to a personal computer and would like to select their own camshafts by introducing CamQuest cam selection software.

Through CamQuest, Competition Cams is hoping to turn confusing camshaft choices into a simple "fill-in-the blanks" process. Competition Cams Project Engineer Tony Leonard says "CamQuest was designed to complement the existing Competition Cams catalog, while giving the 'do-it-yourselfer' one more way to custom design his engine combination."

CamQuest requires an IBM-compatible PC with at least 640K of memory. The user enters specific vehicle and engine information, which allows CamQuest's on-disc database to recommend the best camshaft from Competition Cams Hi-Energy and Magnum series cams. CamQuest also recommends components such as lifters, springs, and rocker arms, along with any precautions (such as piston-to-valve clearance).

CamQuest also features two utility sections to help the user select a camshaft. The first section uses vehicle data to give the user answers to numerous equations, including compression ratio, cubic inches, approximate e.t./mph, and carburetor size. The second section provides answers to common camshaft questions, including the ever popular "Is bigger better?" or the often misunderstood, "What is a lobe center?"

Future CamQuest software will recommend camshafts from Competition's new Dual Energy cam line, along with camshafts designed for newer electronically controlled vehicles. Leonard also mentioned that a CamQuest II version is being developed for full race combinations.

Now that computers can select camshafts, the next thing we need is a computer that can go to work for us, so we can stay home enjoying the camshaft installation process. ☜

Source

Competition Cams
Dept. CC
3406 Democrat Road
Memphis, TN 38118
800/999-0853

EASY HOW-TO

SAVE THAT CAM!

By Jeff Smith

Hot rodding is all about making machines work better. Often, it's also about ensuring that the little things work right. For example, on billet-steel roller cams it's common knowledge you need a "bronze" distributor gear. This softer material is more compatible with the steel camshaft gear. However, when combined with a high-volume oil pump, excessive wear on both the distributor gear and the cam gear will result. Distributor gears are relatively easy to replace, but if the cam gear suffers excessive wear, the only fix is a new camshaft, which is expensive and time consuming.

Crane Cams has come up with a great no-cost solution to this problem for the small-block, big-block and 90-degree V6 Chevy engine families. Crane recommends filing or cutting a .030-inch-wide by .030-inch-deep groove in the lower ring of the distributor housing immediately above the distributor gear. This slot is cut into a ring that seals a main oil passage, creating a spray of oil that is directed onto the distributor and cam gears for extra lubrication. The stock small-block system relies on splash oiling, which may not be effective at low engine speeds, especially when combined with a high-volume oil pump.

The slot can be cut with a three-corner file or a Dremel tool. This slot must be positioned to face the camshaft drive gear. Position the distributor for proper initial timing, then use this position to determine the correct location to machine the groove so it faces the cam gear. This is also an excellent idea for cams with flat-tappet cast-iron gears, especially when combined with a high-volume, high-pressure oil pump. According to Crane, high-volume pumps create additional load when operated at low speeds on engines with stock bearing clearances. These tighter clearances create a back-pressure because the greater oil volume cannot escape past the bearings quickly enough. This additional load impacts the distributor gear because it also drives the oil pump.

This simple modification won't make more horsepower or impress the troops at the local drive-in, but if it keeps your engine running longer, it's worth doing. **HR**

Crane suggests cutting a .030-inch-wide by .030-inch-deep slot in the lower band of the distributor housing to direct a spray of oil onto the camshaft and distributor gears. We used a Dremel tool to cut the slot into this distributor.

Mark a straight-ahead position on the outside of the distributor body to use as a reference mark for the distributor's placement in the engine. Use this orientation to position the oil groove. Remember that the cam is on the driver's side of the distributor.

Crane, Comp Cams and Lunati now offer roller cams fitted with an iron distributor drive gear. These cams do not require a silicon bronze distributor gear. A stock iron gear is compatible. Adding this oiling groove is still recommended if you're using a high-volume oil pump.

SOURCE

Crane Cams
Dept. HR05
530 Fentress Blvd.
Daytona Beach, FL 32114
904/258-6174 (tech line)

Photography: Jeff Smith

SAVE THE LOBES!

BY MARLAN DAVIS

Photos by Marlan Davis

Today's cutting-edge, flat-tappet, full-race cam profiles demand really stout valve-springs, but such stiff springs increase the chance of premature lobe failure. Comp Cams has developed a user-friendly lifter bore grooving tool that solves the problem by cutting a tiny longitudinal groove in the lifter bore that intersects the it's radial oil supply groove. This directs additional oil to the lobes, helping to prevent them from going flat, and is a good idea for making any cam live longer. **CC**

1 Comp Cam's grooving tool includes a T-handle, a mandrel, a cutting blade, a cutter retaining screw, and an adjusting wrench. PN 5003 (shown) fits 0.842-inch GM lifter bores. Similar tools for Ford and Chrysler lifter bores are coming soon.

5 Cut the groove by pulling the T-handle straight up until the wide mushroom end of the mandrel bottoms against the bore's underside. Shove the tool straight back down the bore until you can unhook and re-move the mandrel. Repeat the process for the remaining bores.

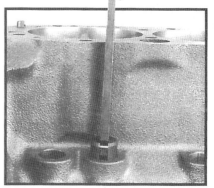

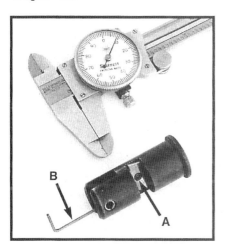

2 Place the double-edged cutting blade in position on the mandrel's radial slot, then tighten the retaining screw (*A*). Adjust the blade so it protrudes 0.009-inch beyond the mandrel's outer diameter by turning the adjusting screw located in the mandrel's longitudinal slot as required (*B*).

4 Rotate the assembly to properly orient the blade. For max lubrication effectiveness, the groove should align with the cam's direction of rotation, so always cut the groove on the side of the lifter bore that's closest to the passenger side of the engine.

3 While holding the mandrel in position at the bottom (cam-side) of the lifter bore to be grooved, insert the T-handle through the top (valley-side) of the lifter bore far enough to engage the hook on the end of the handle with the mandrel's horizontal bar (*arrow*).

6 Here are two freshly grooved bores. You may wish to deburr the groove edges with a piece of emery cloth and then hone them with a paddle-type brake cylinder hone.

SOURCE

COMPETITION CAMS INC.

Dept. CC
3406 Democrat Rd.
Memphis, TN 38118-1577
800/365-9145
901/795-2400
www.compcams.com

Xtreme Performance

By Marlan Davis

In 1965, GM's 327/350hp hydraulic cam was a pretty good high-performance bumpstick. But that was over 30 years ago. Top Fuelers ran in the 7s back then. Today, those times are Pro Stock territory. Racing technology hasn't stood still, and neither have improvements in high-performance street hardware. In fact, many of the advances developed for full-race cars eventually trickle down for use by street guys. That's the case with camshaft technology: Thanks to recent valvetrain design advances, Comp Cams is now able to introduce a new series of street cams that provide increased torque, vacuum, throttle response, and power while still providing quiet valvetrain operation, along with the durability required for a daily-driven vehicle. Known as the Xtreme Energy series, these new flat-tappet hydraulic and hydraulic roller grinds bridge the gap between Comp's classic street Magnum cams and race-only cams. Under development for the past year, the cams went through an extensive test program that included more than 200 dyno pulls and numerous evaluations of valvetrain dynamics.

One of the limiting factors in cam development has always been how far the lobe designer could push a given design before an overly aggressive profile resulted in pushrod, valvespring, or valve durability problems. But thanks to racing's demands, much better ancillary valvetrain components have become available. For example, Comp's workhorse "981" spring is a direct replacement for Chevy's old L79 high-per-

Using experience gained through racing and the latest computer-assisted design concepts, Comp Cams' new line of Xtreme Energy cams incorporates some of the most aggressive lobe profiles ever seen on street camshafts.

PHOTOS BY MARLAN DAVIS AND JOHN BAECHTEL

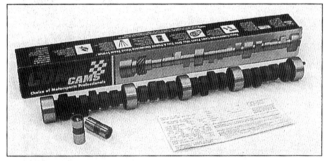

Comp Cams' Xtreme Energy cams offer more power throughout the rpm range with significantly better idle and vacuum characteristics than traditional camshafts—and the price structure is the same as that of Comp's other dual-profile street cams.

An old L79 327/350 cam was run against a modern Xtreme Energy cam on Westech's SuperFlow dyno using a stout Chevy 350 equipped with Air Flow Research aluminum heads.

1. Application Recommendations								
Usage	Grind			Complementary Parts				Power Increase Over Stock
	Xtreme Energy Hyd.	Xtreme Energy Hyd. Roller	Nitrous HP Hyd.	Torque Converter	Intake Manifold	Exhaust	Vacuum Accessories	
Towing	XE 250	XR 252		Stock	Dual-plane	Dual	OK	20%
Heavy Towing or Mild Performance	XE 256	XR 258						
Moderate Street-Performance	XE 262	XR 264	NX 256					
High-Performance Street	XE 268	XR 270	NX 262					
			NX 268					
Street/Strip	XE 274	XR 276	NX 274	2,200 stall	Dual-plane	Headers		
		XR 282		2,500 stall	Single-plane		Marginal	
Light Street/ Mostly Strip	XE 284	XR 288	NX 284	2,800 stall	Single-plane			
Bracket Racing or Pro Street	XE 294	XR 294		3,300 stall	High-rise single-plane		Req. vac. canister	
		XR 300		3,800 stall				115%

2. Test Cam Specs							
Type	Grind or Identification Number	Comp Cams Part No.	Advertised Duration (Int./Exh.)	0.050" Duration (Int./Exh.)	Valve Lift	Int./Exh. Lobe Sep.	Installed Int. CL
Factory Muscle	GM 3863151	12-106-3	320°/320°	222°/222°	0.447"/0.447"	114°	110°
Xtreme Energy	XE274H-10	12-246-3	274°/286°	230°/236°	0.487"/0.490"	110°	106°

The Xtreme Energy's aggressive lobe acceleration mandates premium valvetrain parts—you can no longer slide by with used 50,000-mile pieces. The test engine used Comp's 1.5:1-ratio Hi-Tech stainless rockers, High-Energy hydraulic lifters, Hi-Tech hardened pushrods, and dual valvesprings.

formance street spring; it slips right into the stock small-block Chevy spring pocket with no machining required. Yet, when used with a solid lifter, the 981 will rev to 7,000 rpm without valve float (6,250 rpm with a heavier roller lifter). Combining such improved valvetrain materials with computer-assisted design techniques permitted savvy Comp Cams engineers to quicken the rate at which the valve gets off the seat without adversely affecting durability, which in turn effectively produced a bigger cam with no low-end torque losses or decreases in vacuum output or idle quality. Delaying the intake valve's opening point and then opening it quickly yields a cleaner signal to the intake manifold and carb, which then sucks more air into the engine at low rpm.

Xtreme Energy cams are all dual-pattern configurations. That is, a given overall cam profile combines intake and exhaust lobes with different lift and duration numbers, allowing a specific-

An MSD-6AL ignition combined with Mallory's Billet Competition distributor to light the spark.

A Comp Cams beltdrive was used to ease cam swapping and degreeing chores. The back of the upper sprocket required modification to clear the late factory block's roller-cam thrust-plate retention bosses. The factory thrust plate is not needed when running a flat-tappet cam.

grind cam to better match a particular engine family's cylinder-head characteristics.

Each individual Xtreme Energy lobe design is asymmetrical—the same lobe's opening and closing *rates* are not mirror images of each other. For example, Comp desired a quick-closing valve, but not so quick that excessive valvetrain noise (for a street car) would result. Therefore, the Xtreme Energy's valve closure rate was designed to be slightly slower than the valve opening rate.

Perhaps for the first time in a mass-produced street cam, distinct intake and exhaust design profiles are used on the flat-tappet Xtreme Energy grinds, and (if you're ordering a custom grind) should not be interchanged: A given exhaust lobe closes a little more slowly than would be the case for an equivalent lift and duration intake lobe. Comp found that closing the exhaust at the same rate as the intake costs some midrange torque; apparently, slowing the exhaust closure rate better scavenges the cylinder, boosting midrange torque and horsepower. Curiously, the same effect was not observed during the development of the Xtreme Energy

hydraulic roller profiles, so while the rollers still retain asymmetrical lobes, there are no separate dedicated intake and exhaust lobe profiles. Comp succeeded so well that the new Xtreme Energy flat-tappet profiles achieve opening rates as high as 0.00695-inch lift/degree of duration—nearly at the max theoretical velocity limit for a typical GM-style 0.842-inch–diameter tappet. The hydraulic rollers open the valve at an amazing 0.009-inch/degree.

Right now, Xtreme Energy hydraulic flat-tappet and hydraulic roller profiles are available for the popular small-block Ford and big- and small-block Chevy. The roller profiles include part numbers that replace factory hydraulic roller cams in late-model blocks and work with the original factory-style roller lifter, as well as retrofit hydraulic rollers that fit early (nonfactory-roller) blocks (these require Comp Cams hydraulic roller lifters). The smaller profiles should be compatible with EFI applications, while at the opposite end of the spectrum Comp has covered the Pro Street/bracket-race crowd as well (for detailed recommendations, see Table 1).

Real-world dyno results show just how much of a benefit this new technology is for a modern-day high-performance street engine. To illustrate just how far we've come since 1965,

The 9:1 engine was fed 92-octane pump gas by a 750-cfm Holley double-pumper carb atop an Edelbrock Performer RPM intake manifold.

To simulate real-world street-car performance, Hooker street headers feeding into Flowmaster 3-inch mufflers exhausted the spent mixture.

Westech Performance recently tested a new Xtreme Energy XE274H-10 hydraulic flat-tappet grind against Comp's Factory Muscle L79 327/350 cam, a duplicate of the musclecar era's premier hydraulic street-performance cam (for detailed specs, see Table 2). Comp considers these two cams roughly equivalent in terms of their streetability and operating range. However, as can be seen from Table 2, the L79 cam's seat duration is much larger than the Xtreme Energy profile; conversely, the L79 cam's duration at 0.050-inch tappet lift is much less than the new Comp Cams grind.

The test engine was a Chevy hi-po ZZ4 crate 350 engine converted to use standard flat-tappet cams. Its as-delivered GM aluminum heads were replaced with Air Flow Research aluminum street heads assembled with 2.02/1.60 valves and complementary valvetrain components (complete engine specs, see Table 3).

With the 327/350 cam, the engine made a peak of 349 hp at 5,400 rpm and 380.2 lb-ft of torque at 4,100 rpm. Swapping the musclecar classic for the Xtreme Energy modern-tech muscle netted 43.5 more hp and 4.2 more lb-ft,

Nitrous HP Cams

Nitrous oxide increases horsepower and torque by a set amount over the entire curve. But for most cars, it's hard to use the power gain at low rpm—you'll just break the tires loose and go up in smoke. By trading off some low-end torque for increased top-end horsepower, it is possible to use nitrous more effectively.

Also, when nitrous is injected into an engine along with the needed quantity of extra fuel, the result is the creation of extra cylinder pressure. Higher pressures not only add power, they also add to the volume of exhaust gases that must be scavenged. If you don't "pass the gas" out the pipe, pumping losses increase dramatically. This calls for larger exhaust valves and/or a significantly larger camshaft exhaust lobe than is usually considered the norm for a non-nitrous-equipped engine.

Taking these factors into account, Comp Cams has developed Nitrous HP cams; they use Xtreme Energy technology but are specially tailored for nitrous' unique characteristics. Ground with 113 degrees of lobe separation angle (instead of the Xtreme Energy's 110 degrees), they're not quite as responsive in the midrange, trading off 5 to 10 lb-ft of midrange torque for 5- to 15hp top-end gains. The exhaust lobes also have more lift and duration than the equivalent Xtreme Energy grind. Comp says the nitrous cams work well in supercharged applications, too.

as measured peak to peak. Specifically, the new grind made 384.4 hp at 6,100 rpm and 380.2 lb-ft at 4,400 rpm. But as can be seen from the graph, overall torque and horsepower were up through virtually the entire rpm range tested, with the amount of gain increasing along with rpm. Between 3,000 and 6,300 rpm, the Xtreme Energy gained an average 14.9 lb-ft and 18.7 hp over the 327/350 grind. By the Xtreme Energy's 6,100-rpm horsepower peak, the new cam had increased the horsepower and torque differential to 57.6 hp and 49.6 lb-ft, respectively.

That's power you can feel in the seat of your pants. And best of all, like all of Comp Cams' new Xtreme Energy cams, it's no more expensive than other Comp dual-profile bumpsticks. More power, same price—what more could anyone ask for? Terminate your search for the right camshaft with Xtreme Prejudice! **CC**

3. Test Engine Specs	
Manufacturer	General Motors
Type	Chevrolet OHV Small V-8, Code ZZ4 (*modified*)
Displacement	350ci (5.7L)
Bore × Stroke	4.00" × 3.48"
Block	Cast-iron with 4-bolt main caps (journals 2, 3, and 4)
Crankshaft	Nodular cast-iron with rolled fillet radii
Connecting rods	Forged powdered metal, 3/8" bolts, 5.7" center-to-center length
Pistons	Cast hypereutectic aluminum, 9:1 CR, pressed pins
Cylinder heads	AFR cast-aluminum street heads, 2.02"/1.60" valves, 190cc intake runners
Camshafts	*See Table 2*
Lifters	Comp Cams Hi-Energy hydraulic flat-tappet (PN 812-16)
Pushrods	Comp Cams Hi-Tech, 5/16" od × 7.800" OL, 0.080" wall thk., hardened (PN 7972-16)
Valvesprings	Comp Cams dual assembly (PN 986-16); 0.695" id × 1.437" od; 120 lbs @ 1.800", seat/ 290 lbs @ 1.250", open; 309 lbs/in rate, coil-bind @ 1.100"
Rocker arms	Comp Cams Hi-Tech stainless steel full-roller, 1.5:1 ratio (PN 1104-16)
Carburetor	Carb Shop Stage 2 750-cfm double-pumper, jetted 65/75
Intake manifold	Edelbrock Performer RPM dual-plane
Ignition	Mallory Billet Competition Distributor triggered by MSD 6AL, 35° total timing
Exhaust	Hooker '69 Z28 street headers with 1¾" primaries × 3" collectors into 3" pipes and Flowmaster 3" mufflers
Fuel	92-octane pump gas

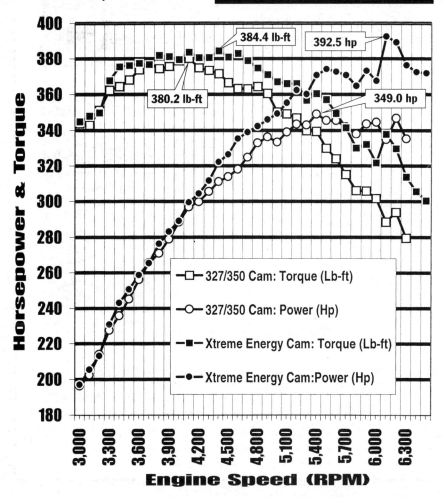